WAR FOR THE HELL OF IT

A FIGHTER PILOT'S VIEW OF VIETNAM

Lt. Col. Ed Cobleigh

United States Air Force (Retired)
Call Sign "Fast Eddie"

War for the Hell of It
A Fighter Pilot's View of Vietnam

Second Edition

This book is published by Check Six Books, Paso Robles, CA

Cover design by Bespoke Book Covers LTD, UK
Interior layout by Veronica Yager, US

All inquires are directed to: Check Six Books, 3750 Sky Ridge Drive, Paso Robles, CA 93446, USA

First edition published by Caliber Imprint of Penguin Books, 2005

Also by Ed Cobleigh;

The Pilot: Fighter Planes and Paris

ALSO BY ED COBLEIGH

The Pilot: Fighter Planes and Paris
An aviation/adventure novel.

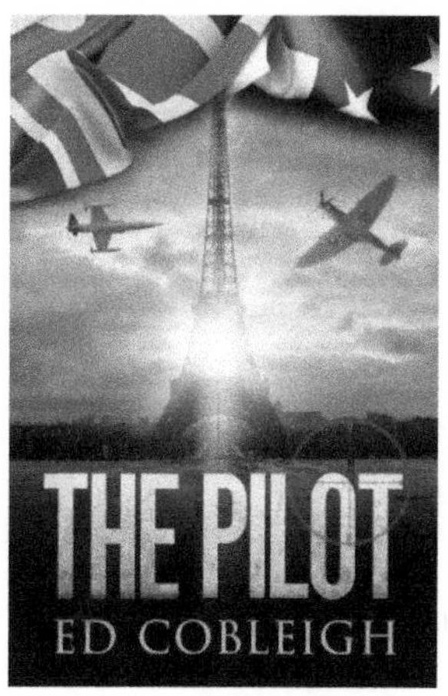

He couldn't shoot down the future,
but his storied past is the key to his present.

Dedicated To

Colonel Edward E. Cobleigh Jr.
United States Army (Retired)

He joined the U.S. Army Cavalry, with horses, serving his country in World War II.

He was proud to see his son fly supersonic jets.

CONTENTS

PRE-MISSION BRIEFING

This book is a series of brief accounts (some would say not brief enough), retelling some of the most significant/interesting aerial combat that I experienced during the Vietnam War as well as descriptions of what happened to me on the ground there. By significant I mean significant to me, not to the overall war effort. I served two tours of duty in "C' flight, the 433rd Tactical Fighter Squadron, "Satan's Angels," assigned to the 8th Tactical Fighter Wing, the "Wolf Pack." My two combat tours were in the late 1960s, each a year long. I logged 375 combat sorties and more than 1000 hours of combat time in the F-4D Phantom II fighter-bomber.

The purpose of this book is not to relate a historically comprehensive or even a strictly accurate view of the whole Vietnam War or of any part of that war, including the war in the air. Nor do I claim to speak for anyone but myself. I don't pretend the episodes I have included are anything more than my own fallible impressions, views, and memories. I had a very restricted view of the war from the cockpit of my F-4 Phantom. I was never based in South Vietnam, but rather at the Ubon Royal Thai Air Force Base in Ubon Ratchathani, Thailand. This book attempts to tell what I saw from that myopic vantage point.

I take some liberties with the calendar in this book. I make no distinction between my first and second tours and have not placed the chapters or events in historical order. The various stand-alone chapters are sequenced so the ideas they represent unfold to hopefully give the reader some insight as to what it was like to be a fighter pilot during that time and at that place in the war. The order is jumbled also because memories return to us, not in an ordered sequence, but as a series of unconnected recollections. The events described happened to me, were witnessed by me, or were caused by my actions. I have tried to remain faithful in tone to what happened, if not in exact detail. No war story is immune to a bit of creative tweaking. No personal account can be completely objective. Remember, my aim is not to provide a textbook or document useful to historians but rather for me to use a series of war stories as a vehicle to illustrate my perceptions and to illuminate my state of mind then. I will vouch for the emotions and thoughts described herein; they are mine and they are true.

There are plenty of books available to the interested reader on the cold facts of the air war over Southeast Asia. Other individuals have put their experiences down on paper, perhaps better than I. Nearly all of these personal accounts fall into the "There I was . . ." school of writing. These are interesting and are often exciting accounts of combat action, of engagements lost, or most often, won. I have not been able to totally resist the siren call of this sort of writing. You will find plenty of accounts of aerial combat in this book, but I hope there is more than that here to discover. I believe there is a dearth of information out there on what it was like to live through such an experience. What did fighter pilots think and feel in the war? What was their state of mind? What were their motivations and frustrations? What did they care about? How did they relate to the men and women around them?

I can't speak for my squadron mates' thoughts and emotions. All I can do is try and express my own. Insomuch as my feelings and values are, I think, typical of most of my fellow aviators, the reader just might get a handle on what it was like to be there.

Instead of trying to add to the existing body of literature in kind, I attempt to tell, by means of a few isolated accounts, what it was really like for me. More important, I try to give the reader my views on what factors made the war experience the way it was. It is always hard to put your emotions and inner thoughts down on paper, particularly those from the way distant past, but I have tried my best. Hopefully the reader will gain some insight on the motivations and feelings of, if not all, then at least one fighter pilot.

For simplicity, I have also taken certain liberties with minor facts, beyond ignoring the historical sequence of events. For example, the members of each flight were given a unique call sign. Even if I could remember all these call signs today their use would confuse the reader and detract from the story itself. So, I have used the call sign "Satan" after my squadron's nickname, as a universal call sign for the flights I flew.

I refer to my navigator not by his real name but instead use the *nom de guerre* "Jack." In fact, the individual described as my friend Jack is in fact an amalgam of several individuals with whom I had the honor of flying.

In my accounts, I show a marked disdain for the senior command elements of the U.S. military who ran the Vietnam War. This goes beyond the normal grousing of military personnel about the top brass. I feel strongly that our politicians horribly mismanaged the war, regardless of the reasons for which it was supposedly fought. However, one can't expect civilian politicians to know anything about fighting a war; that is the job of the generals and admirals. I believe the military folks that ran the war deserve a full helping of blame for not standing up to the Washington crowd when ridiculous orders were sent down the chain of command.

During the decade between the Korean and Vietnam Wars, the country was normally at peace, engaged in only the Cold War with the Soviet Union. Most senior U.S. Air Force (USAF) officers of that era came from a bomber and strategic missile background as former members of Strategic Air Command (SAC).

Personal promotion in the old SAC was based on effective staff work, obsessive unquestioned loyalty, attention to detail, and on not rocking the bureaucratic boat. Few SAC generals knew how to fight a war using fighter planes, or how to fight an extended, non-nuclear war period. Without real life or death combat to roil the organizational waters, the lightweights floated to the top of the USAF personnel pool.

To those of us actually fighting the air war in Vietnam, many decisions made by higher headquarters were patent nonsense. Nonsense that got our friends killed. Even the few fighter pilots who managed to achieve the rank of general, and who should have known better, were co-opted by the bureaucrats and eventually joined them. This is what I believed when I was flying and fighting and what I hold true now. The accounts of this book accurately reflect that myopic viewpoint.

So, what should have happened? How could we have avoided the idiocy? Civilian control of the U.S. military is a cornerstone of our democracy and must not be compromised, no matter how dire the situation. However, any senior military officer can always resign in order to protest grossly stupid commands from politicians if he or she isn't successful in injecting reality into the process. Ours did not, assuming that they did indeed recognize the follies attempted. From my cockpit, it seemed that the senior leadership of the USAF and the U.S. Navy (USN) cared more about their own careers and promotions than about the lives of the men they were sacrificing, throwing away.

I can gratefully say now that the painful lessons of Vietnam were learned and hoisted aboard by all the senior leaders of our military who came afterward. Things are much, much better now. The captains and majors who saw the absurdities of Vietnam, vowed never to let such moronic events happen again. By and large they have been successful and have handed those hard-earned lessons down to their replacements. Lessons painfully acquired are long remembered.

In contrast to the miserable Vietnam era, the American military of today does realistic training. We fight to win. We cooperate and communicate across service lines much more now. Our senior leaders stand up to the politicians and most politicians tend to listen to the experts. Perhaps our elected officials have learned their lessons as well. The positive outcome of the Vietnam War isn't that we prevented the reunification of North and South Vietnam because we didn't; rather, it is that we learned how not to fight a war.

The reunited and benighted country of Vietnam is now enjoying the socialist paradise they have worked so hard to create, despite our best efforts to prevent it. Even with the loss of Vietnam to the forces of political darkness, we did prove the domino theory to be valid. Due to our blood and sacrifice, we kept the dominos from falling, at least they stopped tumbling at Thailand.

Thailand, in my opinion, is the only country in the Southeast Asian region worth saving and we seem to have done that rather well. Continued freedom for Thailand isn't the only accomplishment we can take pride in. We also took another look at who is called upon to fight in our wars.

Since the Vietnam period, the USAF has changed the role of women in uniform. When the events occurred of which I speak in this book, female officers were pretty much limited to a very few military career fields, such as intelligence and nursing. Now, I am proud to say American women are free to undertake whatever they want in the USAF, they fly fighters and command fighter squadrons. They fly and sometimes they die for their country. This is as it should be.

It will not escape even the most casual reader that I, like most male fighter pilots, was not unmoved by a pretty face and/or trim figure, even in the midst of mortal combat and in a hot war zone. No disrespect intended to the female gender; that's just the way it was then and I have to believe that is the way it is now. Some things don't change, nor should they.

This book complains loudly about the ridiculous political and leadership aspects of the Vietnam War. But, it is really about local absurdities. I fought for my life over North Vietnam and returned to air-conditioned comfort at my base. I saw men risk their lives trying to blow up a single truck. Later, I complained when I got chocolate ice cream on my apple pie at the Officers' Club. I fought to the best of my ability in a war that

I knew was unwinnable and I enjoyed doing so. Why I enjoyed such will be revealed in the book.

Lastly, I am well aware that Jack Daniel's is not true Bourbon, but is rather Tennessee Sour Mash Whiskey, a distinction which has only recently become more apparent. During the time frame of the book, the late 1960's, it was considered to be Bourbon by most and thus I have retained that nomenclature. I hope them good ol' boys in Lynchburg, Tennessee forgive me.

I hope you enjoy what is a highly personal view of a strange and exciting time in our nation's history and in my life.

Ed Cobleigh, call sign, "Fast Eddie"

Lt. Colonel, United States Air Force (Retired)

Paso Robles, Calif.

SEWER DOER

Passing silently beneath me in the pitch-black night is the hidden Kingdom of Laos. Overhead, a myriad of stars shines unblinkingly in an uncommonly clear Southeast Asia sky. From 25,000 feet above the night ground, there is no twinkle in the stars; they burn as blue-white points in an inverted bowl of black. The black is reflected below me as well. The low mountains of Laos resemble crumpled velvet heaped against the distant horizon. This velvet land is also speckled with light. The stars are mirrored on the ground, but as angry red dots, not blue-white points. The night sky above is sprinkled with millions of the thermonuclear fires of far-off suns, while below Laos is strewn with hundreds of the small fires of war. The red dots are streamed along areas corresponding to invisible roads and are absent in other more mountainous terrain. The Milky Way is reflected in black and red along the Ho Chi Minh Trail. It is a vivid scene of incredible and terrible beauty, suspending me between the two light fields, one blue-white on the black of space and one angry red on the ebony velvet surface of Laos.

It's two o'clock in the morning and I'm in the sewer yet again. Only this sewer pipe is a U. S. Air Force F-4D Phantom II fighter-bomber suspended in the night sky, traveling at 500 miles an hour. How could a vista of such expansive beauty be sullied by comparisons to a sewer? The fighter jocks in my squadron have read about the U.S. Army's self-named "sewer rats" in action in South Vietnam. These small, wiry soldiers, stripped to the waist, descend into tunnels armed only with a .45 caliber automatic pistol, a Bowie knife, and a flashlight. Their job is to clear the Viet Cong out of the tunnels, or if that is too suicidally difficult, to set off charges collapsing the complex. It is the ultimate in hand-to-hand close combat, mano-à-mano in the dark. We pilots hold such men in professional awe. Perhaps out of rival bravado, maybe hoping we can rub off some of their aura on ourselves, we who regularly fly combat at night dub ourselves the "Sewer Doers" and speak of another night in the sewer.

That combat role analogy may hold true in terms of dark, danger, and aloneness, but not in the world of visual perceptions. The sky and land of Laos are incredibly beautiful tonight. The Phantom jet seems to hang suspended motionless between the immense Milky Way and the long track of fires delineating the Ho Chi Minh Trail. The only visual indication of speed and travel is the inky landscape's slow drifting under the jet's nose; the stars don't seem to move. To preserve my night vision, I have extinguished all the cockpit lights, save one map light dimly illuminating the main instrument panel. If I look closely, I can just discern the indicated air speed of 450 knots. Outside, with my night-adapted eyes I can see the stars as no ground-bound human ever has or ever will. I put my sweat-stained, leather-gloved hand flat against the clear cockpit canopy and I can feel the faint echo of a howling maelstrom of air tearing past the aircraft at a large fraction of the speed of sound. Outside, it is minus thirty degrees Fahrenheit and the air is so thin that, unprotected by cabin pressurization, I would be dead in minutes.

Inside the cockpit, it is peaceful and quiet despite the terrible environment half an inch away on the other side of the canopy. All I can sense is the remote vibration of the engines burning through fifteen gallons of fuel each minute. All I can hear is the sound of my own breathing amplified by the intercom microphone in my oxygen mask. If I hold my breath, I can hear the sounds of my navigator's breathing in the rear cockpit as his soft wheeze is fed into the linked communication system. It is one of life's ironies that modern fighter planes are perceived by nearly everyone to be thunderously loud. There is no doubt that people on the ground 25,000 feet below us tonight can clearly hear the noise of our passage. Yet, all I can hear inside this screaming machine is the soft sounds of two men breathing. My tight-fitted helmet, rubber ear phones, and the efficient insulation filter out the intense noise.

The night cockpit is a secure and safe place; warm, dry, quiet, snug. I would hate to leave it and I wonder how many guys have stayed in their aluminum sanctuary when it was long past time to get out of a dying aircraft. When an airplane is coming unglued, I'm sure the common emotional tendency is to want to stay in it. It occurs to me that likewise when your personal life is coming unglued, flying is an addictive refuge. Many pilots under personal stress hide in the sky. For some, the sour fear of combat is more familiar and more comfortable than the terror of a deteriorating martial relationship. But, tonight, no one is contemplating ejection from the aircraft and there are no personal, ground-bound demons from which to hide.

As scenic as it can be, night flying isn't for everyone, hence the self-defined exclusive clique of us Sewer Doers. It is disorienting and unfamiliar, with precious few of the visual cues which mankind has evolved to use for the maintenance of physical and mental balance. For eons, people have depended on their sense of sight to identify danger, to keep from colliding with things, including the ground. However, tonight the hazards of the jagged terrain are largely invisible; it would be easy to fly out of the sky and into the world. Ground targets are also hard to spot, and intentionally so. The Bad Guys, the guys in the symbolic black hats, move under the cloak of darkness to avoid detection by the Sewer Doers. After dark in Southeast Asia, the weather can be intimidating, with thunderstorms climbing in fury to 50,000 feet. It is not uncommon to have lightning playing over the canopy like a green plasma spider web, the light show known as St. Elmo's Fire. At night it is harder to find the airborne tanker aircraft full of transferable fuel to prolong flying time and life, or are those the same things? On the upside, the sparkle of antiaircraft fire and the rocket motors of surface-to-air missiles are so much easier to see at night. If you believe that what you don't see won't hurt you, then fly in the daytime.

We Sewer Doers also fly at night for another reason; no brass to cope with. Older, more senior officers hate flying at night; it deprives them of opportunities for promotional face time with the local commanders and it is physically more dangerous. Sewer doing may be hazardous to your career as well as to your health. So, with squadron headquarters deserted at night, things are more informal with less saluting. The physical as well as the military climate is also more temperate. These are the tropics; the cooler temperatures after dark make for more comfortable flight planning, pre-flighting the aircraft, and just living. Sewer doing is a kinder, gentler, more informal way to fight a war, at least until the real fighting starts.

But now, it is time to go to work and quit gawking at the celestial light show, we are nearing the target area. I press the radio microphone button with my thumb on the inboard throttle and, summoning my best southern accent, transmit.

"Alley Cat, Satan Flight of two, across the fence, going mission frequency."

No one knows why all fighter pilots are expected to have southern accents; that's just the way it is. Mine is Tennessee bred- in and natural, and there are still universal verbal conventions to be followed. The referenced fence is both a geographical as well as a conceptual one; it is the largest river in Southeast Asia, the mighty Mekong. It is also the border between Thailand, which is mostly peaceful, and Laos, which is anything but.

A hundred miles to the rear over north-central Thailand, a lumbering C-130 Hercules, or "'Herky Bird", a four-engined transport plane, orbits in constant oval patterns. In the cargo compartment sits a large metal box full of radios and sleepy men sitting at glowing consoles. This is the Airborne Command and Control Center, known by the radio call sign "Alley Cat." My transmission arouses a particular major from a mental review of his memories of home. His job is to keep track of all the flights working the southern Ho Chi Minh Trail tonight and to pass along hot target information, weather data, tanker locations, and general encouragement. Satan Flight, that's my wingman and me, has drawn a very good controller tonight, an officer tagged with the nickname "Bruce" by the fighter jocks. Bruce earns his call sign from his lisping, swishy accent. Aurally, he fits all the stereotypes of an out-of-the-closet homosexual. No Sewer Doer has ever met Bruce in person, but we all know him by the sound of his voice in our earphones. As much fun as we make of Bruce in absentia (for example, "I'm excited when Bruce handles me"), he is the best controller going, unflappable, knowledgeable, and highly professional. Bruce is a pleasure to work with and I feel better when he is on the job.

Bruce replies with, "Satan Flight, you're cleared to mission frequency, good luck, and good hunting."

Then he adds the predicted local altimeter setting and signs off. The altimeter setting is important; without it we won't know our exact altitude above the ground and Bruce knows that we will be operating at low level tonight, below the highest mountain peaks. We appreciate Bruce wishing us luck, but we would rather eat a bug than admit it.

I key the mike again and command, "Satan, mission freq."

I hear two clicks in my headphones in reply.

Fifty feet away is another Phantom, floating unseen off my right wing as Satan Two. My wingman has been flying formation in the night, keeping his relative position constant by watching the formation lights on the nose and tail of my aircraft. These are green glowing strips similar to a household night light. Instead of dispelling a sleeping child's fears, these pale, dim panels allow night formation flying without much fear of disorientation. I have turned their intensity down gradually since takeoff to preserve my wingman's night vision and I have extinguished all other external lights on my aircraft for the same reason. My wingie has turned everything off on his jet, including the strip lights. We will soon need all the night vision we can muster, and not just to admire the stars. If I look closely, I can see the outline of his plane only as it obscures the fires far below. Satan Two is slightly lower than my jet and slightly to the rear. Against the inky background of Laos, he is nearly invisible, but there all the same.

Flying as Satan Two tonight are another two Sewer Doers, my wingman and his navigator. I can talk to them on the radio and hear their replies as clearly as if they were plugged into my own intercom. However, I can't see them and even if I could, the blacked-out separation between the two jets hurtling in the dark over Laos at 500 mph makes the other two men as remote from physical contact and sight as if they were with Neil Armstrong on the absent moon.

I know my wingman in many ways better than I know my own brothers. Flying together for many nights has merged our two aircraft and four heads into a seamless, coordinated team. I know what he is doing at most times without asking, and generally where he is in the featureless night sky without ever seeing his airplane. He knows what I am thinking, often before I do. Night flying in the sewer darkly distills aerial combat down to its naked essentials. The large, multiple ship formations assembled and flown in the daytime are unworkable at night; two is the maximum and it is also the minimum number of jets. Operating more than two aircraft in close proximity is dangerous and unwieldy at night. Fewer than two is no better; flying alone at night is a good way to not come back with no one knowing why you didn't.

Our thinking is so aligned that few radio calls are required and such is our familiarity with the attack plan that we will need very little feedback to stay in touch as violent events unfold. The two answering clicks on the radio instead of the USAF standard reply, "Satan Two," are sufficient for me to know that Satan Two has heard me and will meet me on the new frequency.

I wait until my navigator has changed the radio frequency and transmit, "Satan Two. Check. Take spacing."

I hear the same two clicks in reply once again.

Satan Two is on frequency and is starting to pull both throttles back, reducing power, allowing his jet to drop behind my Phantom. Invisibly and silently, he slips off my wing and slides farther and farther rearward. I can never really visually confirm that he is there; I can only trust that he is. Unseen, he drops in trail and I sense, rather than see, his departure rearward. I haven't heard his voice since leaving our base in Thailand, only clicks on the radio.

I have read somewhere that women bond with their female friends by means of frequent verbal conversation, but that men bond by doing guy things together. If this is so, then night combat flying is the ultimate male bonding experience, all doing and no talking.

Without conscious notice, I start keeping track of vitally important spatial relationships in the Laotian night sky. I try to keep a running mental picture of the location of my jet, my wingman, the target, the ground, the borders, and the direction to our home base, even the position of faraway Bruce in Alley Cat. Flying combat at night is like playing blindfolded chess, only with fewer pieces and in three dimensions. Taking a deep breath, I turn off the dimly glowing strip lights and remind myself to ignore the starlight above. It is time to put on our own light show down there on the hostile ground.

Suddenly, a small scope similar to a radar display three inches in diameter on the top of the instrument panel comes to life. A bright green strobe appears on the tiny scope, pointing at the six o'clock position, toward the tail of my aircraft. My wingman has locked his air intercept radar onto my Phantom. Using his radar, he can keep track of my position ahead of him and precisely maintain the planned distance between us. This exact spacing is important for tonight's plan of attack; our respective arrival times over the target must be sequenced exactly right. A less experienced pilot would have transmitted on the radio, "Two's tied," indicating a radar lock-on. However, Satan Two knows I'll see the strobe on my scope and that no radio call is needed.

I pull my own throttles back slightly, reducing power and lowering the nose slightly to begin a gradual descent. The Phantom is a machine with high aerodynamic drag defeated by large engines. It doesn't take much thrust reduction to descend as the drag side of the equation starts to prevail. If I take off too much power, the deceleration would be like running into a wall of black Jell-O. Nothing changes in the cockpit; the noise level remains quietly disturbed only by the sound our own breathing. Slowly the altimeter unwinds, indicating that we are going down. The indistinct horizon climbs in my peripheral field of view, the inky black of Laos grows larger, and the starlit cosmos grows smaller and more distant. The sensation generated by the view outside the aircraft canopy is one of being slowly immersed in a darker shade of black, of submerging into deep water. Sewer water.

I keep busy setting up the armament switches, selecting the weapons, designating the delivery mode, and lastly, activating the master arm switch. The ordnance is now "hot." My leather gloves, palms sweaty with nervous tension, dance around the cockpit, guided by memory, by feel, and by the dim red glow of the map light. I work by touch and long habit, calling out each switch position on the intercom to my navigator for a mental double check. In a few seconds, the Phantom is hot-armed and ready for mortal combat.

The familiar routine of switch selection is somehow comforting despite its lethal intent. Doing something quickly and well which I've done several hundred times before gives me the impression that I can control the developing situation, that the routine will play out this time as it always has in the past. Maybe doing small tasks with precision will endow the larger and more dangerous tasks to be undertaken later with a better chance of success.

Tonight's attack plan is simple in concept but difficult to execute. If the Bad Guys are there and awake, it promises to be an exciting night. I wouldn't attempt this tactic if I didn't trust my wingman explicitly to do his part and to do it well. Our target area is a ford crossing the largest river in southern Laos except for the river border with Thailand, the Mekong. The North Vietnamese are running convoys of trucks up and down the muddy spider web of jungle roads the stateside media likes to call the "Ho Chi Minh Trail." The so-called trail is not one track but a network of single-track dirt roads clinging to the sides of mountains, spanning the local rivers and creeks. Air strikes years ago dropped all the bridges in Laos. There have been no bridges intact since the last war, or perhaps the one before that. The enemy's trucks have to ford rivers where they can. Our job is to ensure they don't survive the crossing. The "trail" is used only at night and our intelligence system has little capability to predict when and where. We have to concentrate our fire on known choke points such as tonight's target.

We will drop down to low altitude, below the tops of the nearby mountain peaks, slopes unseen in the darkness, and will fly down the valley of the equally invisible river. Over the ford I will release a series of. parachute flares. The flares are metal tubes about a yard long and six inches in diameter filled with magnesium powder and suspended from a small parachute. After a short time delay, the flares will ignite in a line straddling the ford, dispelling the Laotian night. Burning magnesium will generate blue-white light projected in circles beneath each flare. There will be a stark line of division between light and dark. Hopefully the flares will flame into life directly over the ford. They should hang underneath their chutes a few minutes, long enough to illuminate the targeted areas of the river crossing and the banks on each side. We will have a few precious minutes to work before the flares burn out and the jungle darkness returns to mask the scene.

With my jet passing overhead the shallow ford at 575 mph, the flares will ignite without warning. The trucks will not have time to complete splashing across the river or to get out from under the flickering light before coming under attack from Satan Two. That is if the ford is in use tonight, which we have no way of knowing. Four guys in two airplanes will attempt a difficult and dangerous task with no assurance of any success.

If everything works out, it will be like walking into the dingy kitchen of a cheap dive late at night and throwing on the light switch. We hope to see dozens of trucks scurrying for the safety of the dense jungle cover like cockroaches running for the sewer drain. The lumbering, Russian-built trucks with their dirty canvas bedcovers look like filthy bugs from the air and their drivers' frantic attempts to drive quickly across the rocky ford will only reinforce the tropical insect image.

Flying a precisely timed distance behind me, my wingman should arrive on the scene just as the flares ignite and before the scuttling trucks can reach shelter outside the flare light. He will have to press his attack before they can escape into the dense foliage or hide in the inky darkness. He will be at a higher altitude suitable for dive bombing and if bugs are beetling, he will light up the night with bomb explosions and the fiery destruction of burning trucks.

However, my immediate challenge is to fly down the river in the middle of the night without hitting the valley walls. Jack, my navigator has programmed his gear, correctly I hope, to give me steering commands on my attitude indicator in the front cockpit instrument panel. Once he activates the proper mode, I will see a needle superimposed on the little black-and-white globe in the display. All I have to do is to fly the actual aircraft so as to keep that needle centered over the little miniature aircraft symbol on the display. If all the navigation calculations are correct and nothing goes terribly wrong, the flares will ignite over the target about the time we are climbing away to relative safety.

As we descend, the Laotian air becomes hotter, wetter, and turbulent. At altitude, the atmosphere is serene, calm, even clean. Closer to the steaming jungle, heat left over from the day rises in thermals that deflect the jet's flight, causing bumps in the night. It gets more difficult for me to keep the needle on the display centered and to fly at the right altitude. Too high and the circles of flare light will be too small to illuminate the truck bugs. Too low and the dripping rain forest will welcome the jet and us. It gets hotter in the cockpit, both from the jungle below and from the exertion required to keep the tossing, bucking Phantom on course. If I could take off my oxygen mask, I'm sure I could detect the smell of slowly rotting tropical vegetation floating in the warm, sluggish river below. The planned airspeed for the delivery is 500 knots, about 575 miles per hour. I have put both throttles full forward and I am much too busy to jockey them. The speed will be what it will be; exactly as fast as a Phantom can go at this altitude.

I know that on each side of our course, vegetation-clad mountains rise in steep vertical escarpments named "karsts." In the daytime, these gray limestone rock formations resemble giant decaying teeth, patchily covered with green plaque and riddled with cavities. At night, they are invisible, but still sensed. I fight the temptation to look for the karsts outside the cockpit; all I could see would be more blackness. But I know they're there. Survival and success depend on making the instrument panel my whole universe, the total focus of my attention. The humid jungle and its beckoning cliffs have to be ignored. I don't have time to let fear be a part of the action. Concern for doing the job right is paramount. I know that if I do my job well and the navigator has done his, this maneuver will succeed.

I hold down the "pickle button" to permit the release of the string of flares; the weapons release computer will order the actual drop. During WWII, the bomb release button on B-17s was indeed the shape, size, and color of a dill pickle and the name stuck. In a modern fighter it is a small red button on top of the control stick.

The flares are not heavy enough to make an impression on the jet when they are forcibly ejected aft; I feel nothing in the bucking cockpit when they leave. After what seems like an eternity of high workload flying, the navigator calls, "Flares away."

Relieved, I make sure the wings are level on the attitude indicator and suck the stick back into my lap. Climbing rapidly away from the foul jungle, we feel the G forces build and both of us sigh, partly from the force of temporarily weighing four times normal, but also from release of tension and from the dank world not so far below the jet. The onset of the G forces seems to have a cleansing effect, it's as if the increased G is pulling out all the strain and danger of flying fast close to unseen ground at night. Fighting mental strain with cleansing physical stress seems to produce a sort of uneasy balance. Most aircrew believe the reason we are so well adjusted and nonflyers are so confused is that a steady regime of increased Gs pulls the bad vibes out, probably through our assholes. This mental therapy is unavailable to the ground-bound.

Happily I spot the star-studded boundary that denotes the ragged black horizon and resume flying the Phantom by visual references instead of by artificial gauges. All fighter pilots like to turn left. It is easier to turn and look toward the left side where your arm rests on the throttles. I complete a climbing left turn and roll out on a heading opposite to the direction on which we laid the flares. I level off at an altitude well above the grasping karsts and take my first relaxed breath in minutes. At least we didn't get shot at; we noted no antiaircraft fire, no surface-to-air missiles, and no enemy action of any kind.

As I get my bearings, I re-establish my mental picture of the night air battle space. Satan Two should just now be approaching the targeted ford. One by one, the flares ignite and I can see the meandering path of the lazy river as the steely gray water reflects the flare light. I can make out the dirty foam waves caused by the shallow ford and the sticky mud road that leads to and from the river crossing. The images below dance in the night as the flares dangle and sway under their parachutes. Anxiously I scan the circles of light cast by the flares and diffused by the jungle humidity, looking for scurrying trucks and waiting for my wingman's ordnance to start detonating among them.

Unexpectedly, my attention is diverted to an area south of the river, among the jagged karsts. An oblong flame path erupts in the middle of the darkness giving a bright texture to the broken ground. It isn't the sharp flash followed by total darkness of an exploding bomb. It isn't the white sparkle of a swarm of cluster bombs. It isn't, although I want it to be, the greasy red smear and persistent orange flames of napalm. The fire burns crimson and yellow; a small mushroom cloud of hot gas and flame rises a few hundred feet in the air and then fades out. The inferno doesn't light up the surrounding area as one would expect, but rather seems to burn in isolation against an pitch-black background. The burning ovoid lives for a few seconds, maybe ten, and then just as quickly dies, leaving a scattering of glowing embers in the Asian jungle night like a poorly doused campfire.

My navigator instantly spots the smeared fire when I do and comes up on the intercom with his voice only slightly elevated in pitch.

"Holy shit! What was that?" he asks.

He knows very well what it was and I know that he knows, but some routines must be obeyed, no matter what. Following established norms, even to the point of expressing pro-forma profanity, is a good way to keep calm. Instead of replying, I push the microphone button to call Satan Two, even though I don't want to and I don't want to a lot. I transmit, in what I hope is my best controlled, almost bored, southern accent.

"Satan Two, your position?"

Neither one of us in my plane is surprised when there is no reply on the radio, only silent blackness in the night and the sound of our breathing amplified over the intercom. My solar plexus feels like I was sucker punched in the gut by Mohammed Ali. There is a sinking feeling inside me that is almost sickening. I want to throw up. I try to raise Satan Two on the radio a few more times, including using the emergency channel, and then reluctantly start a climb to higher altitude to better make contact with Bruce in Alley Cat.

The fire on the ground is almost gone now, with only a few scattered embers left alive in the night. As I climb, those become even dimmer and farther away. Suddenly, I feel totally alone over southern Laos, with only my navigator and myself to cope with shitty life in the sewer.

As calmly as I can manage, I notify Bruce in Alley Cat that I have lost contact with my wingman, referring to our target's coded location. I have to be careful when relaying information over the radio; the Bad Guys monitor our frequencies. Bruce has already heard my emergency channel radio calls and is ready for the bad news. At his command, a well-oiled search-and-rescue operation swings into action across Thailand and into Laos. The rescue people have done this before; the drill is not unfamiliar.

At an air base on the Thai/Laotian border, by the river, a crew runs to another Herky Bird and the four propellers start to spin. This aircraft, call sign "King," will launch immediately to assume the role of rescue coordinator. King is a flying command post as well as an aerial refueling craft. The slow, lumbering Herky Bird is perfect for refueling helicopters and can remain on station for half a day if required. The crew manning King are search-and-rescue specialists; they have done this more times than they or I want to think about.

At the same base, a flight of two A-1E Skyraiders is preparing for a predawn takeoff; the sleepy pilots are studying the target information relayed to them by Bruce. They don't need much study; they know this section of Laos like their own hometowns. They too have been here many times before. The Skyraider, call sign "Sandy," is a relic of the Korean War. It is a single piston engine, propeller-driven attack plane that flies about as fast as a Phantom does on takeoff. The Sandys are armed to the teeth with a nasty variety of guns and special antipersonnel munitions, some of which I don't want to know about. It is their job to orbit the area of the intended rescue and keep the Bad Guys' heads down while the rescue helicopters pick up the downed aircrew. With many hours of fuel on board, the Sandys will be overhead the target area at first light.

The search-and-rescue helicopter used in these sorts of operations is nicknamed the "Jolly Green Giant," call sign "Jolly." They work in pairs, but are now waiting, they won't get airborne until there is some indication that there are indeed survivors to pick up. The Alley Cat, King, Sandy, and Jolly team is well oiled, trained, and ready. They do this a lot, unfortunately.

In the aircraft now closest to the action, I serve as the on-scene commander until the rescue team arrives overhead the crash site. My flight time is going to be extended by aerial refueling until I'm relieved on station. It looks like a long night in the sewer.

I jettison the flare dispenser pods to save drag and thus fuel, bombing them off the wing stations with the pickle button. I then enter a racetrack flight path over the location of the now unseen ford at 25,000 feet. Suddenly, the night sky over Laos has become a lonely, empty place for one solitary Phantom to fly. There is nothing to do but orbit, watch the fuel gauge, and listen for any radio transmissions from the ground. Candidate survivors (that would be us) are trained to maintain silence on their survival radios until dawn to prevent the Bad Guys, who also are listening, from pinpointing the rescue site. If either of the crewmembers of Satan Two was able to eject from the jet, he may be on the air at dawn. The ultimate good news will be to hear two voices on the personal radios.

As my navigator and I bore holes in the sky, the cockpit intercom is silent. We are no doubt thinking the same thing. With no antiaircraft fire seen and no indication of hostile action, this tragic episode looks like a case of what the official after-action report will refer to as "cause of loss unknown." This usually means flying into the ground. But there is always hope.

After two more long airborne hours interrupted by a trip back to Thailand for an aerial refueling, we are done for the night when King arrives in the area to take command. The pros onboard the Herky Bird will maintain the radio listening watch until fuel or hope run out.

King comes up on the mission frequency.

"Satan One, you're relieved. We'll take it from here. Tough luck tonight."

I don't want to leave this scene and yet I want to get away from here as quickly as I can. I turn the Phantom to the memorized heading that will take us to our base in Thailand and push the twin throttles forward.

The landing, an hour before dawn, is uneventful. I taxi the jet to the bunkered shelter and shut it down. As I open the canopy, the warm moist air of Thailand, fragrant and sticky, envelops me like a friend's hug. Slowly, the engines wind down to silence and the Phantom goes to sleep. The crew chief on the ground beneath the cockpit refuses to look at me as he chocks the wheels and puts up the access ladder. Normally, the enlisted troops like to hear a brief account of the mission and joke about the condition in which I've returned their precious airplane, but not tonight. At the line shack, I fill out the maintenance forms, the senior sergeants standing there are also silent. It is the silence of a death in the family that no one knows how to discuss. They lost one of their pampered airplanes, the object of their attention during most of their waking hours. They lost an aircrew and an airplane. I lost two close friends.

On our solitary trudge down the flight line back to the squadron, no one returns my gaze. No one says hello. No one acknowledges our presence as my navigator and I walk by. There is none of the camaraderie that makes life in a fighter squadron so intense and so enjoyable. People step aside and let us pass by a wide margin. This is due in part to the looks on our faces and partly due to the situation. When there is a loss, an aircraft shot down, word gets around the base like wildfire, even in the wee hours of the morning. Some otherwise well-meaning guys just don't know what to say to a crew that just lost their wingmen. Others fear that sudden death might be contagious and that bad luck rubs off. I guess that we are walking reminders of mortality and of the short odds of wartime survival.

We spend what seems like an eternity debriefing the somber, female intelligence officers about what happened, what we saw and heard, and what we didn't. We go over the maps again and try to locate the fireball on the ground and from that point attempt to extrapolate where an ejection could have occurred. We try to discern where the crew of Satan Two might have bailed out, where the winds carried the parachutes, and thus suggest where the rescue forces should start their search. All three of us think this is an exercise in futility, there is little hope that anyone ejected before that fireball blossomed, but once again, certain norms have to be obeyed and certain forms have to be filled out. When there is nothing more to say, we depart the cluttered rat's nest of the intelligence shop and make our individual ways back to the squadron. My navigator and I are miles apart, walking together. When we get to squadron headquarters, he disappears into the fading night without a sound.

Each USAF fighter squadron has a logbook where pilots sign out for each flight, a relic from the days when you actually signed for possession of the aircraft. Upon returning, you fill in the logbook with your takeoff and landing times, flight time, and other administrivia. At the end of each line, there is a short space for a few words to sum up the flight. Most guys put "successful" or "weather bad" or maybe "mission complete" or some such homily.

There, below my sign-out signature is the line containing the printed name of my wingman and his signature, his last act of bureaucratic compliance. After I complete my entry I note his takeoff time and draw a line through the rest of the blanks. At the end, I add, "Satan Two did not return from this mission," and close the book. That is the last entry for tonight. The admin sergeant will start a new page for the coming day.

I store my flight gear in the personal equipment shop, hanging my parachute harness and my many-pocketed survival vest on their pegs, strip off my anti-g suit, balance my helmet on its own shelf, and secure my automatic pistol, cartridge belt, and Bowie knife away in my locker. The personal equipment (PE) shop is full of guys preparing for the early day missions, the "dawn patrols." They have woken up at 0430 and are preparing for flight while it is dark outside order to take off at dawn. The atmosphere on a normal morning resembles a college sports locker room. The rows of harnesses, helmets, and lockers add to the athletic analogy, but the games we dress for in this locker room are played for keeps.

Even at this ungodly hour, our conversation usually runs to sharp banter and relentless kidding. This is the verbal means men use to achieve intimacy, without seeming to do so and without admitting what they are doing. Wisecracks and jokes also tend to take the edge off the situation; banal conversation masks the deadly seriousness of what we are about to do or what we have just done.

This morning things are much different. The mood is somber, the banter forced and artificial. The day flyers ask a few cursory questions about what happened. Did I see any flak? What about the weather? The questions and the corresponding answers are less detailed than one would predict. There is no mystery here; all the guys are only too knowledgeable about this sort of action. Given a few facts, they can fill in the blanks. There is also the contagion aspect; no one wants to think too much about what can happen, knowing that blind, uncontrollable luck is also at play here. If the confidence that lets you take these sorts of risks depends on believing that you have a high degree of control over events, you don't want to think about luck. While bad luck isn't contagious, crippling fear may very well be, so why risk it? Finally comes the payoff: did I think the two guys in Satan Two got out of the aircraft before impact? All I can do is shake my head: The words won't come, they're stuck in my throat.

Some questions reflect morbid curiosity, some a desire to gather self-preservation data, and some are clumsy attempts to emotionally connect. I do my best to answer, but mostly I'm treated as if I have a case of the plague, the lost wingman disease. Silently, the guys file out of the PE shop en-route to briefing their day sorties and I am once again alone.

In a front corner of the crowded PE shop is a well-worn Government Issue fridge. It harbors a line of bottles of Bourbon whiskey and multiple cans of cold cola. This stash is provided by a regulation on the books since World War I in the days of the U.S. Army Air Corps. Back then, pilots endured long flights in open cockpit biplanes, experiencing freezing temperatures at high altitude. After their missions, the effect of a shot of alcohol on a half-frozen body was perceived by them to be warming. We know now that the opposite is true, booze only makes you feel warmer; actually it is chilling you. The increased circulation of blood caused by the alcohol radiates precious body heat. However, the medical officers of the day wrote into the books a rule stating that every aircrew member was entitled to three ounces of free whisky immediately after every flight. During World War II, conditions had improved a bit with closed, heated cockpits, albeit at higher and colder altitudes, but the regulation remained in the manuals. The mandated tradition of free mission booze was carried on in Korea. but was largely forgotten during the Cold War when no official combat sorties were flown.

During the first days of what became known as the Vietnam War, some USAF pilot, long returned to the States, found this obscure regulation on the books and brought it to the attention of the powers that be. This unnamed airman is now acclaimed locally as a genius. Consequently, the United States Air Force is required by its own regulations to furnish the PE shop with "Post Mission" booze for the warming and the enjoyment of combat aircrew. That's the good news. The bad news is that the USAF procurement channels are compelled to buy goods, including booze, from the lowest bidder. So, the fridge is amply stocked with the cheapest rotgut available, bought at $1.75 a fifth, tax free. Most of the guys won't drink it on a bet, but this early morning I will. I could go to the Officers' Club; the bar is open 24/7. But social interaction is not on my personal agenda just now. Also I feel that my morose presence at the club would put a damper on human spirits there.

I take out a cold can of cola, pop it open, and drain half of it in one gulp. I refill the can with mission booze and close the fridge.

A local Thai contractor who knows how to build Thai-style buildings and nothing else constructed the squadron building. So, the structure is raised on short pilings to keep the floors dry in the monsoon flood season and it is ringed with a covered porch, complete with railings and government General Accounting Office metal chairs. It is a welcome change from the stateside uniformity of government architecture. The porch is always inviting, even now.

Coming down from a prolonged adrenaline high, I slump with the weak-boned weariness of defeat in a waiting folding chair and prop my legs up on the wooden railing, staring with unfocused eyes out into the breaking dawn. Dawn is Thailand's best time. I'm glad I'm still here to see it. The oppressive heat hasn't built yet and the humidity is still soft and friendly. Sometimes, the rising sun backlights thunderstorms left over from the previous night, but today's new sky is cloudless and barren. The air base is strangely quite just before dawn with no howling jet noise. The Sewer Doers have landed and the early daylight flights have yet to fire up. Watching dawn break is a relaxing way to end a night of high energy flying and I usually welcome the opportunity as a deserved reward. You have to relax fast in the tropics, as the sun seems to leap vertically out of the eastern sky to take command of the day. None of this registers this morning as I swill my cheap Bourbon and cola and stare out into a mental void. Other guys, who I would normally greet and exchange insults with pass silently, letting me be. I am clearly not in a talkative mood and they all know why.

I run the mission over and over again in my head like an endless loop on a tape deck. I mentally review the mission planning, the maps, the briefing, the data, looking for something I could have done better, some error of omission or commission. What started the fatal chain of events that ended with the impact of an F-4 against the Laotian karst? What could I, the Flight Leader, have done differently? What went wrong? Who screwed up? I am reluctant to blame events on bad luck and even more loath to chalk the crash up to a mistake made by Satan Two. Either explanation has profound implications on my own chances of living through this shitty war and I don't want to run either of those root causes out to their logical conclusion. Try as I might, I can't find any rational, correctible reason why there are almost certainly two fewer crewmembers and one less aircraft now in the squadron.

Some place else I don't want to go is to allow thoughts of my wingman's early life to pop into my consciousness. His life now has only a past and no future. The images of a childhood, of loving parents, of schoolmates, and of graduations keep interrupting my dedicated mission analysis. I envision him as a college student and then as a junior officer, although I didn't know him then. I remember the times we ravaged the bar at the O Club and the poker games in the officers' quarters. All that has been "terminated with extreme prejudice" and the experience he gained has been wasted. Two vibrant lives have been thrown away trying to torch a few junk trucks which cost the Red Chinese $800, max, to build.

I hope the venal politicians and careerist senior officers who sponsor, plan, and run this sorry excuse for a war are losing as much sleep over it as I am. Do they know they are throwing away the cream of our nation's manhood bombing $800 trucks? If they know, do they care? What sort of industrial-strength rationalization do you have to dream up which allows you to send guys out night after night on a fool's mission? Finally, the free booze does its job and I can no longer mentally focus on tonight's failed mission. The images that I am trying in vain to suppress become dominant and this conversation with myself turns in Lufbery circles inside my head.

I crush the cola can with my shaking hands and throw it as far out into today's dawn as I can, hearing it splash into the green scum-frosted canal paralleling the squadron porch. I had better get back to the officers' quarters and get some sleep. I'll need to start breaking in a new wingman. The newly updated squadron scheduling board says I'm back in the sewer tonight.

Weeks later, after a few drinks, my navigator tries to verbally express what we both saw. His imaginative description is all the more surprising coming from him, normally a taciturn and inarticulate man. Imagination is not a quality highly prized among navigators as imaginative navigation is dysfunctional in the extreme. More importantly, when you trust your life to the flying skills of another guy in. the front cockpit, too much imagination can be worrisome. But, from somewhere down deep inside himself, my navigator tells me the fireball impressed him at the time as resembling two vaporous souls trying to hold on to this world, to survive and to not leave it. The mushroom cloud of hot gasses represented the spirits of two human beings unwillingly torn from their physical bodies, but not willing to go quietly into the long night. As the fire burned itself out, he perceived they were at last consumed and lost forever to this world, floating away into the stinking wet air of the Laotian jungle.

Also later, during one of the sleepless days that substitute for my nights; I am in my bunk holding the nightmares at bay. In my mind's eye, I see for the umpteenth time the image of a huge gash on the black surface of the night world, opening up a momentary glimpse down into hell itself. I see an earth wounded by the impact of 50,000 pounds of fighter jet. But as I watch from overhead, the gash is healed from below to scab off and close the wound. The peek into an incandescent underworld lying just below the sweating jungle fades with the dying fireball.

Which image is more accurate, the one of my sleep-deprived imagination or that of my navigator's, which he gathered in real time on the spot? I don't know and I don't know if it matters. All that counts is that we both have to deal with what we remember.

MIG NIGHT CAP

A gray-dark aluminum cloud is suspended above me, obscuring the staring stars. It is the night of a full moon and I am flying in the moon's shadow cast by the metal overcast just above my jet. I have stuck my F-4 Phantom underneath and slightly behind the large, dark airplane. While looking upward through my canopy, I am flying close formation on a KC-135A Stratotanker, the military version of the Boeing 707, a flying gas station in the sky. The Phantom is a large aircraft, particularly for a fighter, but as the KC-135 hovers over me in the night, it seems huge by comparison. The 707 is blanking out the moon and stars. But, I can see rays of moonlight illuminating the silhouette of the large transport above me in ghostly pale blue light.

My navigator and I are on a night MiG CAP. Our mission is to fly Combat Air Patrol, or CAP, looking for enemy aircraft. MiGs are known by the acronym identifying the Russian factory where they are built. For us Sewer Doers, used to hurling our pink bodies at the black ground night after night, a CAP mission is a welcome change of pace. We get to stay up at high altitude, use different weapons systems, maybe get into some air-to-air combat, and generally enjoy ourselves. Of course, the ultimate objective of tonight's flight, or any other combat mission for that matter, is to shoot down a MiG.

The North Vietnamese only fly MiGs and only they fly them in the combat zone over their own country, so any one we find is fair game for a kill. The concept of a CAP or of a free-ranging aerial sweep is an old one, dating from the dawn years of military aviation. Biplanes flew the first CAPs during WWI. This tactic was conceived and developed by the likes of Capt. Eddie Rickenbacker, the original "Fast Eddie", of the U.S. Army Air Service and Col. Manfred von Richthofen, the real Red Baron, of the German Air Force, albeit without the aerial refueling which we are to perform tonight. The weight of flying history is absent and forgotten in the immediate necessity to get my jet filled with fuel at 22,000 feet over northern Thailand at one o'clock in the morning.

Aerial refueling has been the subject of faltering experiments ever since the days of the WWI aces, but was really perfected during the 1950s by the USAF Strategic Air Command. SAC wanted to base its huge jet bombers safely on the U.S. mainland and not on unreliable overseas airfields. However, the bombers of the day couldn't reach the Soviet Union and return to the United States without running out of fuel. There are those of us who believe returning home from a thermonuclear war sortie is quite unlikely no matter how much fuel you have. However, the requirements of aircrew morale dictated that the bomber crews be given a fighting chance to do just that. This concept of operations required the perfection of the techniques of aerial refueling and the development of specialized aircraft to make it possible. Hence, the dark metallic cloud flying thirty feet over the top of my canopy tonight.

Once SAC's bombers and tankers perfected the art and science of refueling in midair, it didn't take the fighter guys long to grasp the possibilities this offered. Always alert for a good deal, the fighter force realized SAC's tankers could allow fulfillment of one of the cardinal objectives of flying fighters; more flying time. You can get more flying time and have more fun doing it if you don't have to land to refuel. Seriously, this new capability reversed a tactical setback caused by the jet age. During WWII, piston engined, propeller-driven fighters such as the P-51 Mustang and the P-38 Lightning had enough fuel to escort bombers almost to the limits of the bombers' own range. This was the fabled "long reach" that gave bombers a fighter escort from their bases in England to Berlin and back, an eight hour mission. In fact, my current outfit, the 8th Tactical Fighter Wing, the "'Wolf Pack," earned its spurs and nickname on long-range patrols in the European theater of WWII. My ass hurts just thinking about sitting on a lumpy parachute for eight hours. However, things changed radically during the Korean War. The new jets with their greedy fuel consumption reduced fighter missions to an hour or two, not long enough to fly an effective CAP or to satisfy the jocks' need for flight time. So, all modern U.S. fighters are capable of aerial refueling. Whether their pilots are capable of pulling this off is another question.

Aerial refueling is simple in concept, but difficult in practice. It is the hardest thing I have ever tried to learn to do on the short list of things which I eventually succeeded in doing. I never did learn how to play third base well. My plan is to fly the Phantom in steady formation slightly below and to the rear of the KC-135. On the top spine of my fighter, behind the rear cockpit, is a receptacle hidden behind a remotely controlled trap door. I have opened the door and the locking ring of the receptacle is ready. Attached to the rear underside of the KC-135 is a flying boom, a pipe about fifty feet long. The boom is free to move up and down, left and right within certain angular limits. It is flown by two attached wing-like elevons controlled by a crewmember in the tanker, the "Boomer." The Boomer lies on his stomach on the floor of the KC-135 and peers at the action out a window in the belly of the tanker, while flying the boom with his own joystick. The boom also retracts and extends over a fifteen-foot range. It has on its tip a plug-in nozzle that exactly fits into the receptacle on my jet.

Each of us involved in this action has specific duties, which we must accomplish flawlessly. The tanker pilot's job is to hold a steady course and altitude, holding his big plane rock solid in the sky to give me a fixed reference on which to fly formation. My job is to fly precise formation, holding the relative position of my Phantom constant with reference to the tanker, keeping within an imaginary box defined by the reach limits of the boom. The boomer's job is to fly the boom over the top of my canopy without hitting and smashing the Plexiglas. He will then position the nozzle over the Phantom's receptacle. Once we all achieve precise alignment, the Boomer extends the tubular boom, thrusting the nozzle into the receptacle, where the locking ring will grasp it. My navigator's job is to worry a lot and monitor the whole scene. He is the only one not totally focused on a particular flying task and can be alert for danger, of which there is plenty. Once a solid linkup is achieved, fuel flows automatically from the KC-135 through the boom into the F-4's nearly empty fuel tanks.

The sexual analog to this process is obvious and the source of a zillion jokes, most of them bad and all of them old. However, neither sex nor jokes are on my mind tonight, only getting this refueling done and done well.

I will be aided in my formation flying by two rows of lights on the tanker's belly up toward the nose of the KC-135. One indicates my fore and aft formation position relative to the tanker, the other my up and down placement. Unfortunately, these lights take their cues from the boom and illuminate with the hookup. Until then, I am on my own. Also, the boom extension has color-coded bands on it, green through yellow to red illuminated from within the boom, to let me know how much distance I have left for the boomer to plug in. Once hooked up, a lighted chevron in the middle of each track of belly lights and a green doughnut on the boom extension will indicate the formation sweet spot I will try to fly. It is like the perfect sex act, but one designed by the Strategic Air Command.

But, none of this immediate gratification can happen until I get into position. SAC's lumbering bombers and unwieldy tankers have a fixed set of maneuvers, positions, and radio calls that they must perform during the hookup process. They think this is needed to safely fly their huge aircraft in close proximity to each other. We fighter guys think the SAC brass has a psychological need to specify directions to the nth degree, orders for orders' sake. In fighters, we learn to refuel in the States on training missions where SAC requires us to follow the entire set of bomber regulations and procedures. However, once in the war theater and out of the grasp of SAC micro-management, we have distilled the action down to its essentials. All the aerial kabuki dance mandated stateside is no longer operative. We just fly up and get the gas, or at least try to.

Now is the time I have to do just that. The ground-based radar controller, call sign "Lion", has given us vectors to the tanker's fixed orbit, known as the "Orange Anchor." Once released from ground control by Lion, my navigator has used his airborne intercept radar to position us behind the Orange Anchor tanker by giving me verbal steering commands such as "turn right thirty degrees" over the cockpit intercom. When I spot the tanker visually in Thailand's clear night sky he turns the jet's radar to standby; you don't want 300 watts of energy transmitting while flammable jet fuel is flowing between aircraft. I have completed the intercept, matched the tanker's speed and altitude, placing us in the pre-contact position. All I have to do now is move my F-4 a few feet forward into contact range.

Flying formation is an exercise in ignoring all visual and sensory cues but one. It doesn't matter if you are on a training mission over west Texas, flying an air show with the USAF Thunderbirds, or trying to link up with a tanker over Thailand; the technique is the same. My entire focus is on the tanker and all my flying is done relative to the KC-135 and nothing else. The tanker can turn, climb, or descend and I will barely notice. My cockpit gauges are ignored. All that matters to me is my position relative to the tanker.

At 300 knots indicated air speed (about 350 miles an hour), my fully loaded Phantom handles like a clapped-out garbage truck. It feels as if the hydraulic fluid has been drained from the flight control system and has been replaced with molasses. Response by the aircraft to control stick inputs is sluggish and slow. Power delivery, as in all jets, similarly lags my throttle movements by a noticeable amount. I have to plan my position changes in advance and rock the twin throttles, one backward and one forward, to get the precise formation station keeping required. With no position lights yet on to assist in formation flying, my whole world is the moonlit silhouette of the KC-135 above me. I fly solely by reference to the tanker, without noticing or caring about my instruments, the world far below, or anything else.

I'm too far back; I can see too much of the tanker. So I push the right throttle up a hair and pull the left one back a bit. This moves me forward a few feet, but I have to return the throttles back together before I reach where I want to be, allowing for the lag in power change. Now I'm too low and I raise the nose an imperceptible amount to climb up three feet, no more, and stop there. Left and right look good, that is the easy part, no rudder inputs needed. Climbing, getting closer to the tanker is hard to make myself do. Every aspect of my sense of self-preservation wants me to escape the tanker's embrace, to drop away. I get the visual impression that I am flying directly under another giant aircraft only twenty feet way at 300 knots and 22,000 feet. The effect is suffocating, like sticking my head into a dark clay pipe, maybe a sewer pipe. It took me a long time to get used to this feeling. In training, I had to just make up my mind that I was going to stick my plane in under the tanker, no matter what. I learned to ignore the anticipation of an imminent fatal collision, to stuff that fear back into the furthest reaches of my mind and just do what needed to be done.

I modestly believe that I am the best pilot in the squadron, maybe the wing, at flying formation; no brag, just fact. If I didn't believe this, I shouldn't be in the squadron as it is a safe bet that every other pilot member feels the same way, that he alone is the best. But it took me quite some dedicated effort to learn to achieve and hold the contact position smoothly and quickly. Now, I have it nailed and I see the illuminated tip of the boom floating slowly three feet over the top of my canopy. It seems weird that between my head and the boom three feet away there is clear night air flowing past at 300 knots. It looks as if I could open the canopy and touch it. But, I ignore the passing nozzle; you can't fly off the boom, only the mother ship, as the Boomer reaches, reaches for the receptacle. He gets it, thrusts it in, and I feel a faint click as we are, as preachers often say, "joined as one" in another context. Standard procedures dictate that the Boomer transmit on the radio "Confirm good contact" as he can tell by his gauges when fuel is flowing. But we all have done this many times and SAC procedures are once more ignored tonight, maintaining radio silence.

Now, the position lights are on, and I can make small flight corrections to light up both center chevrons and freeze the doughnut at the perfect spot on the boom. It takes imperceptible movements of the stick and throttles to move the few feet required. I relax maybe 10 percent and take a deep breath of the cool, metallic flavored oxygen flowing through my mask. The whole linkup process has taken about thirty seconds, a lifetime. I continue to focus on flying immobile formation on the KC-135 as I feel the jet get heavier and even more sluggish as its weight grows with the added fuel load. Finally, after a few minutes, the boomer notes that fuel flow has stopped. He retracts the boom and stows it. I wonder if he'll call or write.

I can't relax just yet; I have to slowly reduce power and slip back in trail out from underneath the KC-135 before I do anything else. A one percent throttle reduction does the trick and I see the KC-135 getting smaller, invisible in the night. I take a deep breath and feel like I have just pulled my head out of that clay sewer pipe.

The tanker pilot comes on the air and transmits, "'Was it good for you tonight, Satan One?"

That's an old one, but I push my mike button on the inboard throttle and reply 'That's affirmative, thanks for the gas, Satan One is going mission frequency."

I hear in my earphones, "Good luck, Satan One, see you in an hour or so."

I close the refueling receptacle with a toggle switch, confirm that the fuel gauges are reading full, that the drop tanks are feeding, and turn the Phantom north toward North Vietnam and hopefully to the MiGs to be found there.

The tanker navigator is a real pro, despite being crewed with a pilot with a juvenile sense of humor. He has planned his turns so that he has dropped me off at the north end of Orange Anchor right at the border between Thailand and Laos. A less experienced tanker crew could have left me at the southern end and made me use fuel to transit northern Thailand before I got to the CAP zone. It is a pleasure to work with people who know what the hell they are doing.

Before I go to full combat readiness, I have to check in with Bruce in Alley Cat.

"Alley Cat, Satan One is across the fence."

The Mekong River, the fence, is the border between Thailand and Laos even as far north as we are tonight.

Bruce responds with the weather report in the patrol area, severe clear with a full moon, and relays the local altimeter setting. He signs off with "Good luck, Satan One" and probably returns to ogling his Playboy magazine.

Laos curves around northern Thailand in an inverted "L" shape. Tonight's CAP position is over the far northern regions of Laos, over the mountains northeast of the Plain of Jars. We will be out of range of radio contact with Alley Cat most of the time. Bruce's good luck wishes are his way of telling us we are on our own and to write if we find work.

As I fly the Phantom northward, the moon illuminates the jungles and plains below with a ghostly pale blue light. Only the brightest stars are visible above, the rest are blanked out by the intense moonlight. It is indeed very clear as Bruce predicted. I can trace the Mekong wandering and shimmering brightly in the moonlight. I see the dark folds of the foothills and patches of ground fog, low-lying, wisp-like, ethereal. It is a great night for an airplane ride. We drift over the Plain of Jars, its rolling, brown grassland a lighter shade of dark, rimmed with low, blue-black mountains. Unlike the Laotian southern panhandle, northern Laos is not pockmarked with the angry fires of war or at least not with many. I see a few dimly lit hamlets tucked into shallow valleys. The visible lights indicate that the inhabitants aren't at all worried about being bombed.

Scattered over the Plain of Jars are a few fires, with fewer still in the surrounding mountains. These are probably campfires of the Hmong tribal people, fierce warriors ethnically and temperamentally distinct from the more laid-back Laotians. As we fly farther north, the campfires become fewer and fewer as the terrain becomes more rugged. Now, I pick up the mountains across the border in North Vietnam, silently black, totally devoid of any lights of any kind.

I climb up to 33,000 feet to save some fuel. The cockpit grows colder and I am still soaked with sweat from the effort required for the aerial refueling, so I turn up the cockpit temperature. With little to do but sightsee, I remember that CAPs flown during WWII were at this altitude as well. I have a hard time grasping what it must have been like spending hours on end in an unpressurized, noisy, vibrating, and very cold piston-engined fighter at 33,000 feet. Those old birds were airplanes you had to fly all the time, with no autopilots and no systems to coddle your body. What about those intrepid guys in WWI, flying CAP at 20,000 feet over France in the winter in open cockpits? All they had between them and the elements, a 90 mph slip stream, and below zero temperatures, was some wooden sticks and doped fabric, without even a parachute to sit on. The very thought of such misery makes me turn up the temperature of the air-conditioning another notch.

The moonlight in the cockpit is almost bright enough to read the instruments. I keep the internal lights on anyway, but dimly. I won't need super-sharp night vision tonight, as we won't be trying to find targets on the ground. I have the radarscope in the front cockpit on and I can see the return of the radar beam scanning from side to side on the display. That information is more valuable than trying to capture with my retinas the last few photons from outside. I don't have to set up the armament by feel tonight; I can actually see the switches. For a hardened Sewer Doer, this is real luxury.

My Phantom tonight carries a full air-to-air combat load. Three disposable fuel tanks for maximum endurance, four AIM-7E Sparrow radar-guided missiles and four heat-seeking

AIM-9D Sidewinder short-range missiles. My F-4D has no gun; a later version of the Phantom, the F-4E, has a twenty-millimeter Gatling gun in the nose for close-in work. Ordinarily, I would sorely miss not having a gun on a CAP mission, sort of like walking into the Oriental saloon in Tombstone, Arizona, circa 1880, sporting an empty holster. But tonight I would rather have the extra fuel and less weight. Any air combat that occurs tonight will be fought at long range on the radar scope. I won't see my opponent until I spot the distant fireball of his aircraft exploding from the impact of my missiles, maybe.

Before there can be any fireballs, I have to arm and ready the missiles. I select "radar" and "CW power on" with toggle switches on the missile control panel. This "tunes" the Sparrow missiles to the exact frequency of the aircraft radar, The Sparrows are semi-submerged into recesses in the bottom of the jet's fuselage and are blind at launch. If and when I pull the trigger, they will be ejected in sequence and start looking for the target onto which the Phantom's radar is locked. After a few seconds, I get four green lights indicating the Sparrows are awake and tuned.

The next switch on the missile panel is labeled "heat." This gets me four green lights from four Sidewinders, two on each wing, hanging on pylons. The "heat" toggle switch has a six-inch extension on it jury-rigged from rigid plastic tubing. This lets me cycle through all four missiles without looking down into the cockpit in the heat of battle. All I have to do is slap the tubing with my left hand to select another missile. Sidewinder operation is indicated by a growl, like a rattler's hum, in my earphones. This will tell me before launch that the missile's seeker sees the heat generated by the target. With nothing visible outside the aircraft but the far, frozen moon, there are no growls tonight, yet. To ensure that each Sidewinder is coiled, aggressive, and alert for action, I could have selected them as I joined up on the tanker, using the tanker's engines as ersatz heat sources. Understandably, the tanker crews are not very enthusiastic about having live missiles locked onto them, but what they don't know probably won't hurt them. Still, accidents happen and ever since some hapless fighter pilot shot down the B-52 bomber he was practicing against, using the tankers as surrogate targets is strictly forbidden. So, all I can do is hope the 'Winders are well. The last switch remains off. It is the "missile arm" toggle and allows the missiles to launch. It will remain off unless things heat up both literally and figuratively.

Our CAP station is near Laos' northeastern border with North Vietnam. The flight orders say we are to orbit at least ten nautical miles from the border and await the presence of the MiGs. Translation: "Be prepared to spend a couple of hours boring holes in the sky. Enjoy your night airplane ride, then go home." We are escorting an invisible airplane on an unknown mission. We are to protect this unseen aircraft from threats that don't exist. Our job is to prevent an invulnerable plane from being shot down. Success is expected.

Tonight, a SR-71 "Blackbird" reconnaissance aircraft will be crossing North Vietnam to gather intelligence data. The location of the targeted data is has not been revealed to us lowly fighter pilots, nor has the method of collection, we only know what type of aircraft is coming. The SR-71 was designed by the famous Lockheed Skunk Works in the late 1950s to be the highest-flying, fastest manned aircraft in the world. It still is. I am not trusted with any of the details of tonight's Blackbird flight profile, other than it will occur well above 60,000 feet and involve speeds in excess of Mach 3. Indeed, we are instructed not to lock our jet's air intercept radar onto the Blackbird if we can find it. To do so might reveal its conditions of flight on our scopes and we mortals are not authorized to know that data. Also, the navigator in the rear cockpit of the SR-71 might interpret our radar signal as that of an enemy and soil the space suit he is wearing. Above 50,000 feet, and the Blackbird flies way above, all aircrew are required to wear full pressure suits, capable of preserving life on the moon. I guess it is uncomfortable to be scared in a space suit.

We will have no contact with the SR-71; the two-man crew will take off from an undisclosed base far away from the theater of war (We all know it is Andersen Air Force Base on the island of Guam, but nobody's telling). It will refuel from a special tanker containing unique fuel and zorch across North Vietnam like a manned comet. We don't know the exact time of passage, the course to be flown, any of the flight details, the call sign, the radio frequencies used, or anything else. Why should we? We're only the escorting MiG CAP weenies with the live missiles. I wonder if Bruce in Alley Cat knows any of. this? Probably not; such secrets are not shared with anyone who lives anywhere near the Bad Guys, and Bruce's base is in northern Thailand.

The SR-71 is a long, thin, black airplane with two giant afterburning engines. It moves at the speed of heat. I have never seen one, but I built a plastic model replica once. That's as close I have ever come to the jet that I'm supposed to protect from being shot down.

The premier interceptor of North Vietnam's air force is the MiG21. It was designed in the early 1950s to be a light, cheap interceptor to attack lumbering bombers at medium altitude. It has a rudimentary radar, a single crewman, limited range, and no radar guided missiles. The North Vietnam Air Force rarely flies at night. Takeoffs and landings in the dark challenge its low-time pilots, not to mention the lurking danger of much more capable night fighters such as my Phantom.

I know that if I employ all my skill, use every ounce of performance I can wring out of my jet, and if my missiles work perfectly, I could still never shoot down a Blackbird. The chances of a primitive MiG-21 with an ill-trained pilot doing what I cannot are precisely zero.

So, why are we here at 33,000 feet over northern Laos in the middle of the night? The SR-71 belongs to SAC, which has the mission of Strategic Reconnaissance, or SR, from the plane of the same name. Since SAC took over this mission early in the Cold War, there has been a standardized operating procedure which dictates all reconnaissance flights are to have fighter cover. This requirement stems from the time when such flights were by conducted by unarmed, modified versions of common aircraft. The introduction of the SR71 did not generate any rethink of this policy, despite the vast difference in performance between the escorts and the escorted.

The commanding generals of SAC are fighting the Vietnam War from their impregnable redoubt, a deeply buried bunker at Offutt Air Force Base on the outskirts of Omaha, Nebraska. By orders of God and SAC, every SR-71 flight will have fighter cover and that is the end of that story. So, my navigator and I will have a prolonged scenic night view of northern Laos, log some more flying time, and get to practice our night aerial refueling. It will be fun, but if I were a taxpayer, which I am, I would be pissed off at me for burning up several hundreds of thousands of tax dollars on a fool's mission.

Our only hope is that the generals running North Vietnam are as obtuse as ours seem to be. Maybe they will send a MiG-21 up tonight for the pilot to prove that he can't shoot down a SR-71 either. Maybe my navigator will spot the impotent MiG on its futile mission with our radar Maybe we will get cleared to fire from whatever command authority there is in the region tonight. Maybe the target on the radar won't be a lost U.S. Navy pilot from the Gulf of Tonkin (lost Navy pilot, isn't that redundant?). Maybe the moon will fall out of the sky. Bruce was right; we will need lots of luck tonight. We will need it to keep from drifting off to sleep and crashing.

Since the time of Julius Caesar, soldiers have complained and groused about duties that seemed to them to be senseless. I'm sure some Roman Centurion bitched and moaned that he should be whooping it up in Paris instead of freezing his butt off manning an outpost on the edge of Gaul in the middle of a winter night. All you can do is hope the guys running the war know what they are doing. However, I do know more about what I am doing than any swivel-chair general in Nebraska. Far too many of the missions I fly are similar to the one tonight. I fly CAP for aircraft that can't be shot down. I drop bombs on targets that don't exist. I employ ordnance that doesn't work. I take off in stinko weather that is unworkable. Despite all this, when my squadron mates and I have the enemy on the ropes, the politicians call a bombing halt and let him climb back into the ring. The soldiers of North Vietnam try their best to kill me, while airhead movie stars and biased journalists visit Hanoi from the States. Why does this madness continue? Lowly fighter jocks such as my navigator and me, lay our asses on the line night after night to accomplish what? We rather get the impression that the whole war and the individual decisions which make up the that war are being scripted by people who don't know what they are doing, or who have hidden personal agendas unconnected with victory, however it is defined. That is the charitable view. The truth is probably crazier.

I have no doubt that we are here over far northern Laos at two o'clock in the morning because our top Air Force commander in Saigon doesn't have the guts to tell the other generals in Omaha that tonight's mission is stupid. Being bold enough to point out unpleasant facts to the higher-ups can be harmful to your career.

But hey, what am I complaining about? It is a spectacular night to be flying. Am I a small part of the problem? Should I have told my squadron commander that tonight's mission is a waste of everyone's time and refused to fly? Should my boss have told the Wing Commander to take a hike on launching the night MiG CAP? Should the Wing Commander have called Saigon with his regrets? Where does the buck start? Never mind where it stops. Rather than confront this ethical dilemma, I chose to enjoy the scenery, the night sky, and fly my airplane.

I should have brought my binoculars tonight to look at the moon; it is really clear and bright at 33,000 feet with less than half of the earth's atmosphere above us to obscure the view. As we turn endless racetrack-shaped patterns in the night sky we have no contact with anyone. Bruce is out of radio range. The Blackbird crew won't speak to us mere mortals. Lion and the Orange Anchor tanker are way too far away. There are no other flights in the north tonight. Likewise it seems there are no air strikes in northern Laos either. We would have seen the red blossoms of exploding bombs and perhaps the ground fire trying to stave off the explosive rain. It is hard not to feel very alone. I wonder if this is what astronaut Mike Collins felt when the Apollo 11 command module passed behind the moon while the other two crewmen were down on the surface? Mike couldn't talk to Houston or the lunar lander. Mike knew (hoped?) he was going to emerge from behind the moon and reestablish radio contact. Eventually we will have to fly south, find the tanker, and get some gas to get home. But wait a minute, all Mike had to do was let Newton's laws of planetary motion work. I have to fly this jet back to Thailand.

I know I'm daydreaming and that can be fatal, but what else is there to do?

Suddenly a bright purple fireball streaks across the sky above the Phantom's canopy. It is moving from the southeast to the northwest and it is really hauling ass. The brilliant incandescent light illuminates the cockpit as bright as day, destroying what little night vision I have built up. I crane my neck and swivel my head and helmet trying to get a better view of the flame-trailing object. I yell into my inter-cockpit microphone to the Navigator.

"'What the hell is that?"

Instantly my brain goes into data processing overdrive, examining all the possibilities. Instinctively I shove both throttles forward to their stops, commanding full military power from my jet's engines. My leather-gloved left hand slaps down from the throttle to the missile arm switch; the missiles are hot. In the time this takes, my brain has considered several possible explanations.

Has the Blackbird blown up overhead our jet on its Mach 3 run? No, I have seen jets blow up in the air and this looks different. A destroyed plane slows down rapidly as it disintegrates and loses its aerodynamic form. This fireball is definitely not slowing down.

Is it a Surface-to-Air Missile, a SAM, fired at us? I don't think so. SAMs are the size of telephone poles and much slower traversing the sky. The only way a SAM could light up the night sky like this thing is if the booster rocket was still attached and burning. But, this apparition is above us, above 33,000 feet, and SAM boosters drop off much lower. Thankfully, it isn't a SAM.

'What about an air-to-air missile fired by someone trying to bag our Phantom and us? That's not it; the Soviet-supplied missiles the Vietnamese use are much smaller and burn white, not purple. We aren't to be someone else's kill tonight, at least not yet.

My adrenaline-fueled brain considers and rejects all these possibilities in the one or two seconds available, then comes up with the answer. It is a meteor, larger and brighter than any I have ever seen. A rock, probably the size of a grapefruit, is entering the earth's atmosphere from outer space. Its kinetic energy is being converted to super hot gases by air friction as the rock burns itself out, maybe fifty miles up. Everyone who flies at night, all the Sewer Doers, see meteors. Nearly always, they appear as they do on the surface of earth, only brighter. This one is a luminescent monster with a visible size and odd color, but it is totally harmless.

My navigator thinks otherwise. Jack yells into the intercom.

"Leave it alone!"

Leave it alone! I think. This rock is going God only knows how fast and is fifty miles straight up. If I can't shoot down a SR-71, how in hell am I going to even begin to bring missiles to bear on a meteor?

All I can do is to say, "Don't worry about it, I'll leave it be."

I am laughing so hard that I can barely fly but I turn off my microphone so as not to embarrass my navigator. Leave it alone I shall.

I settle down, get my heartbeat rate back into double digits, and see that our time on station is over, it is time to head back south to Orange Anchor and get enough fuel to make it home. Our night MiG CAP is over. I wonder if the SR-71 crew saw the meteor. If they did, SAC will probably put them in for a hero's medal as a reward for avoiding it.

Somehow, tonight's mission all makes perfect sense now. We spent a gorgeous evening flying over an exotic land. We accomplished a night aerial refueling to burn jet fuel for no apparent reason. We kept an invulnerable aircraft from harm's way. We didn't shoot down the MiGs that weren't there. Finally, we left a meteor alone. It makes a fellow proud to be a soldier.

IN THE ABSENCE OF FEAR, BRAVERY IS NOT REQUIRED

Fear comes in various assorted flavors. The trick for long-term survival is to not let yourself become too comfortable with any of them. Fear can become habitual, a familiar presence, once it is established in your gut or perched on your shoulder like a raven. However, once you have tasted fear on your tongue, found it to be too bitter, and spit it out, it will become harder and harder to swallow in the future. But beware, like all strong flavors, fear can be addictive. Once addicted, there will be hell to pay to kick the habit.

Pilot training and combat fighter aircrew training are each year-long exercises to develop your taste buds until you are a connoisseur of gourmet fear. Through constant sampling, I have learned to feed off certain varieties of fear and to shun other flavors. The first day a junior officer in the USAF straps on an airplane the desensitizing process begins and it continues without respite as long as landing gear continue to retract and jets become airborne. I have been taught and I have gleefully learned how to master the most basic and primeval of fears.

The fear that once stuck in my craw is the fear of death, of injury, of crashing. For any sentient human, this is the meat and potatoes of fear. It is the choking, vomiting fear of non-survival. I first learned to fly in a Cessna propeller-powered bug smasher with a top speed of maybe 125 knots with the throttle fire-walled. Even if improperly flown, the T-41 could barely kill me. Emboldened by the perceived invulnerability of extreme youth, I learned not to fear anything that primitive Cessna could do. This mastery was hard-earned, imprinted bit-by-bit, flight-by-flight.

The next aircraft on the training menu was the T-37 "Tweety Bird" a tiny two-person jet also built by Cessna. The "Tweet" got its name from its diminutive size and the piercing shriek of its engines. It could have killed me with ease, as it did one of my classmates. Again, each sortie, each flight, each new challenge instilled in me more and more confidence. Fear of non-survival faded into some remote, recess of my brain, perhaps in the reptilian stem. I became comfortable with jet speeds and used to higher performance flight. I found myself blithely doing aerial maneuvers that only a few months before would have scared me shitless.

My basic pilot training culminated with many flights in the T-38 "Talon" a true high performance jet machine. The "Talon" nickname was inspired by the smooth curve of its fuselage, which resembles the outstretched talon of a raptor in the stoop, diving to pluck prey from the air. The T-38 could and did achieve supersonic flight, faster than the speed of sound, with me at the controls. I was on my way to being a fighter pilot. Fear was well under control.

Indeed, the Northrop Corporation converted the Talon to a real jet fighter, the F-5A "Tiger." The Tiger is even now being flown in combat by the South Vietnam Air Force, the VNAF. Never mind that pilots in the USAF say that VNAF stands for "Very Nice Air Force" due to the lack of aggressiveness exhibited by most of its pilots. The F-5/T-38 can be considered to be a fighter plane of sorts. In learning to fly the Talon, I shoved the fear of non-survival further down into that mental cache. The T-38 took me and my rapidly expanding ego quite literally into the stratosphere.

The F-4 Phantom was a whole 'nother feast of mastery over fear. The ugly, dirt-brown F-4 is nothing if not a purebred fighter plane, a machine whose sole purpose in life, and death, is killing. It is the world's top-of-the-line fighter, the best jet flown by anyone, anywhere. By the time I became comfortable in the spacious cockpit of the F-4, I wasn't worried at all about dying, only about failing.

The USAF pilot training process is designed not to eliminate fear entirely, but rather to replace one type of poisonous fear with the flavor of one more palatable. The substitute taste is the fear of failure, of not hacking the program, to be considered a wimp by one's peers. This is the fear that drove me on, that made me burn the midnight oil studying, focusing my senses onto the tasks and missions assigned. Fear of failure is a rancid, sour taste; the opposite complementary flavor is the taste of success, of doing well at a supremely difficult and exceedingly dangerous task. That job is flying fighters for the United States Air Force.

Over the months and years, during training sortie after training sortie, the fear of non-survival was baked out of me. Or, at the very least, it is buried so deeply that it takes extraordinary danger to summon it up. Even the sick fear of failure is suppressed and latent. I believe now I can hack the fighter pilot program. Today my operative worry is a concern about not doing well, the fear of not excelling. If and when I do excel, the taste is very sweet indeed. After hundreds of combat missions, I have come to believe, I have to believe, that nothing the enemy can throw up in the air at me is going to cause me to fail, or die, assuming there is a difference between the two.

No training program can replicate the fear cooked up by combat. In training, lots of things can go wrong. The weather can be stinko. You can fly too low and too fast or too high and too slow. The aircraft can malfunction, blow up, and burn out from under you. Your wingman can collide with you. If grossly mishandled, the F-4 can be an evil pig of an airplane, repaying ineptness with a spin, crash, and fireball. However, all these fearsome risks are known, quantified, and predictable. Being predictable, training risks can be calculated and then either be taken on or avoided.

Combat flying forces you to operate on another level. In combat, dedicated, brave, and occasionally skilled people do their dead level best to kill you. The risks are unpredictable and hard to calculate. There are no rules in an aerial knife fight. Most times, the danger can't be avoided or ducked. You have to perform; no rain checks are allowed in this game.

The unquantified, unpredictable risks generate fear of another, unknown, unfamiliar flavor. In combat, you can do your best and you still may not excel, or even survive. Sometimes, even the Bad Guys win.

Some guys never really come to grips with the unique, intense fears of combat. The Major was one of them. He came to fly the F4 Phantom from the USAF Air Defense Command, where he flew the F-102 Delta Dart. The Air Defense Command is charged with defending the airspace of the continental United States. The Major was stationed in southern California, with its relaxed attitude and usually good weather. His duty days were filled with hours on alert status, flying training sorties, and living the good life. His stateside flying was very predictable, with canned mission scenarios and compliant, pretend targets flying predictable flight paths. The risks were few and well known. The F102 is a straight and level interceptor which uses its radar and long-range missiles to engage lumbering bomber-type targets. The risks and dangers of combat were miniscule; no airborne enemy has attacked the mainland United States since WII.

That is if incendiary balloons launched from Japan constitute an attack. If the Japanese ever try that again, even an F-102 should be able to shoot down a converted weather balloon without much risk to the aircraft or its pilot. A greater risk to that pilot is the USAF bureaucracy.

Suddenly the Major was folded, spindled, and mutilated by the USAF personnel system. He was given a minimum time checkout in the F-4 and soon found himself in Thailand fighting the Vietnam War. He did not adapt well. Instead of boring holes in the safe upper sky of California, he was dive bombing Laos, his windscreen filled with views of nothing but rapidly approaching dirt. People were trying very hard to kill him. The nights over Laos were inky black and deadly, not like the shining and friendly skies of Los Angeles County.

We all could see the Major was overwhelmed by the danger of it all. Fear ate at him like a parasite in his brain. Instead of feeding off the fear, using it to spur himself on to cope, he let it consume him like malevolent tapeworm. He never learned the difference between the subtle taste of well-done fear and, the choking bile of panic.

I once read a book by an airline pilot, Earnest K. Gann, who categorized two types of fear. I don't know what reasons an airline pilot has to be fearful. Perhaps he worries that his aircraft's coffeepot will conk out or that the stewardesses will be fat and ugly. In any case, this airline guy nailed his analysis spot-on. He postulated a distinction between fear and panic. I have found these categories to be accurate.

Fear sharpens your reflexes, focuses your attention on the essentials, and eliminates extraneous, time-wasting thoughts from your gray matter. Time slows down under the influence of a well-founded fear. Fear-driven, your brain calculates various courses of action at warp speed and selects the one most likely to lead to survival and/or triumph. Your hands move of their own accord on the controls, the aircraft melds itself into your reflexes which are operating in quick time. Your immediate cockpit environment fades away as you become one entity with the jet, a man/machine hybrid. I have returned from stressful missions with over six Gs on the recording G meter and I couldn't remember exactly when the extreme G loading occurred. You would think that instantly weighing 1100 pounds would stamp the event on your memory, but not when your memory banks are flooded with startled fear.

Things are different in the air with fear absent and only lurking nearby. One minute you are flying, yet at the same time a portion of your thoughts is ruminating over what you intend to do once you land. Or more likely, whom you intend to do later tonight. A fighter pilot is a guy who, when he is flying, thinks about girls. When he is with girls, all he talks about is flying. However, it only takes a few rounds of antiaircraft fire over the top of your canopy to erase any thoughts of physical or social interaction with the opposite sex flooding your head with an intense desire for actions intended to allow you to live a few seconds longer.

Panic, the other side of the fear omelet, short-circuits your brain's wiring. You do stupid, irrational things. You make critical, life-threatening mistakes. You focus on trivia, ignoring life or death matters. Under a panic attack, your body betrays you. Your breathing labors, your heart jumps out of your flight suit, your hands shake. Panic is an enemy that must be defeated, dealt with, before you can begin to cope with the real Bad Guys.

The Major never panicked, or at least not for long and not so as anyone could tell. If he had, his backseat navigator would have had a quiet word with the Squadron Commander and the Major's flying career would have been terminated then and there. But, he never learned to deal with the fear of combat either. He never learned to forge his fear into a goad for higher performance. He was always flying his first ten missions, over and over again.

The first ten combat missions are when fear tries to reign supreme. More guys are lost, shot down, or crash on their first ten missions than at any other time in their combat tour. The first ten flights are when fear tries to mutate into panic and before experience has had time to jell into proper self-preservation instincts.

After the first ten, you reach a fearsome crossroads in your mind. One fork often leads to chemical addiction as you become fonder and fonder of fear's highly addictive chemical by-product, adrenaline. You learn to relish fear, anticipating the shot of adrenaline that always follows. As time goes on, like all junkies, you have to have deeper and deeper doses of fear to get the adrenaline high you have learned to crave.

The other fork, if taken, numbs your tolerance and reverses your craving for adrenaline. On this path, fear is a constant companion, one who must be defeated daily. The guys on this path are the real heroes. If you crave your daily danger high, fear is a friend; bravery is not required. Otherwise, if fear is always there for you, it takes daily bravery to function.

The pilots who live with fear and who are afraid of. fear itself, to hijack FDR's nicely turned phrase, tend to outwardly manifest their inner emotional turmoil. Some develop facial tics, usually around the mouth, as if the taste of fear was related to that of jalapenos. Others lose weight with worry. Others get skinny by constantly shitting; not all diarrhea come from the local spicy Thai food. Self-medication with booze is always popular, as is whoring in the local town, usually done in some combination. There is a myriad of comely Thai girls readily available, who are only too willing to help you get out of your troubled mind for one hundred Baht. The one-hundred Baht bill is known, semi-affectionately, as a "love note." Love has less to do with it than fear and the tension it generates. Even commercially acquired sex is a great reliever of tension for some.

The Major didn't drink that much and he was ever faithful to his wife back in the States. He didn't really enjoy drunken singing or poker games. For him, there was no easy outlet for the fear showing around his darting eyes and no release for the tension roiling in his gut. Thin when he reported to the squadron, he continually lost weight he couldn't afford to. Perhaps worst of all for him was the shunning. Guys who had outwardly seemed to have conquered their own fears but worried about re-infection, distanced themselves from him. The few who were still not immune to the fear virus shunned him as a carrier. The major was cut off from the emotional support and camaraderie that makes life in a fighter squadron so intense and makes combat more possible.

A lesser man would have requested a transfer; others before him who couldn't defeat the fear demons have gone down that escape route. All it takes is a private meeting with the base chaplain. A few days later, a transfer to a staff job in Saigon duly turns up in the daily orders. A few more straightforward guys have dramatically tossed their insignia wings on the Commander's desk and ended their tour of duty safely running the Officers' Club, never to fly again.

A unique privilege possessed by fighter pilots is the luxury of opting out of combat. We aren't like the poor grunts slogging through the sodden rice paddies of South Vietnam who can't call in sick or scared. Why can we quit when we feel like we must while others under equal pressure cannot? There are two answers to that troubling question.

The first is practical. You cannot fly a fighter plane under the influence of the stomach-churning sickness of fear. Fear causes mistakes, errors of judgment, inept actions in the heat of combat. Fear causes important switches to be left inactivated, targets to be missed, and wingmen to be unsupported. Panic, the ultimate manifestation of fear causes a once steady hand on the control stick to snatch too many Gs on the aircraft, grabbing too much angle of attack. This ruptures the sensitive aerodynamic relationship between the curved wing and the encompassing airflow, snapping the jet over into a fatal spin. A fearful aviator is a danger first to himself and to his navigator, then to his wingmen. You can trudge through a rice paddy while scared witless dogging mines, snipers, and shit-covered punji sticks. You cannot successfully operate a supersonic jet with teeth clenched in fear.

The second dispensation is ethical in nature. A fighter cockpit can be the loneliest battleground in the world. It holds one, sometimes two, souls. You climb into the cockpit alone, there is no one there to lean on, to provide moral support, to quiet your fear. A fighter pilot volunteers for personal, intimate combat every time he straps in. You step out alone onto the dusty main street of Dodge City at high noon with no posse, no deputy, no townspeople, only a sidekick in the rear cockpit. At least Gary Cooper had Grace Kelly to protect his six o'clock. In fighters, we fight alone and when we die, we die alone. It is too much to ask a man to fight by himself if he doesn't believe he can win and survive. That is why we have the ability to quit by various means.

The Major availed himself of none of those remedies. He stubbornly, or bravely, stayed on the flying schedule. Too shaky in the air to be a Sewer Doer, the major flew daytime missions and brooded late at night.

Often, as I made my way back to my quarters in the small hours just before dawn, I would see the Major sitting motionless on the porch of the BOQ, staring soundlessly out into the hot, humid night of Thailand. He would sit bolt upright in a folding metal chair, his back rigid, his hands on his knees. The Major was unable to sleep longer than an hour or two at a time. So, he sat there night after night, waiting without speaking. For what? For his tour to be over? For a nocturnal gift of something to defeat his fear? For someone to mercifully take him off the flying schedule? I suspected he was waiting for something, anything, to end his torment.

Last night, my mission was a short, early one. I wrapped up the debriefing just before midnight, wolfed down a plate of scrambled eggs and fried rice mixed with hot chili peppers. For dessert, I had a double shot of Tennessee whisky before hitting the sack. About 0300, I had to heed the call of nature, due no doubt to some weird gastric reaction between the Thai chilies and the sweet, brown whiskey. In the dark, I stumbled down the porch from my room toward the latrine at the center of the building.

It was raining, a tepid drizzle of water from a damp night sky too hot and too humid to retain any more moisture. Across the dark courtyard, through the misting rain, I dimly perceived the Major sitting on the opposite porch in his usual spot. As always, he was staring with fear-pinched eyes at the night. I thought nothing of it, I had seen him there too many times before. The dripping rain and the late hour stifled any thoughts I might have had of a greeting or conversation; I really never knew what to say to him anyway. Nothing I could say would have exorcised his fearsome demons.

I relieved myself and quietly made my way back to my bunk. The Major was still there sitting and staring.

★★★

This morning, as I walked to the squadron, I remembered seeing the Major in his usual place last night. The vivid mental image made my stomach do a quick barrel roll, as the Major has been dead for over two months. His Phantom took a direct hit by ground fire over Laos. The jet trailed red fire and left a black smoke trail as it tumbled end over end into the jungle below. His wingman saw no parachutes.

One of John Wayne's movie characters once said, "Bravery is not the absence of fear. It's being scared to death and saddling up anyway."

The Major was the bravest man I ever met.

FIRECANS AND SPECTRES

I'm back in the sewer once again and I have a raging lunatic in the rear cockpit of my jet. My navigator, who goes by the call sign of "Crazy Jack" is absolutely wacko. In his more lucid moments, he improves to the status of a mere homicidal psychopath. However, his bloodlust doesn't hamper his navigation and weapons systems skills. As a GIB, or Guy In Back, Jack is a piece of work.

'We are just crossing the Mekong, flying alone into Laos at 23,000 feet and 400 knots, about 450 miles per hour, Tonight Satan Flight consists of just one lonely F-4; that would be us. It is eleven o'clock and the night is pitch dark, with the moon not yet risen. The Southeast Asia skies are hazy tonight, with thin clouds far above us and a broken layer of wispy clouds below. Only the brightest stars are visible through the icy stratospheric haze on top. The ragged cloud deck below is barely discernible against the dark black Laotian terrain. A full moon will be up shortly to illuminate the scene with its stark blue light, but until moonrise, we will have to cope with the inky blackness masked by torn clouds.

Knowing Jack's unstable mental state, I had fun winding him up earlier as we walked to our waiting Phantom. I hummed, then sang, the current hit by Credence Clearwater Revival as we carried our flight gear down the flight line, the vast concrete lake still hot from the day's heat:

Don't go out tonight,
Well it's bound to take your life,
There's a bad moon on the rise,
Hope you've got your things together,

Hope you're quite prepared to die,
Looks like we're in for nasty weather,
One eye is taken for an eye,
There's a bad moon on the rise.

Predictably this got Jack's brain juices flowing and he is wired for action. For Jack, action is the elixir of life. After USAF navigator's school and the award of his navigator's wings, Jack's first assignment was to the Strategic Air Command as an Electronic Warfare Officer, or EWO, due in part to his civilian technical education in electronics. For four long years, he rode around in the back of B-52 bombers, bored out of his mind. This painful history explains his current precarious psychological condition.

An EWO's job is to listen to the electronic signals emitted by an enemy's radar and then to identify the signals and thus the radar. In response, he turns on corresponding electronic countermeasures such as radar jammers, or releases radar-masking bundles of shredded aluminum foil, called "chaff." However, peacetime B-52 training sorties rarely encounter enemy radars. There are no such radars within hearing distance over the continental United States, and when Jack was on overseas flights, the Russians were reluctant to reveal the locations and characteristics of their radars by illuminating an offshore B-52. EWOs can't actually practice deploying their countermeasures in peacetime as jammers and chaff work equally well on civilian radars, such as those operated by the Federal Aviation Authority, or FAA, air traffic control system. Shutting down the FAA's ability to track civil airliners is strongly discouraged by the USAF. Thus, during his numerous long training flights, Jack had absolutely nothing to do. This was very upsetting to a man of Jack's natural energy and aggressiveness, to the point of unhinging his military mind.

Jack's highly negative job satisfaction index was exacerbated by the lack of status awarded to EWOs. An EWO isn't the bomber's pilot or its copilot. He isn't the navigator, the radar navigator, or the bombardier. He is definitely the low man on the bomber crew totem pole, save for the enlisted tail gunner. Additionally, the B-52 is the lowest aircraft on the USAF macho pecking order. The EWO is the lowest status officer on the lowest status aircraft. Accordingly, Jack spent four years lower than whale shit, professionally and mentally. Being the butt of SAC jokes finally pushed poor Jack over the edge; he volunteered for fighters and asked to be sent to the war.

Crazy Jack now thinks he has found his niche in life and in the USAF. He loves the prestige of flying the USAF's top-of-the-line tactical fighter (don't we all?). The nightly combat action turns him on. Jack digs dropping bombs and mixing it up with the Bad Guys. He loves contributing and being an essential aircrew member instead of enduring twelve-hour B-52 airplane rides fighting to stay awake. Thriving on combat and danger, his natural aggressiveness is totally off the charts.

Aggression is never lacking in any fighter squadron, only the degree is in play. Fighter pilots tend to be way out there on the aggressiveness scale, to the point of self-endangerment. Self-confidence is also not in short supply. It takes full measure of both confidence and aggressiveness to strap on 50,000 pounds of fighter jet. Another helping of both is required to go out night after night to mix it up with dedicated people who would like nothing better than to kill you. In a group of aggressive, supremely self-confident guys, Crazy Jack stands out as being over the top.

Most navigators serve as essential voices of reason, curbing the wilder instincts of the jocks in the front seats of the Phantoms. When the pilot is caught up in the heat of battle and intends to press an attack when prudence and self-preservation would dictate otherwise, it is usually the navigator that calms things down. Without the responsibility to actually fly the jet, the GIB can devote more time to thinking instead of reacting emotionally.

Jack, on the other hand, is always pressing for flying lower, getting in closer, dueling with antiaircraft guns, stretching the fuel reserves, making multiple weapons deliveries, and generally sticking it to the Bad Guys. This attitude comes through the cockpit intercom loud and clear despite Jack's general lack of verbosity. if he says anything at all, it usually to point out that I am not being aggressive enough. If I hear nothing from him in my earphones, I know that he is pleased with how things are going. This always makes me wonder whether we are getting in too deep. If I suggest a bomb release altitude of 7,500 feet, he counters with 5,500 feet. When I want to deliver all the bombs on one pass and get the hell out of there, Jack wants to stick around and stir things up, one bomb at a time.

Tonight, with no moon yet up for visual reference and no wingman to help watch for ground fire, I am resolved to play things cool. I tell myself that I won't listen to Crazy Jack this evening. I'll ignore him at least until the moon rises to shine some welcome light down into the dank sewer.

For a change, tonight we are escorting an AC-130 gunship, call sign "Spectre." Gunships were invented a few years ago in South Vietnam. Some bored but ingenious transport driver, probably related to Jack, dreamed up the idea of mounting three mini- Gatling guns sideways in a twin-engined, propeller-driven C-47 "Gooney Bird." The "Goon" was first used in WWII as a troop transport. It has long endurance and a very slow airspeed. The mini guns are all pointed out the left side windows and are aimed with a mark made by a wax pencil on the pilot's left side cockpit window. The pilot circles the combat area in a left hand orbit and places the wax pencil mark, the "death dot", over the intended target. When the geometry is right, he fires the guns through an electric trigger and adjusts the fire storm by observing the visible stream of the tracer bullets. The tracers are clearly visible, as this is a plan that only works at night. The Gooney Bird would be a sitting duck, or rather a circling duck, to ground fire if flown in the daytime. These lethal C-47s are nicknamed "Puff the Magic Dragon" and can put a 5.56-millimeter bullet into every square yard of a football field in three seconds. They operate under the call sign "Spooky." A few transport aircrew members welcomed the invention of the gunship. This ingenious modification to their lumbering airplanes allowed them to actually fight in the war, putting ordnance on target. The gunship mission was judged to be way more rewarding than spending a combat tour flying boring cargo from point A to point B.

The success of Spooky in South Vietnam generated a similar idea for the more demanding air war in Laos. Various automatic guns, from 7.62-millimeter mini-guns, to 20-millimeter Gatling guns, up to 40-millimeter cannons are mounted in the cargo hold of a C-130 Herky Bird. Instead of a wax pencil dot on the windscreen, the Herky has infrared scopes and low-light sensors for target acquisition and a real computing gunsight near the pilot's left shoulder.

These flying gun platforms are proving to be devastating to the truck convoys on the Ho Chi Minh Trail. In our fast-moving fighters, we are lucky to be able to attack two or three trucks at a time at night, when we can find them, which isn't often. The Spectres orbit slowly for hours at medium altitudes and watch the dirt roads that make up the "trail" through their night-piercing, all-seeing sensors. When a convoy of trucks is spotted, a sensor is locked on to the front truck and multiple rounds are sent on their way with a single pull of the trigger. Tracers are not needed. The sensors and the computers that drive the gunsight are so good, the first truck is usually torched with the first burst. Then the last truck is blasted to bits, preventing the others from escaping back along the single-track, muddy road. Once the convoy is trapped, the Spectre can pick off the doomed trucks at will. It is not unusual for one Spectre to kill 100 or more trucks in a single night.

The expensive AC-130 gunship is a valuable war machine and the USAF employs fewer than a dozen. Each giant plane also carries twelve to fifteen crewmen; pilots, navigators, sensor operators, and gunners. Thus, an order has been given from on high that they will not be shot down. Each Spectre flies every night with constant fighter escort. Tonight, that would be us.

The black-painted gunship is invisible from the ground while flying at medium altitudes. The Bad Guys can and do fire blindly toward the droning sound of its turboprop engines or failing that, shoot wildly into the air hoping for a lucky hit. Slow, big, and a converted transport plane with no armor plating, Spectre can't take much ground fire and still survive. Tonight, Jack and I have the mission of enhancing the odds of survival for Spectre and its crew.

My jet has six cluster bombs on board, three under each wing. These bombs are canisters about the size and shape of a large garbage can fitted with tail fins. Each cluster bomb is stuffed with hundreds of bomblets the size and shape of baseballs. My job is to try to pinpoint the location of any gun firing at Spectre. I will attempt to do this by visually following the trails of Bad Guys' tracer bullets back to their point of origin on the night ground. Then, I will have to make a dive bomb pass targeting the gun site and release a cluster bomb. As it falls, the cluster bomb reads its altitude above the ground with a radar fuse. At the right altitude, about 2,000 feet, the fuse blows open the canister and the bomblets fall free like a dense cloud of iron baseballs. Each bomblet detonates when it hits the ground, spraying a hail of shrapnel. The swarm of bomblets covers a wide area; all the better to place at least one inside the pit containing the offending gun. An exploding baseball won't destroy the gun, but it will kill the crew, damping the enthusiasm of other gunners for further target practice on Spectre. Or at least that is tonight's plan. What isn't in the plan is what happens to Jack and me before we release the cluster bomb.

We'll be dive bombing toward the muzzle of a gun specifically designed to shoot down aircraft. I guess the trade-off is judged acceptable, risking an expendable F-4, an aggressive pilot, and a nut-case navigator in order to keep the convoy's nemesis, Spectre, safe.

We are entering the Laotian area of operations patrolled by Spectre and I raise the pilot on the radio. After checking in, I set up my own left hand orbit above 20,000 feet and look down into the night for the gunship. I can see off to the west the first dim glow of the rising moon. It will slowly appear out of the unseen South China Sea like a one-eyed Chinese lantern in less than an hour.

To allow escorts to see and avoid the Spectre, the AC-130 displays a cross of low intensity lights, similar to the green-glowing formation lights on my Phantom. The circular lights are mounted in a line down the top of the fuselage, crossed with another line of lights transversing the wing's upper surface. I spot the slow-moving green lights far below. They are invisible from the ground, only from above. The pale cross drifts silently beneath me through the night searching for prey along the unseen trails.

The Spectre gunship is emulating its pagan namesake while displaying the universal symbol of Christianity, the cross, on its black wings. The communist masters of North Vietnam are suppressing the dominant religion of the country, Buddhism. No competing allegiances are allowed in the north. If we defeat the commies, Buddhism will flower in the north as it does now in the south. Tonight, and every other night, a deadly ghost plane flown by Christians and Jews, marked with the sign of the cross, is trying to make the world safer for Buddhists. I can taste the irony on my tongue. Or is that metallic residue from the oxygen system?

I have my armament switches set up, the bombs are armed, the cockpit is dim, and the gunsight is on. Now, all it takes to rain a hail of deadly baseballs is a tap on the pickle button. When and if I do pickle off a cluster bomb, the light show will be spectacular. Each bomblet detonates in a bright white flash. The hundreds of bomblet going off in a circular pattern on the ground will resemble an oval football stadium full of sparklers during a rock concert.

The low cloud deck is periodically obscuring the trail and Spectre has to work in and out of gaps in the misty coverage. From my position high overhead, I can see the first circle of the rising moon in the east; it is up, almost out of the South China Sea. Already blue-white instead of moon-dawn orange, it is now cresting the Laotian mountains. Once the moon breaks the tops of the hills, Spectre will have to be more careful, as the big, black AC-130 is easily silhouetted against moonlit clouds. That's all the gunners will need to direct their fire. But for now, things are quiet. Even Jack is more silent than usual. He is probably trying to spot the muzzle flashes of guns for us to dive toward.

Spectre calls on the radio that he has a good target and he sets up a left-hand orbit. I can see nothing but the pale formation lights on top of the slowly turning gunship. Suddenly a red fire flares on the ground like a struck match. It flames angrily and then is reduced to a dim pinpoint of embers. Spectre calls, "Lead truck." His sensor operators have found a blacked-out convoy on the Ho Chi Minh dirt road headed south. After another ninety degrees of turn by Spectre, another fire sparks into existence on the ground. This one keeps burning brightly. The first truck was carrying ammo that exploded all at once when struck by Spectre's first shots. This second one looks like fuel burning, probably the last truck, carrying diesel fuel for the convoy.

Spectre will have to work quickly to get the rest of the trucks before the moon is any higher. Already I can see the flat tops of the cloud deck shinning like white cotton instead of the previous dirty black wool as the moon's rays climb more overhead and ever brighter.

One by one I see individual trucks flare as invisible shells hit them, raining down from the big gunship. Some burn for a few seconds, some for a minute or two, and some are only revealed in the instant when Spectre's rounds hit home. After three full firing orbits by Spectre, I can see a line of burning trucks laying in a serpentine curve, indicating on the dark night ground the path of the road where they are dying along with the men driving and riding in them.

The burning, destroyed convoy looks to me like a strand of pink pearls hurriedly dropped on a lady's hastily discarded black velvet dress in a darkened motel room. The rising moon is casting its pseudo blue-neon glow to add more fantasy to the image. This sexually suggestive carnal scene pops into my head because I haven't seen anything like it for real in months and months. I had better bear down and concentrate on the here and now or I won't live to see it again.

Without warning, my earphones erupt with the frenetic sound of a desert rattlesnake, a big one, but not very loud.

Jack yells into his microphone, "Firecan!"

I don't know if the Spectre has picked it up, but if he hasn't, he should. I push my radio mike button and try to speak calmly, slowly.

"Spectre, Satan's got a Firecan on the air."

The reply comes back, "Roger, Satan, nothing here."

I ask Jack, "Are you sure?"

He replies in a tone of voice reserved for little children, simpletons, and fighter pilots.

"Of course I'm sure, that's a Firecan, no shit."

Firecan is the NATO code word for a Soviet-built, ground-based fire control radar. It is used to lock on to and to track airborne targets when those targets can't be seen in an optical sight, as at night. The radar's tracking solution is fed to automatic anti-aircraft guns, allowing accurately aimed fire at unseen aircraft. During his days in SAC, Jack was drilled for hours and hours on the identification of a wide range of radars using only the sound their emissions produce on an aircraft's electronic receivers. To keep in practice, he frequently lies on his bunk in the officers' quarters and listens to cassette tapes of those sounds. These aural workouts keep his senses sharp and allow him to practice identifying the rattles, beeps, and squawks. That's what an EWO does. If Jack says it is a Firecan, who am I to argue? Even so, there has never been a report of a Firecan in Laos; this sophisticated sensor is normally reserved for the defense of North Vietnam itself.

If the electronic signature we hear is really that of a Firecan, if it is in this area, and if it is linked to the guns we know are already here, this is very bad news for Spectre. Very bad news indeed. The big gunship's survival is dependent on it being invisible in the night sky. The barn-sized transport with its four rotating, radar-reflecting propellers makes an excellent radar target. The dumbest Firecan operator in the North Vietnamese Army could lock on to an AC-130 in nothing flat. The size of this slow airborne target doesn't require pinpoint shooting accuracy. If the guns are in range, Spectre will take deadly hits on the first burst from the ground.

I transmit again, a sense of urgency creeping into my voice, "Spectre, Satan's still getting a Firecan signal."

I get back, "Roger, Satan, nothing here."

Maybe we are getting a stray Firecan emission leaking from inside North Vietnam, not from Laos. At our altitude, we have a clear line of sight across the border. The mountains shield the Spectre in its lower orbit. However, the green dashed strobe on the ECM scope in both our cockpits points to the target area near the dying convoy as we circle, and not from the east.

Maybe the Firecan isn't linked to the guns yet. Maybe this is a test: "This is only a test; do not adjust your set."

Maybe the Spectre crew is too busy shooting to notice the sinister rattlesnake sound or to even turn on their ECM gear. With Gatling guns spitting fire and lead next to your ears, it would be easy to miss a radar signal, particularly one not supposed to be there. Maybe the Firecan is out of range of the low-flying Spectre's ECM gear even if the set is turned on.

On the other gloved hand, maybe Spectre is about to get nailed. The trucks are certainly getting their asses handed to them. Even from my altitude, I can see two dozen or more aflame and Spectre is circling for more, firing all the while. Every truck torched is one less load of war material destined for use against our troops in the south.

The Bad Guys are in a helluva fix and justly so. They can do nothing and watch their convoy go up in flames truck by truck. Or they can use their Firecan in Laos, which they have never done before, and escalate the war to a new level. Or they can shoot blindly at Spectre. The last two options get them bombed by Jack and me. I have left on my green-and-red navigation lights, the red flashing beacon on the tail, and the white lights under the jet. There are few guns that can reach to 20,000 feet;

we are relatively safe up here. But the Bad Guys can see us orbiting and thus know that Spectre has an Phantom escort. My lights are intended to announce our presence and bad intentions. Hopefully that message will deter them from shooting.

No such luck. I see a burst of 37-millimeter AAA fire climb up from an area of black nothingness near the line of burning trucks. The Bad Guys have cracked. The line of tracers climbs quickly into the night sky, probing, searching for the vulnerable gunship. The Firecan isn't aiming these guns as the shells miss the Spectre by a fair distance. They fire another clip of seven rounds and more red tracers climb into the night sky like lethal lightning bugs. This was a big mistake on their part. The first clip attracted my attention to the general area, but I didn't have time to locate the gun site. The second burst allowed me to follow the thin red line of tracers back to its origin on the ground.

Now, I'm flying by feel alone, my eyes "padlocked" on the amorphous ink spot on the surface of Laos hosting the gun site. I can't look anywhere but there. I can't take my eyes off the spot for a second. If I do, I'll never reacquire the target. I try to triangulate the position of the gun site in relationship to the string of flaming trucks.

Waiting is not an option either. The next burst may be more accurate. Worse yet, the lethal Firecan might lock on. I have to make my dive delivery now before bursting rounds impact Spectre and the fifteen guys inside. I know the gunship pilot has spotted the ground fire and is wondering what I, his trusty escort, intend to do about it. I push my mike button and transmit.

"Spectre, Satan has the gun. I'm in from the west, got you in sight."

The Spectre pilot replies, this time with his voice slightly rushed.

"Roger, Satan, you-all take care now, you hear?"

This is going to be tricky; a ragged shelf of clouds is partially obscuring the target, drifting over from the Laotian mountains to the east. I'm west of the gun site and I have a good view of where I want the cluster bomb to hit. If I run in from this direction, I'll have to pull off my dive up into the clouds. That's not so bad, except the moon is up far enough now to skylight my jet against the layer of gray fluff with grazing illumination revealing my jet to the gunners. However, if I wait until I'm further around the circle, I may lose the target and Spectre may get shot down in the meantime.

Crazy Jack asks me from the rear cockpit what I'm waiting on. I think, "What the hell, who wants to live forever?" I roll the jet to the left and let the nose drop toward the imaginary point in the blackness where the gun site is theoretically located. This won't be pretty; there is no time to set up a classic dive bomb run. The dive angle, airspeed, and G loading will be whatever works out. All I have to do is to get the oval pattern of the bomblets somewhere around the gun pit, maybe nobody gets killed, but the explosions should stop them from shooting at Spectre.

Holy shit! They may not be shooting at the gunship, but they're sure as hell shooting at me! In my peripheral vision I see the ECM scope showing the Firecan to be directly on my nose, the rattlesnake burr in the headphones is relentless. I see tracers stream over the top of my canopy, some from the left and more from my right. More are rising up in front of my flight path; I'll have to dive through them. The Laotian night sky is lit up like the Fourth of July.

Jack yells, "Shit hot, go get them, Fast Eddie."

That's just what I need now, a navigator with a death wish. We go down the dive chute with tracer bullets on all sides, plunging through a thin wisp of cloud. I see white, green, and red lights reflecting off the milky vapor flowing past.

Shit! I've forgotten to turn off the external lights on my aircraft. Every gunner in southern Laos can see us bright and clear. They all do just that and all start shooting like mad fiends. In my peripheral vision, I can see tracers and shell bursts all around the jet. I can't reach over now and turn off the lights; the switch is out of reach on the left console. I can pull off and abort the run, but then the cluster bomb will fall ineffectively short. All this shooting is making me angry. I really, really want to kill these guys now. My instantly revised plan is to try to complete the bomb run and pull off into the sheltering clouds.

It's funny what getting shot at does to you. My logical reaction should be one of. fear and a heightened sense of self-preservation. However, in a fighter jet, the psychologically comforting effects of being in a protective cockpit and the illusion of being in control predominate. The effect of having many folks trying to kill you isn't what you might think. It isn't terribly frightening as much as it is tremendously annoying. What do those jerks think they're doing? Don't they know whom they are dealing with here? My immediate reaction is anger and the desire to hit back, "First-est with the most-est" as J.E.B. Stuart said. Ordinarily, I would expend one cluster bomb on one gun site, saving the rest for the remainder of the mission, but these guys are really pissing me off with their guns. They get the full whammy.

Jack calmly says, "Ready, pickle."

I hit the pickle button on the top of the control stick six times in quick succession. I want lots and lots of bomblets down there doing their deadly thing while I attempt to make it to the clouds unscathed. I also want to teach these North Vietnamese bozos a lesson. The jet bounces upward slightly when each eight-hundred pound cluster bomb leaves. When the last canister falls away, I bury the stick in my lap and lay six Gs on the airplane. As the nose comes up, I scrunch up my leg muscles to keep from blacking out and my vision tunnels down to a circle in front of the airplane. My blood is draining from my overheated brain toward my boots, starving my retinas. Even through my visually dark tunnel, I can still see tracer bullets streaming in front of the Phantom. A fully lighted target, a Phantom with all its lights on, is inviting these guys to zero in.

As quickly as the shooting started, it stops, and the tracers disappear off somewhere into the night. When a cluster bomb canister is explosively split, it announces its airborne arrival with a single bright flash in the sky. The live gunners know this well, the ones that didn't get the memo are dead. The smart ones realize that in three or four seconds a shit-storm of bomblets and flying fragments will blanket the area. Each bomblet contains dozens of bird-shot-sized pellets that will deluge the target area. The gunners, seeing the first canister's opening burst, dove into their shelters to escape the incoming steel rain and stopped shooting at us.

As soon as its nose is twenty degrees above the horizon, the Phantom pops into the cloud deck. The canopy is enveloped in a dim white fog illuminated by those dammed navigation lights that almost got us killed. I can see the red flashing beacon reflecting in sharp pulses off the clouds. The effect is very disorienting. I relax the Gs to get back more night vision. As I let the stick ease forward, the jet starts feeling slightly sloppy and loose. The flight controls are slackening. I glance down at the dimly lit airspeed indicator to see it coming down through 300 knots. That's way too slow for a combat mission.

Not content with already making one life-threatening mistake tonight, I decide to compound the situation with another screw-up. I shove both throttles past the detent into full afterburner, trying to keep the airspeed from decaying further. Instantly twin plumes of white-hot gases shoot thirty or forty feet behind the jet's engines and I feel a kick in the butt signaling extra thrust is reporting for duty. If the gunners aren't still cowering in their holes, they have an even more visible target to aim at. Two J-79s produce huge torches in the night sky. The afterburners light up the inside of the cloud, clean white flame reflecting off dirty white vapor. What little night vision I had is now gone, I can't make out the instruments, the inner lit cloud isn't bright enough and the instrument lights are too dim. It is like flying inside a giant frosted light bulb. A second later, someone turns on the light. Below in the jungles of Laos, thousands of bomblets are going off, each with a white fireball the size of a basketball. It is the sparkler show from Hell. The detonating bomblets light up the underside of the cloud deck, big time. The incandescent light surges through the clouds and illuminates my cockpit like the photo flashguns of a thousand paparazzi. I am totally messed up, having no idea which way is up or more importantly, down. With no visual references inside the cloud, no visible instruments, and no vision, I am not flying this jet as much as I am going along for the ride. Swiftly we burst from the ragged, flat top of the cloud layer pointed more or less into the absolute vertical. Both afterburners are still howling, but the airspeed is rapidly decaying toward zero. I can tell we are above the clouds and I can see the moon somewhere, but the bomblets' flashes dashed any hope of me making out the horizon.

Into my mike I manage to say, "Uh."

Instantly, Not-so-Crazy-Now Jack replies firmly, "I've got it."

I relax my grip on the control stick and hope for the best.

Jack is not a rated pilot, but he knows how to recover the jet from what are whimsically called "unusual attitudes." We practice this in the daytime. I tell him to close his eyes and then I roll, dive, and turn the jet, trying to tumble his internal gyros and disorient him. Then I say, "You've got it." After many repetitions of this basic flying exercise, I trust him explicitly to recover the airplane.

'We have a pact, when one of us says, "I've got it," that guy gets control of the airplane, no matter what. His job then is to open his eyes, focus on the attitude indicator and flight instruments in his rear cockpit, take over the stick and throttles and recover the jet to straight and level flight, despite whatever his inner ear says the jet is doing. After numerous practice maneuvers, each more violent than the last, my navigator is a whiz at recovering from unusual attitudes. During dive bomb runs at night, as soon as he calls "pickle," his attention goes directly to the instruments. He has been staring at the black ball of the attitude indicator, the altimeter, and the airspeed indicator all during our rapid passage through the clouds and as we erupted from the top like a sailfish broaching in the Sea of Cortez.

Jack rolls the jet toward the nearest horizon, pulls the nose down to level, if inverted, flight, and then rolls right side up. As the airspeed builds to over 300 knots, he pulls the engines out of afterburner and says,

"You can have it any time."

I couldn't have done it better myself. As a matter of fact, I probably couldn't have done it at all.

I take a few deep breaths of pure oxygen from the rubber mask around my face, turn up the cockpit lighting so I can see something, and check the airspeed and fuel. I glance outside at the horizon now clearly defined by the full moon. One look down at my leather-gloved hands confirms they have stopped shaking.

I tell Jack, "Roger, I've got it," and take control of the jet, resuming the job of flying.

The Spectre pilot comes on the air, his voice dripping with sarcasm.

"Satan, that was a pretty spectacular show."

I reply after another deep breath to lower my voice pitch down to the manhood range.

"Roger that. The things we do for you guys."

Jack, reverting to crazy once again, asks, "How many cluster bombs do we have left? Let's go back and get those guys."

I tell Spectre, "Satan is Winchester (out of ordnance)."

Jack sighs the sigh of a man dealing with a wimp over the intercom as he hears my transmission to Spectre.

Spectre comes back, "Roger that, this area is getting too hot anyway, we're RTB (Returning To Base)."

As I point the jet westward to Thailand, I look back at the red line of burning trucks and the white. glowing residual embers of the cluster bombs on the black ground. This night in the sewer is one to remember. We cross the Mekong River "fence" with the moon shining brightly in our rearview mirrors.

★★★

Jack and I are debriefing tonight's mission in the rat's nest that is the Wing Intelligence office. All USAF intelligence shops are incredibly messy, with papers, books, charts, manuals, and general-purpose trash stacked everywhere. This one is no exception. You have to have a Top Secret clearance to enter the cipher-locked room, no janitors or houseboys are allowed in. No self-respecting intelligence officer is going to do mundane house cleaning, so the piles of stuff grow and grow.

At two o'clock in the morning, the duty Intelligence Officer is a male lieutenant. The cute female intelligence officers are only assigned to work in the daytime so the senior wing staff officers can ogle them. This male chauvinism is another less-than-good deal for us Sewer Doers. We are having a hard time getting through to this guy.

Jack says, "I tell you I picked up an ECM cut of a Firecan near tonight's target area in Laos. They nearly nailed us."

The intel weenie replies, "There are no Firecans in Laos. Seventh Air Force HQ in Saigon is quite adamant about that."

Jack presses on, "I heard the rattle, I identified the signal, the ECM scope correlated the pattern. As we orbited, the strobe pointed to the same point on the ground."

The lieutenant is unmoved. "You must have been mistaken, sir. There are no Firecans in Laos."

Now we are well into the Crazy Jack mode. Jack, his voice rising, fires again, almost shouting.

"Listen here, Sonny. I was tracing Firecans when you were still in three-cornered pants. If I say there's one in Laos, it's because I'm sure there is."

The veins are standing out on Jack's neck. This green intel guy has just insulted Jack's professional expertise as an EWO. If he had called Jack's mother a whore, the impact wouldn't have been worse. I am getting worried that this debriefing may end up in Fist City.

I interject, "Lieutenant, your job is to write up the after-action report as we tell it to you. All you need to do is to put down that we think a Firecan radar in Laos illuminated us tonight. If you do, Saigon will schedule an ECM recce bird to check it out. End of story. Then we can all go to the bar."

The lieutenant sticks to his guns. "Saigon says, "No Firecans in Laos" and that's what I have to report. I can call them on the secure phone and you can hear it for yourself, sir."

Jack is getting apoplectic. I fear violence in the intel shop. But by now, I have gotten the picture. I'm not dumb, just slow. The wing intelligence officers have been told to not forward any reports of a Firecan in Laos. If they do, the current Rules of Engagement require that the slow, vulnerable gunships be withdrawn from the danger zone. If Spectre doesn't work the trails, hundreds of trucks will escape getting racked up on the combat tally board. This will be a blow to the war effort, but a bigger blow to the staff officers who have sold the expensive gunship program to the brass. Also, the brass won't be able to brief the media in Saigon about all the trucks the USAF is killing every night.

I tell Crazy Jack, "Jack, let me handle this alone. I'll meet you at the bar."

Jack spurts a further protest but I continue.

"If you don't haul ass right now, I'll never let you fly the jet again."

That does it and Jack stalks out, slamming the security door behind him. I turn to the intel officer and stare him right in the eye, trying not to blink. I strive to speak in cold, measured tones, knowing that the underlying fury will burn through.

"Lieutenant, you can put whatever the hell you want in the after-action report. I have no control over what you transmit to Saigon. You can put in whatever you have been told to put in. To be more accurate, you can omit what you have been told to omit. However, there is a Firecan radar in southern Laos. I heard it and Jack identified it. If and when the Bad Guys link that radar to their guns and judging by the flak we took tonight, they have; there will be hell to pay with the Spectre gunships. There will be a trail of blood that leads from this shop all the way to Saigon. Is that clear?"

I get back from the chagrined intel type, "Yes, sir."

Now, it is my turn to stomp out. For once, I'm glad that this intel officer is male. I don't know if I would have been able to make that point as forcefully to one of his distaff counterparts. I walk to the bar by the light of the full moon, trying to shed some light on the difficulty of reconciling official policy with hard facts.

★★★

It's two nights later and I'm at the Officers' Club, enjoying a rare night off and a rare steak. Man lives not by Thai food alone. I intend to wash the steak down with plenty of the adult beverage distilled in Lynchburg, Tennessee. I'm still steamed by Jack's and my inability to get the USAF command authority to admit that there is a Firecan radar in southern Laos. My brain has obsessed with this issue so intently, all I can think of is a child's ditty, suitably modified:

"Firecan, Firecan,
Burning bright,
In the jungles
Of the night."

Credence probably won't make a hit out of that one, but I can't get the doggerel out of my head.

My meal arrives, served by a cute, curvy Thai waitress in a long slinky dress. She is tightly wrapped in the kind of thin dress that covers all but reveals everything. I wonder how she gets bright Thai silk to cling like that. Her skin-tight dress begs my overheated imagination to mentally picture its contents. It displays everything she has. As she walks away, there is no doubt in my mind that there is nothing under that dress but her. At least that's what I want to believe, therefore it's true. To me, she's nude but covered with gossamer silk. Some things can be hidden in plain sight. I guess some people see only what they want to see and others are blind to things they are told not to find.

My beef and brown whisky meal is interrupted when a squadron mate sticks his head in the side door of the club.

He yells, "Spectre is inbound to crash on the runway."

An AC-130 gunship has been hammered by anti-aircraft fire in Laos and is limping back to the base with two engines out, hydraulic system trouble, wounded men on board, and many holes in the airframe. The crew has radioed ahead to prepare the field for a crash landing. They want the fire crews and medical personnel ready and waiting.

Everyone there dining piles into the squadron jeep and we make it to the perimeter of the airfield just in time. With no warning, in the dark we hear the grinding, sliding noise of sheet metal scraping on hard concrete, like a ten-second auto crash. The big turbo prop has landed wheels up without lights, grinding its soft belly away on the runway.

I see a shower of sparks erupt into a raging fire as the wrecked airplane finally slides to a stop. The wing fuel tanks rupture and ignite, sending flames hundreds of feet straight up into the night sky. The inferno doesn't catch gradually but erupts instantly like a can of gasoline thrown on a campfire. I can make out the black outline of the AC-130, silhouetted against the flames with one wing broken down, the flat-bladed props twisted by the impact, and the wreckage skewed sideways off the runway into the adjacent mud.

Helplessly, I watch as men frantically climb out the shattered cockpit windows, black stick figures running through the flames. Maybe some of the flight deck crew escapes, but if there was anyone in the cargo compartment, they are doomed to incineration. Now, the whole aircraft is engulfed and the base fire trucks have reached the crash scene. There is no wind tonight, allowing the flames and smoke to boil straight up. The crash crew stops close in front of the burning wreck, their fire truck silhouetted in black like Lucifer's chariot against the fires of Hell.

Before the fire-smothering foam squirted from the truck has a chance to beat back the inferno, the dead gunship's ammunition starts cooking off, the cartridges detonating in the heat of the fire. A Spectre carries thousands of rounds of high explosive shells and the flames are consuming most of them. It sounds like the Devil's own popcorn popper as the rounds cook off in bursts of ten or twenty in close succession. The bullets fly in random directions out of the fire like crazed swarms of bees.

I shouldn't be this close to the carnage; I could easily get tagged with a wild round randomly launched by the fire even at this quarter-mile distance. But, I can't run. I have to see this tragic scene played out to its fiery end. Not only morbid curiosity holds me here. Agonized with guilt, I ask myself if Jack and I could have done more to head off the catastrophe unfolding in front of me. We alone were certain of the growing peril faced by the Spectre gunships and their crews. I can't stand not to watch. God help any men still trapped inside the Spectre.

The firemen abandon their truck in front of the crumpled AC-130 and run for their lives toward me and away from the exploding ammunition. I can see their fleeing forms struggling in their silver turnout suits against the still-raging fire as they keep the sacrificial fire truck between them and the lead-spitting inferno. The burning fuel, with sharp flashes embedded, lights the night scene even brighter as more rounds detonate inside the black hulk. I can see through the gaping holes in the plane's fuselage to the fire burning on the other side. Dante himself couldn't have pictured anything like the death of a Spectre.

It seems that Jack's analysis of the existence of a Firecan fire-control radar in Laos might just be more accurate than the careerists in Saigon have admitted, until now.

The waning moon hasn't risen over Thailand yet. I drive back to the O Club bar with the jeep's lights on. I hope my steak and drink are still there at my table. If not, I won't mind waiting as my replacement meal is served and watching again as the waitress' round butt stretches and pulls her sprayed-on skirt. Watching men die makes me think I should enjoy life while I still can. Can I eat, drink, and lust after the sexy waitress so soon after seeing what I just saw and remembering my part in the tragedy? Is that cold and heartless on my part? Or am I shoving those feeling of sympathy away as an act of mental health preservation? Maybe an orgasmic interlude will stifle the still, small voice in my head saying, "You could have done more, fought harder to sound the alarm." If Jack and I had snuffed it on the runway tonight, would the Spectre crew be at the bar? Damn right they would.

I think I'll order another steak, two more drinks (both in the same glass), and hit fast erase on my memory.

"Waitress, Honey, what time do you get off?"

TROUBLE IN PARADISE

On the shaded, screened-in veranda of the USAF Officers' Club at Clark Air Base on the Philippine island of Luzon, the living is easy; at least it's supposed to be that way. The Officers' Club occupies one corner of a rectangular green parade ground. The Visiting Officers' Quarters (the VOQ), at which I am a temporary guest, is on an adjacent corner. The flat expanse of the parade ground is carefully mowed and groomed, surrounded on all four sides by tall shade trees. These trees aren't the vertically towering oaks or the elms of more temperate climes, but are some sort of branching mangrove, shaped like inverted leafy triangles, nearly as wide at the top as they are tall. Even shade trees in the tropics are weird and different, but effective all the same.

From my comfortable deck chair on the porch, I can see the short circular drive from the parade ground leading to the club and back; the VOQ is hidden in the trees down the perimeter street to my left. What I can't see is the waiter who is supposedly fetching my drink.

At midday, it is already in the mid-80s, tonight, the temperature will fall all the way to the low 80s, now the ordered pina colada will hit the proverbial spot. Where is that guy?

I am in a cranky mood for a variety of reasons, ranging in magnitude from major to minor. My airplane is broken, a good friend of mine was shot down last night in the sewer, and my drink is nowhere to be seen. So, why am I here tying to relax on the veranda?

Clark has specialized aircraft maintenance capabilities not available at my combat base in Thailand. Our Phantom jets are flown to Clark on a periodic, routine schedule to have their vital systems, such as the fire control radar, checked out and maintained. It is an easy two-hour flight from northwest Thailand across Laos, Vietnam, and the South China Sea to the Philippines. It is unreal to think that a short flight not even requiring aerial refueling can transport my navigator, Jack, and me in one morning over a hot combat zone to the tropical paradise that is Clark. Such is the magic carpet of jet aviation. Usually a short stay at Clark is a welcome respite from the rigors and pressures of daily combat operations, but not today. Not while a buddy is on the ground in Laos. I want to be back at the war, in the air, armed to the teeth, assisting the search-and-rescue troops. I want to help get my friend up out of the jungle and safe from rotting to death in some hellhole of a prison camp in North Vietnam or worse, tortured to death by the Pathet Lao.

At last, my frosted drink arrives cold in its wasp-waisted glass, and I tell the Filipino waiter to put the charge on my incipient tab. I'm running a tab because sitting and drinking is all I am apt to do today. I can't fly back to the war until the mechanics fix my busted bird and thus I can't help my good friend in his rescue. I realize that my buddy on the ground in Laos is even now probably sitting and wishing he were drinking as well. Undoubtedly, a swig from a hot canteen would taste as good to him as my rum-based fruit concoction does to me. One of Southeast Asia's little ironies is that there is little available drinking water in the rain forest. It is even harder to procure a drink there, where it rains 200 inches a year, than on this veranda.

I am acutely sympathetic to my friend's thirst plight due to firsthand knowledge I gained in the local jungle surrounding Clark. This is the home of the USAF Asian Jungle Survival School. Attendance and graduation is required of all USAF pilots stationed in this theater of war. To survive in Latin American jungles, you have to go to another school in the

Panama Canal Zone. I'm not sure if the requirement for two, count-'em, two, jungle survival schools is due to marked differences in flora and fauna between South American and Asian jungles. The existence of two schools is probably generated by the fact that each school is administered by a completely separate USAF organization. The difference lies in bureaucratic jungles and not in actual rain forests.

In any case, water is very hard to find on the ground in Laos. It rains constantly, but the thirsty vegetation and the muddy soil soak up the falling water on impact. There are few streams and no lakes or ponds in the jungle highlands of Laos. The Bad Guys, hoping to nab a downed airman when he comes to cop a drink, tightly patrol what running water that does exist. It must be maddening to be dripping wet with sweat, rain, and fear in a land where the precipitation totals over 200 hundred inches a year and still not be able to find a sip of fresh water.

The dueling USAF jungle survival school bureaucracies haven't been able to agree on the design of a canteen to provide to pilots, one suitable for carry in fighter cockpits. Thus, we all employ our own improvised water containers. The current favorite is the plastic baby bottle, mailed from the States by wives and mothers. These are filled with tap water and capped without the nipple. I carry four, in shades of pink and blue, in the ankle pockets of my flight suit. On the veranda, I take a long sip of my pina colada from its tall, curvy glass and I wonder if my friend is now sipping some of his precious and dwindling water from a baby bottle, and if so, I speculate on the color of his improvised canteen. It is either blue, pink, or yellow. I'm at the Officers' Club drinking iced rum and coconut milk from a glass shaped with a definite feminine profile and he is sipping warm water from a baby bottle in the Laotian jungle. For the life of me, I can't quite make the Freudian connection that surely exists in these parallel situations.

At the daily Command Post briefing, I learned this morning that a Phantom with a familiar call sign was shot down while "sewer doing" over southern Laos late last night. The intelligence briefing listed the names of the two downed crewmembers. One of the guys was from my class in pilot training; I have flown on his wing and he on mine many times. I know his wife by her nickname, I have been to their house for dinner, and we exchange Christmas cards. I got on the military phone network and called my squadron in Thailand. The duty officer was prevented by security regulations from filling me in on the details while using the unsecured phone line, but he was able to tell me that the rescue effort was under way, which I already knew, but that no pickup was imminent. He couldn't tell me if the rescue forces had made radio contact with the two guys on the ground or not. I hope so, and I hope the waiter will hurry with my second drink as I hand him the now empty first glass, after eating the fresh pineapple wedge floating in the foamy bottom. I hope my pal is remembering what he learned in survival school, that the practiced techniques and instructions are suppressing the panic and fear in his mind.

The instruction at Clark's jungle school is dispensed by two-man teams of instructors made up of USAF enlisted troops and Negrito Pygmy warriors from the Philippine jungles. From them, I learned how to find water pooled in palm fronds, to cut jungle vines and suck the watery sap, and how to tap a "water tree" with my Bowie knife. This was all great fun here in the local jungle. I once cut a creeper vine and swung across a ravine like a clumsy Tarzan, only to crash into the anchor tree on the far side. The most fun was being winched up out of the jungle like a fish on a line by means of a cable dangling from a search and rescue helicopter.

I wonder if my friend is using any of the knowledge shared by the Negritos. I wonder if he is able to, or are the Bad Guys too close and he can only hide from view? Is he too stressed to think clearly? Is he hurt? Are the jungle water sources as plentiful as the helpful Negritos demonstrated? Will that pineapple wedge make my tongue break out? I've had fresh pineapple in jungle school, but I can't remember if it affected me then as the Negritos cooked it in rice.

The Pygmies here are an entirely different race from the other native Filipinos, with dark black skin and curly hair as opposed to light brown skin and straight black hair of the more numerous Filipinos. They stand about four and a half feet tall. Negrito Pygmies are some of the most quietly competent, impressive men I have ever met. They are soft spoken, polite, and dignified people with a personal knowledge of the jungle that I find staggering. They never volunteer information to us huge Americans, that would be rude, but they answer any question with great patience. Natural-born instructors, they have a long tribal tradition of passing on jungle lore using detailed demonstrations. They are proud of their know-how and are eager to transfer even a tiny fraction of it to us ignorant pilots. They are inherently proud people with a quiet reserve and, a keen sense of humor. I get the firm impression they are not easily angered, but that they would not suffer a serious affront gladly.

Every male Negrito carries a primitive wooden sheath holding a ten-inch bolo knife with a hand-carved wooden handle. It is a rite of passage for a Pygmy warrior to forge his own knife out of a leaf spring salvaged from a junked jeep. Using his homemade knife, he can extract a splinter from your finger, skin a snake, and chop down a tree, hopefully in that order.

Despite their competence in the tropical jungle, or perhaps because of it, the minority Negritos are much despised by the majority of Filipinos. I'm sure racial prejudice is at the bottom of the situation. There is constant friction between the two groups usually to the detriment of the Negritos. However, occasionally a Filipino will cross the fuzzy line between a verbal slight and a serious insult. That foolish individual runs the risk of disappearing into the jungle at the hands of the Pygmies.

I don't want to know what else the Negritos can do with those razor-sharp knives. Negritos are not allowed on the main base at Clark. The top brass (or more likely, their wives) are of the opinion that the routine appearance on base of half-naked black Pygmies with big knives would disturb the tropical tranquility. Hence, the waiter scurrying forth with my next cold libation is a more familiar subservient, light skinned, taller Filipino. The service at this club needs improvement. An idyllic setting should generate impeccable service.

If life at Clark AB, the Philippines, doesn't make you a believer in colonialism, nothing will. Clark was established as a U.S. Army base after our country took over the Philippines from Spain shortly after the turn of the current century. It was "You may fire when ready, Gridley" in Manila Bay and we had ourselves a colony. Generals Douglas MacArthur and his father, Arthur MacArthur, served here. This is the place which MacArthur *fils* referred to when he theatrically announced in the dark days of WWII, "I shall return." A half century of U.S. military presence here (with time out for the Japanese occupation) has slowly transformed an airfield carved out of the jungle in the middle of the island of Luzon into an idyllic wonderland of transplanted Americana.

Unlike the combat bases in Thailand and Vietnam, dependents, wives, and children of military personnel are allowed, even encouraged, to live and live well on Clark Air Base. A posting to Clark means three to five years of easy times. In contrast, assignments to the war zone are for one year, without dependents, and the living there is not at all easy. The presence of so many women and children here at Clark has generated a weird kind of tropical suburbia, Asian colonial style. The streets near the parade ground are lined with large, square houses built on six-foot pilings allowing air, floods, and snakes to circulate freely underneath. Each house has screened porches on all four sides and a tin roof. These officers' family quarters were probably built between World Wars I and II.

Each family has a Filipino maid, a cook, and a houseboy/gardener. The senior officers have personal drivers as well. The USAF provides most of the physical comforts of home and on the cheap to boot. A well-stocked Base Exchange and Commissary has all the food and consumer goods from back in the good ol' USA. The local produce and personal services are also very affordable. I can hear dozens of kids splashing in the Officers' Club pool behind me. Next to the pool are the tennis courts where Filipino tennis pros give lessons to officers' wives for a dollar an hour. In their immaculate white tennis outfits, the adept pros will serve, volley, or lose as many games to you as you wish.

Which reminds me that I have no plans for tonight. My jet is awaiting replacement parts from the States and I am at loose ends. The social opportunities on base are limited. I could have dinner in the main ballroom of the club. A decent dinner there will be highlighted by the performance of a fifteen-piece orchestra right out of the big band era. They put out those Benny Goodman tunes six nights a week and do it perfectly. The lead singer is a Filipino version of Frank Sinatra without the mafia connections, but with the tux and patent leather elevator shoes. A local girl singer, gorgeous in a sprayed-on ball gown, accompanies him. She is Manila's answer to Abby Lane. This scene is very popular with the senior officers and their wives. As I am scheduled to be slightly drunk tonight, dinner in the ballroom might be a career-limiting choice. Besides, gaping at a curvy Filipina poured into a skintight dress would be damaging to my morale, if not my morals.

In the basement of the club, there is a casual bar appealing to a younger crowd. The service in the "Pit" includes steaks, fries, burgers, beer, and booze, not necessarily in that order. The formal entertainment downstairs is provided by a rock and roll band whose lead singer sounds more like Elvis than Elvis does. Visiting airline stewardesses, the nearly grown daughters of senior officials, and the lonely wives of absent junior officers often provide the informal entertainment. But somehow, the loud, smoky bar scene doesn't fit my current mood either.

On the hill overlooking the main base is the Clark golf club. The attendant staff serves a Mongolian barbecue on the patio of the clubhouse to the accompaniment of an authentic sounding Filipino country and western band. That will do nicely tonight. There is nothing like well-prepared barbecue washed down with a drink sporting a little umbrella on top of the glass, even if the barbecue owes more to Nanking than Nashville. In any case, I can savor my meal to sad music dripping with hillbilly despair. Songs about time in jail, dear old Mama, trains, and cheating lovers will suit my current mood just fine.

I wonder who will be next to get shot down in combat. The wing from Da Nang lost an F-4 three days ago. The second loss was my friend who got tagged last night. The rule of three will not be denied. Fighter pilots as a rule are not a superstitious lot. I believe in luck, both good and bad, but prefer to rely on my eyesight, reflexes, and skill rather than some nutty superstition. However, most of us believe that aircraft losses come in groups of three, despite all data to the contrary. As one of my squadron mates pithily put it, "Shit sandwiches come in three bites." Who will be next?

On my way into the main bar to make a reservation tonight for the patio, I pass the rank of slot machines and feed in a nickel, but to no avail. I think that it is somehow fitting that the Officers' Club has these one-armed bandits readily available to instruct the casual observer on the fundamental role that luck and the odds have in determining our fate. This gaming luck that doesn't seem to respond to superstition rituals.

I'm here in the lap of tropical luxury furnished by the US government while my friend is hiding in the jungles of Laos. Of course, his immediate predicament was also furnished by the government. Why did his airplane come unglued over the Ho Chi Minh Trail and why did mine break down at Clark? It could have just as easily been me now running for my life and hoping to stretch that life another day. He could have been here deciding between rock and roll and country and western. I guess this time, I hit the situational jackpot and he came up with snake eyes.

At least my broken airplane can eventually get me back into the air again, as soon as the parts arrive from the States. Normally a busted jet is no big deal at an operational fighter base. If the airplane I am scheduled to fly is down for parts, I just walk down the ramp and pick out another one. However, if there is only one Phantom on the base and it belongs to you, when it's broken, it's personal. It seems that some key part of my personality, maybe even my manhood, is nonoperational. What is a fighter pilot without a fighter plane, an ordinary guy? Phantoms aren't supposed to break; they are supposed to fly me around with speed and style. That is, if the word "style" can be applied to a double-ugly F-4.

There are some who would say that a Phantom looks broken, even when it isn't. The designers bent the wing tips upward, apparently as an afterthought. The fuselage is both humpbacked and cola-bottle shaped, leading to a bulbous black nose. The dual canopies are small, too small to see out of well. The horizontal tail stabilators droop down to an alarming degree and the top of the vertical stabilizer is cut off. If there was ever an airplane designed by feuding committee members, it is the Phantom. The brown, green, and mud-colored camouflage paint scheme doesn't help either.

Sometimes, I envy the guys who fly other more comely jets. I'd love to drive the stiletto-thin F-104 Starfighter or the aptly named F-106 Delta Dagger, Even the spear-shaped F-105 "Thunderchief" wouldn't be too bad. Those are pretty airplanes, fashioned with sleek lines, pointy noses, and harmonious curves.

The Phantom has one thing going for it. The airframe is immensely strong and solid, with size and weight aplenty. It is wrapped around two huge engines that ram all that metal through the air with dispatch. It totes a larger bomb load than the B-17 Flying Fortress of WWII and mounts more missiles on one wing than the effete F-106 carries internally in its whole airframe. With its butt-ugly lines, shit-colored paint, yawning air intakes, and dangling armament racks, the Phantom is the consummate war machine. It can bomb, strafe, launch missiles, and return me home at the speed of heat.

However, it is not reassuring to remember that my awesome fighting device is now laid low, grounded, by the absence of a small greasy part, whose replacement is rumored to appear any day now. Oh well, I guess those pretty jets break sometimes too. Until the missing but crucial bit arrives, there is nothing to do but kick back and live like a colonial Englishman while my friend is living like a hunted rabbit over in Laos.

I ask myself, "Do I feel guilty, living like this, while my ex-squadron mate is trying to simply carry on living?" The answer comes back from inside my head that I don't feel that way at all. The one-armed bandit of war has spun me triple sevens while my buddy got dealt junk under the pay line. I have to believe this or else it would be very hard to strap on that airplane and go back to combat. I could go crazy trying to make sense of why things happen the way they do.

If combat survival depends only on skill, who has enough skill? Some of the most skilled guys in the USAF are now eating pumpkin soup in the Hanoi Hilton, while lesser pilots are already back home safe in the United States. There is no doubt that skill is important, but there is something else at work in determining who lives and who dies. If a God is calling the shots, why does He bag some guys and not others? Who knows what you would have to do to curry favor with such a capricious God? And which God do you choose to suck up to? My mental well-being requires me to attribute the random outcomes of war mostly to fate and the odds. You can't predict or question either fate or slot machines, both wheel and deal and all you can do is cope or enjoy.

I guess there are many ways to enjoy Asia and it is my turn of luck to experience one of the better ones. All I have to do is sit back and breathe deeply. The essence of Asia is floating in through the screens of the veranda.

Asia is, above all, a smell, an aroma, an odor. The smell of Asia is unmistakable. Once that bouquet hit into my olfactory nerve the first time, I knew it was captured there forever, like a sensual virus. The smell assaults your nose with your first breath of Asian air wafting through the open door of a commercial airliner after landing in Singapore. That sensory effect is replicated when you raise a Phantom's canopy on the ramp of a USAF base in Thailand. I'm sure the Navy guys smell it on board ship long before landfall at Cam Ranh Bay, Vietnam.

The smell of Asia is omnipresent, from the fragrant harbor of Hong Kong, to the jungles of the Philippines, to the Chao Phraya River in Bangkok. It is the smell of rotting vegetation, of constant heat, and dense humidity. It is fetid jungles and brown-water rivers. It is too many people in too small an area. It is rice paddies and banana groves and mangrove swamps and rain forests. It is jacaranda trees and bamboo thickets. But, the smell of Asia is also pungent sesame oil in a hot wok, of fresh fruits too numerous to identify. It rises from fermented fish sauce and lemongrass. It is exotic flowers and strange food laced with unfamiliar spices. It is the aura of mind bending perfume and of radiant Thai silk sliding on bare brown skin. It is dust and mud and incense burned in a temple. It is sweet-and-sour sauce with the fiery hot chilies the Thais call "rat turds." It is the floral output of decay, of parasitic growth, and of incredible beauty. If orchids had an aroma, that would be the smell of Asia.

I have read that your brain remembers a particular smell longer and more distinctly that any other single sensory input. It seems that the return of a long-forgotten but once-familiar odor will trigger old memories and will bring to your mind's surface thoughts long buried. I also remember reading that Napoleon said he could smell the fragrant shrubs of Corsica sixty miles across the Tyrrhenian Sea from his exile on Elba. The aromas of his birth island made the little emperor homesick. I wonder if I will be able to remember the smell of Asia once, and if, I return home? Or will I have to return to Asia to breathe it in again? Will I want to?

The screened-in porch of the Officers' Club filters the smell of Asia and mixes it with scents of fresh-mowed grass, of chorine from the swimming pool, and the antiseptic spoor common to government buildings, but the screens don't change the fundamental aroma of Asia. The presence of Clark Air Base in the Philippines has temporarily altered the makeup of the islands. We have brought our food, our lawn mowers, our crystalline pools, and the smell of our spilt blood. Once we Americans leave, the smell of Asia will return unfiltered and unchanged. The impact of our western culture on the overpowering smell of Asia will fade like footprints in the muddy jungles of Laos.

The presence of Asia, which totally surrounds Clark Air Base, seems to only minimally affect the American subculture within the perimeter fence. However, the reverse is not true. Outside the base lies the local town of Angeles City and if there was ever a city more inappropriately named, it is not on this planet. There are no angels in Angeles City. There are bars, restaurants, nightclubs, casinos, liquor stores, whorehouses, cheap motels, and drug dens. Usually all these businesses seamlessly occupy the same building. An American can enjoy any pleasure of the flesh, any drink, any drug, or any sexual preference in Angeles City and save money doing it. Sin is cheap in the Philippines.

On the air base, the crime rate is zero and the sin rate only slightly higher, depending on whose definition of sin is being applied. Things are buttoned down on Clark AB. Outside the base, anything goes and the local mobsters make it happen. Yesterday, the Mayor of Angeles City was cut down by machine-gun fire on the steps of City Hall. Despite the large crowd present, no witnesses have come forward. Rumors on the motive for the mob hit are rampant, but none include overdue parking tickets. As a matter of fact, the mayoral murder probably didn't stem from any previous breach of the law, as almost nothing is illegal in Angeles City.

As wild as Angeles City is, conventional military wisdom holds that the Philippine town of Olongopo outside the U.S. Navy base at Subic Bay makes Angeles City look like Davenport, Iowa. I guess those anchor clankers are ready to party hearty after six months at sea and for sure the local entrepreneurs are only too willing to accommodate them. In Olongopo, it is rumored the booze and sex flow like rainwater down the middle of the streets, as opposed to the relatively sedate social life outside Clark Air Base.

As I relax on the veranda, I wonder once again why it seems we manage to export only the indulgent portions of our American culture to Asia. Why don't we spread the ideas of democracy, the rule of law, of individual rights, and freedom? Instead, we seem to pass along only the concept of the honky-tonk. Instead of teaching the locals, be they Filipino, Thai, or Vietnamese, how to vote, we teach them how to sing like Elvis. Maybe the problem isn't so much with the transmittal of our culture, but rather with the ground on which it falls. Is this a cultural case of Gresham's law, where the counterfeit currency drives the real gold out of circulation? There are no crummy honkytonks outside our bases in Europe. The mob doesn't run towns bordering USAF facilities in Iceland. Why do Asians embrace our baser values and not our best aspects? Are we not trying hard enough, or are they not receptive? Who teaches them these things? What they seem to be receptive to is our money given in exchange for a good time.

The readily available local debauchery doesn't appeal to me, at least not yet. However, my navigator has tasted of the fruit of the vine in the garden of sin and has found it favorable. He tossed his duffel bag on the bed on the VOQ when we arrived a week ago and split for the fleshpots of Angeles City.

A few months ago we took another airplane for a major overhaul to Taipei on the island of Taiwan. Jack pulled the same disappearing stunt. He returned later that night with someone who he called an "ornamental girl" (instead of "Oriental girl") in tow. Whenever he has found enthusiastic feminine company, he has always suggested that I would be much more comfortable vacating the room and sleeping outside on the patio hammock. It's touching when he wants his pilot, that would be me, to enjoy the cool night smells of Asia unscreened and outdoors.

For a change on this trip away from our home base, I have had the room all to myself. Jack checks in from time to time to see if the jet is still broken, to top off his aftershave supply, and to tell me how much he has won at the crap tables. He seems to have taken the recent shoot down in stride, not knowing either of the crewmembers. I wish I could be as blasé. Maybe a night with a willing Filipino girl snuggled up naked next to me in the VOQ would take my mind off what is happening on the ground in Laos, but probably not. I think I'll just cry in my drink tonight in time to a Hank Williams ballad of lost love.

Even if I wanted to enjoy having a lithe brown body next to me tonight on base, I couldn't. The USAF is looking after my morals for me; no local talent allowed in the VOQ. The thought of a government bureaucracy being in charge of the strength of my moral fiber causes me to drain the last dregs of my second pina colada in one gulp.

My navigator's sexual and gambling adventures (not unrelated activities) occur exclusively off base here in the Philippines. In what seems to me to strongly suggest yet more racial prejudice, Filipino girlfriends are not allowed on Clark by the U.S. Air Force. Female maids, house girls, and cooks are permitted, but not social companions, not even in the "Pit" at the O Club. The USAF Air Police stop any local female without a permanent work badge, escorted or not, at the gate. The senior powers that be, and/or their wives, don't want cute brown ladies of questionable morals readily available. Perhaps the American women can't stand the talented competition.

There are few single "round-eyed" women on Clark, which is one of the reasons that, as George Thorogood sings in his rock classic, I drink alone. A handful of schoolteachers, a few teenaged daughters, and the visiting airline stewardesses (married or not), that's about it. Far too few single girls are available to provide social opportunities for the many male bachelors. This could be easily rectified, but not according to the USAF. Above all, conservative western moral behavioral norms must be upheld.

It is tolerable, even applauded, to bed the wife or daughter of someone stationed on base as long as they are white or black and American. That sort of thing happens all the time. However, it is forbidden in the interest of morality for two consenting adults to conduct a commercial transaction involving sex if the female half of the pair is Filipino. It is not even allowed to couple for free with the locals. Free and extramarital is OK. Paid and single is not OK. Even free and single Filipino sex is not OK. Go figure.

Not that all, or even most, of the town girls are pros. There are plenty of nubile young Filipina ladies who would like nothing better than to hook up with a GI to taste the wedded bliss of matrimony. A marriage certificate is a surefire ticket to the land of plenty back in the United States and away from the tropical poverty of the Philippine Islands. I guess this is why all the waiters in the Officers' Club are male. Uncle Sam is once again looking out for my best interests. Having dozens of mini-skirted waitresses readily at hand might lead to something untoward.

I guess the moral police would rather my navigator take his chances in some mob-controlled fleabag motel in Angeles City than in the safe VOQ. While I'm not in the commercial dating game, yet, it frosts my ass to think that my government trusts me with a multimillion-dollar jet, but doesn't trust my choice of female companions. I can easily get shot down like my buddy and spend the rest of my nights with the rats in the Hanoi Hilton for my country. But, I can't bed a willing Filipino for even one night in the VOQ whether she is doing it for love or money. Supposedly, we are fighting the Vietnam war for our way of life, but our way of life seems to lose something, to get debased, when transplanted into Asia. How does the message get mixed up? I can't teach these people to vote if I can't even organize a sleepover.

The thought of forced celibacy drives me to drink, not that far a journey, and I order another one from the nearby waiter. I ponder what all this means while contemplating my newly empty glass shaped like the hourglass figure I won't be seeing tonight.

Jack and I are theoretically fighting for the land of the free and the home of the brave, as another famous song goes. The version of this one that I prefer is not by George Thorogood, but was performed by ex-paratrooper Jimi Hendrix at Woodstock. I think we have got the brave part covered, or at least my buddy Jack does. After all, he flies with me. It seems the freedom part needs a little work. When we joined the military, in exchange for the opportunity to fly jet fighters we agreed to give up certain freedoms. We have forgone living where we want and we gave up the idea of getting rich. We gave up the freedom to run when we're scared and we agreed to risk giving up the freedom of life itself. It seems that we have also given up the freedom to sleep with who we want, where we want. I'm sure this enforced morality makes sense and if that waiter would get his ass in gear with my next drink, I could figure it out.

I hear footsteps behind me and turn to take pina colada number three, but find my trusty navigator instead, flashing a big, shit-eating grin. He tells me that he has just come from the base Command Post and that the Jolly Green Giant helicopters have fished both crewmen out of the Laotian jungle and that they are en route to Thailand, safe and sound. I didn't know Jack was querying the CP several times a day.

I break into my own version of his grin and reply, "Shit hot!" That is a load off my mind and all my intentions of analyzing the USAF version of sexual purity evaporate instantly.

Jack invites me into Angeles City tonight to celebrate, but I decline. My almost-lost buddy is heading for a wild party of his own at the Officers' Club at his home base, as is the custom after a successful rescue. I'm still scheduled solo for some high lonesome sounds on the hilltop patio. Now, I can really get seriously into sad country songs without some well-rhymed and nasally expressed emotions spilling over into what passes for my reality.

AND TO ALL A GOOD NIGHT

There is only an hour to go until midnight and the blessed arrival of Christianity's holiest night of the year and the beast is waking up. The beast in question is an F-4D Phantom II strapped firmly to my butt. The ground crew and I are about to roust it from the slumbering security of its flight line revetment. Until we do, the beast is nothing more than 50,000 pounds of inert metal. The keepers of the beast are ready; it's time to go to work.

With my left hand, I push the two battery toggle switches behind the throttles to "on" and the instrument panel leaps to life, each black dial containing a white-glowing needle. By the red cockpit lights now illuminated I can see that many needles are flaccid and limp against their lower stops, but some are erect and ready to perform. In the rearview mirror suspended inside the canopy top arch, I can see my navigator with his helmeted head down in the rear cockpit. He is busy aligning the jet's inertial reference platform and preparing to perform his own pre-flight checks.

The yellow auxiliary power cart is screaming away just off the left wing tip. Its own tiny, noisy jet turbine is spinning a generator, pushing electric power through a fat black cable into our Phantom energizing the aircraft electric system. Also attached is a six-inch air hose, a yellow fabric corrugated umbilical. It runs underneath the aircraft to the center of the fuselage, connecting the hard-working start cart to the navel of the Phantom. The cart is howling, ready to pump compressed air to the onboard starter turbines.

I raise my leather-gloved right hand over the windscreen, high enough to be seen by the ground crew chief, with my index finger pointing at the hot night sky of Thailand. I spin my finger and hand in a tight spiral, telling the chief,

"Start number one."

The sergeant pushes a large red button on the side of the start cart. I feel the drowsy jet quiver, as the starter turbine is force-fed hot air, spinning to life one huge J-79 jet engine buried in the aluminum belly of the beast. As the left rpm gauge reaches 10 percent (the tachometers are calibrated in percentage of maximum rpm's, not with the actual number of revs) my left hand pushes the massive right throttle forward past the lockout detent. At the same time, I push the ignition button on the base of the throttle's handgrip and hold it down with my thumb.

At about 45 percent rpm, the beast starts to grumble, roused from its slumber. A fire is lit in its gut, as a drink of JP-4 jet fuel torches off in the combustion chamber. The rpms climb to about 75 percent and I feel the engine thrust report for duty, straining to move the Phantom forward against the chocked wheels. Engine oil pressure, fuel flow, and exhaust gas temperature are normal, according to my gauges.

The ground crew scrambles underneath the plane to move the air umbilical connection over to the right engine. When they all emerge into view, I raise my right hand once again, with two fingers up and rotating,

"Start number two."

I repeat the process and the right J-79 whines up into fiery life. I make an unplugging motion with my hands and the crew yanks off the air hose and the electrical cable. The airplane is now on its own power, truly wide awake and growling with malevolent energy, leashed by wooden chocks propped against the main landing gear wheels. The beast is awake, but what sort of nocturnal animal am I riding and hopefully controlling?

Some fighter planes seem to me to be feline in profile, made up of smooth compound curves with sleek-flowing lines. This category includes all fighters designed in France, where esthetic form evidently dictates aerodynamic function. The French company Dassault's Mirages imitate enormous Persian cats with their dark color schemes, sleekly faired bodies, and pointy noses. The slanting lines of their Plexiglas cockpit canopies seem particularly like clear feline eyes. Eyes with humans in their pupils, that is. In the air, French Mirages are all about agility and grace, with tiny, sharp missiles, the claws of the airborne cats.

English jets invariably resemble ungainly dogs, maybe Basset or Walker hounds, with gangly discordant parts assembled with no thought to visual esthetics. The English Electric Lightning, the British Aircraft Company's Buccaneer, and the best of breed, the Hawker Hunter, are like a disparate pack of enthusiastic canines of different breeds. British jets are friendly and functional, almost lovable in their apparently uncoordinated designs and unconventional configurations. English fighters are dogs of uncertain lineage and dubious pedigree, but they're appealing all the same.

American jet fighters are typically not feline or canine in nature, but most are decidedly of the equine persuasion. They tend to be large, rawboned, strong, but not terribly refined in form. A good analogy is a faithful, but homely, cow pony aircraft such as the F-100 Super Sabre remind me of a quarter horse, with sturdy lines and a short stature. The F-105 Thunderchief is certainly not an Arabian or a Clydesdale, but a Thoroughbred with long legs and rippling muscles. A Thoroughbred with a brown-and-tan pinto colored paint scheme to be precise. American fighter jocks unconsciously buy into the cowboy/horseman scene with our talk of "mounting up" and "top guns." I have heard of an F-105 pilot who, when he releases the brakes and plugs in the afterburner for takeoff, always announces in true rodeo fashion, "Coming out of chute number one, Stoney Burke."

The F-104 Starfighter pilots even proudly wear what they call "spurs," which are really metal clips strapped to the heels of their flying boots. These high tech rowels allow the ejection seat to reel in their feet, better to clear the instrument panel when explosively ejecting from a stricken aircraft. The F-104 has to be an Arabian horse, small, elegant and responsive to subtle inputs, but treacherous for the unschooled pilot/rider.

Unfortunately, the Phantom fits none of these noble animal-toaircraft analogies. It is nothing if it is not a generic primal beast, ugly but immensely powerful. Seen from the front of its steel and concrete revetment cave, it looks like a large ill-tempered monster lurking in its lair. The F-4's thick wings with their upturned tips, the downward drooping tail, the big black nose, are the couching limbs and peering face of some mythic, evil creature, ready to pounce on the unwary.

What of the MiG fighters flown by our enemy, the air force of North Vietnam? MiGs are like rats; crude, small, and sloppily built. Their cockpits are probably dirty inside. They have droopy, pointed noses and long tails dragging in the air behind them. The Russian-built aircraft are dangerous, in a vermin sort of way. Without effective air-to-air missiles, they try to gnaw you to death with machine gun and cannon fire. MiGs are fit only for extermination.

Whatever feral animal it resembles, the Phantom beast must be tested, tamed before flight. I perform a kind of pas de deux with the crew chief using the cockpit stick and rudder to check out the flight controls. I move the stick and he responds with hand signals indicating what the control surfaces are doing. Stick full left-left spoiler up, right aileron down, rudder left. Stick full right-right spoiler up, left aileron down, rudder right. Stick full forward (in the "makes houses look bigger" position)-stabilator leading edge up. Stick full back ("makes houses look smaller")-stabilator leading edge full down.

Foot pedals full left and right-rudder full left and right. Speed brakes are tested to open and close with a switch on the inboard throttle. The beast's major muscle groups are limber.

My navigator comes up on the intercom. "Cleared primary and synch."

This means the inertial navigation platform is aligned with the local vertical direction and with true north, where it will remain throughout the flight. I synchronize my heading indicator with the platform. A deep breath and I point both thumbs outward on each side of the cockpit, telling the crew chief to pull the yellow wooden chocks blocking the main gear wheels from creeping forward under the engines' power at idle.

The chief replicates my thumbs outward signal and waves me forward, out of the chocks. I inch both throttles forward and the beast starts to emerge from its protective cave. I tap the wheel brakes by rocking the rudder pedals forward slightly and the nose dips, signaling the brakes are OK. A touch of right and left rudder moves the nose correspondingly; the nose wheel steering is operative.

I think to myself, "Quick! Which way do I turn?"

The Phantom can travel at 1500 miles per hour in the forward direction, but it can't back up at all. There are two identical lines of revetments facing each other in a "I' configuration on the flight line. If I turn the wrong way, toward oncoming aircraft traffic, I'm screwed. I'll have to shut the engines down, have the jet pushed back into the revetment with a tractor, and redo the start process. My squadron mates will then gleefully ride my ass about my fighter pilot faux pas for the rest of my life. Thank God for the crew chief; he is on my left side using hand signals for a left turn out of the revetment. I head the jet left, using a touch more power and a tap on the left brake to make the sharp turn. Heading off to war, I flash the chief a big thumbs-up sign, thanking him for a highly professional start. In return, he whips a snappy hand salute.

The crew chief and his assistants service and care for the Phantom I'm flying tonight, working twelve hours a day, six days a week. They give the ugly jet TLC outdoors, in monsoon downpours and burning Thai sun. The beast is their pet.

I know as the chief salutes me when I taxi by he is speculating about the condition in which I will return his plane. Will major aircraft systems be broken, requiring hours of repairs? Will there be battle damage, bullet holes? His worst fear is that it will not come back at all, that his beast will die. He worries that I will scatter the object of his mechanical affections in little pieces over North Vietnam tonight. As he handed me my helmet, standing at the top of the boarding ladder, He told me,

"Good luck tonight, Sir."

Translation, "Don't bring my precious airplane back shot full of holes that I have to fix."

I make a mental note to try very hard not to do that.

My navigator checks out his cockpit systems as we taxi to the arming area at the end of the runway. On ground control frequency, my wingman comes up on the radio to tell me that his jet is broken. He is aborting tonight's flight, as there is no spare aircraft available. Ordinarily, I would also cancel out as well. Flying ground attack sorties solo is not a plan for long-term survival. But tonight, the primary danger will be intense boredom. Satan Flight, now a flight of one, is scheduled for a Combat Sky Spot. We will not venture below 20,000 feet.

Parked in the arming area with the engines again humming at idle, the Nav and I extend our hands clear of the cockpit, showing the munitions crew that we are not fooling around with any switches or flight controls as they arm the weapons.

The arming crew scurries underneath the jet, checking for leaks and pulling the safety pins with their attached red flags from the bomb racks, drop tanks, and missiles. Finished, they show me hands full of red streamers confirming the jet is now lethal to someone beside us. Tonight's load is twelve 500 pound bombs, a total of 6,000 pounds of cast steel and high explosives, along with two Sparrow air-to-air missiles.

Jack and I lower our canopies and he changes the radio to tower frequency. I ask for and receive permission to take the runway and I'm cleared for takeoff, when ready, by the air traffic controller.

Pointed down the strip of dark concrete, I douse the bright white taxi light to start acquiring some night vision. The black runway is visible only in outline, lit by amber edge lights. The wing flaps move down to the one-half position in response to a small yellow flap-shaped lever on the left wall of the cockpit.

I push both throttles to the first stop and the engines quickly wind up to 100 percent thrust, pushing the nose down, straining mightily against the locked wheel brakes. It takes nearly all my foot strength to hold the brakes against the engine thrust; the beast is raring to go. A quick check of the gauges shows all is normal. I release the brakes and the nose bobs up, the beast is unleashed. I push the throttles past the first detent into the afterburner range and feel a boot in the ass as the extra thrust kicks in. A quick glance at the gauges confirms what my butt has already told me; both burners are lit.

Despite 5,000 pounds of iron bombs, an equal weight of fuel in two drop tanks, and full internal fuel, the Phantom accelerates briskly. Thirty-five thousand pounds of jet thrust will not be denied. I work the rudder pedals to keep the plane straight on the narrow, high-crowned runway.

Unlike most jets, which demand some finesse with the controls to be coaxed safely off the runway, a Phantom takeoff is a no-brainer. When I release the brakes, I pull the control stick all the way back against my lap, hold it there and wait. As the nose comes up to ten degrees above the invisible horizon, I start the stick forward to hold the nose steady and we "slip the surly bonds of earth." as the poem says. The runway lights recede in my peripheral vision and we climb into the dark Thai night. I raise the flaps and slap the landing gear lever to the up position. The gear lever on most jets is a small handle, maybe six inches long with a lighted wheel on its end in case you forget what it is for. Not for the F-4 such a wimpy handle. The Phantom's gear lever is all of a foot and a half long, thick in diameter, with a large red-lighted wheel on its end. It looks as if it belongs on a steam locomotive, not a flying machine.

As the flaps retract, I get a definite sinking sensation due to the loss of extra lift they produced. At 300 feet in the air and only 200 knots with nothing ahead but soggy rice paddies, a sinking situation is unsettling, but normal. I instinctively pull the stick back another inch and the sink rate stops. This is the only time I ever feel the Phantom's full 50,000 pounds of weight; once the airspeed builds, the jet feels solid and agile.

Tonight's liftoff isn't as hairy as the ones the U.S. Navy pilots experience when they are shot off their aircraft carrier at night into a totally black abyss. They leave the boat only seventy feet above the water, just barely flying. They can have that experience all to themselves; a night takeoff from a runway with a fully loaded jet thrills me quite enough, thank you very much.

I confirm the landing gear and flaps have retracted with a glance at the gauges and pull the engines out of afterburner as we accelerate through 350 knots. The engines settle down at 100 percent power and our rate of climb slackens. The fuel flow assumes a more reasonable rate of consumption now that the greedy afterburners are shut down. Fading unseen into the black behind us are the lights of the air base and of Ubon City as we continue to climb into the night. The dark lands of Laos and North Vietnam are ahead of us, in front of the nose.

Over sleeping, Thailand, it is five minutes to midnight on Christmas Eve. Soon, it will be the twenty-fifth of December, the holiest day in all Christendom. For two of the last three Christmas Nights, I have been airborne, delivering explosive presents of death and destruction to atheists, trying to win the freedom for the Buddhists of South East Asia.

As we climb to cruising altitude, I activate the cabin pressurization and adjust the cockpit lights. I am too busy to contemplate the theological significance of tonight's action. Without me asking, Jack gives me a course to steer toward the extreme southern panhandle of North Vietnam.

I pull the power back to establish a 400-knot cruise at 20,000 feet, headed northeast, and leave the cockpit lighting turned up. We won't be dive bombing tonight. Having good night vision is not so important, but performing the switchology correctly is vital; I need to see and confirm every switch position in the cockpit.

We will be blind bombing straight and level from this altitude, a night mission which would seem familiar to the

Royal Air Force pilots led by Air Marshal Arthur T. "Bomber" Harris during WWII twenty-five years ago. The RAF specialized in night bombing, alternating with the US Eighth Air Force who pounded Germany by daylight. Hopefully our delivery accuracy will be better tonight than it was back then. The RAF only had to hit the city of Dresden, Germany, with thousands of bombs from hundreds of planes. We are trying for a truck park, maybe two acres in size, with about half of the bomb load of only one of the four-engine, propeller-driven Avro Lancaster bombers of the RAF in 1943.

Tonight's orders call for a Combat Sky Spot delivery. The Sky Spot device was originally used by the Strategic Air Command as a bomb scoring system. SAC's huge bombers would conduct atomic bomb practice runs on known targets, tracked precisely from the ground by the Sky Spot radar. When the bomber ceased transmitting a tone on the radio, signifying a simulated bomb release, the ground-based Sky Spot computer would calculate where in relation to the pretend target a real nuclear bomb would have impacted. Early in the current war, some technoid had what (at least to him or her) seemed to be a great idea. Why not run the problem backward through the Sky Spot computer? The ground radar could steer the aircraft toward the target with the aid of voice commands and tell the pilot when to drop the ordnance for a perfect hit on a target whose location was known.

I guess the scoring system worked well enough for nukes, where pinpoint accuracy was not required. Any thermonuclear detonation within a quarter of a mile radius will thoroughly vaporize most targets. If we were dropping even a small nuke tonight, the chances of successful target destruction would be very high. But we aren't. Uncorking the nuclear genie would usher in an entirely different sort of war, much shorter in duration. Wisely, nobody calling the shots in Washington wants that, yet. Instead, we have twelve, count-'em, twelve iron bombs each with a kill radius measured in a few hundreds of feet, not large fractions of a mile.

Tonight's target is a anonymous stretch of jungle suspected to be harboring a truck park. The intelligence troops think it is just north of the political boundary drawn on maps as the border between the theoretically independent countries of South and North Vietnam. Actually, the existence, or not, of this political border is the public rationale for the war, used by both sides. As is usual with all intelligence data, the location, or even the existence, of the truck park is also somewhat suspect. However, for the purposes of tonight's aerial argument, I will trust that the promised truck haven does indeed exist and, like Dresden, it should be torched.

That is, if the unguided iron bombs can be delivered anywhere close to their desired destination. The odds of this occurring are not high. A bewildering number of fundamental errors infest the Combat Sky Spot system. Our bombs' impact point in relation to the target will be affected by unforeseen winds, natural ballistic bomb dispersion, inherent radar tracking inaccuracies, by my limited ability to fly the jet precisely, by target location uncertainty, map errors, computer settling time, my reaction time on the pickle button, the rotation of the earth, and gravity. We'll be lucky to get the bombs close enough to wake up, much less blow up, the sleeping North Vietnamese truckers.

Outside in the night, I see the Mekong River pass far below us in the hazy moonlight. It appears to be a silvery ribbon slowly wandering in a flat black landscape. We are across the watery fence now and over southern Laos. With my left hand, and without looking, I set up the armament switches, practicing for missions when the cockpit lights can't be this bright. A quick confirming glance shows amber lights on the panel between my legs at the two inboard wing and the centerline stations.

Jack has already checked in on the radio with Bruce orbiting in Alley Cat. The navigator changes the frequency to one assigned to the Combat Sky Spot site and reports in, ready for action.

Earlier, a wing intelligence officer told us the target is in the De-Militarized Zone, the DMZ. This is a twenty-kilometer wide strip of land that runs parallel to and on each side of the imposed artificial border. It was delineated by the United Nations at the end of the French Indochina War (they lost). All military activities, including fortifications and troop movements, are forbidden in the DMZ. It says so clearly in the treaty signed by all concerned parties in the late 1950s. The UN's intent was to provide a safe, peaceful area to separate the two Vietnams. The demilitarized zone is now one of the most highly militarized stretches of real estate on the planet.

The DMZ is a hellish wasteland of bunkers, minefields, tunnels, gun emplacements, fortified outposts, bomb craters, ambush sites, burned-out vehicles, wrecked bridges, torn-up rail lines, concertina wire, and graves. What little jungle that remains in the DMZ offers cover for troops of both sides and supposedly one truck convoy carrying ammunition southward tonight. I'm glad the zone is de-militarized; God only knows what would be in there if it weren't.

The Sky Spot site comes up on the radio and Jack tells them the particulars of our mission and location. Soon they have a radar lock-on and begin giving us steering commands. Once we are stabilized on the desired heading for the bomb run, the operator instructs,

"Confirm armament switches set," to remind me to get my shit together.

I flip the red guard up and raise the large toggle switch labeled "master arm" to the "on" position. My action is rewarded by green lights appearing over the three stations holding the bombs.

Now, verbal commands from the ground site are streaming constantly into my earphones. I am totally focused on the heading indicator in front of me on the instrument panel, trying to fly smoothly. The projected descent path of the bombs is profoundly and instantly affected by changes in heading. Small adjustments in the direction of our flight path produce large differences in the forward-projected impact point of the string of bombs. Minor errors in altitude and airspeed are not as important; the Sky Spot computer can cope with these.

The night air is smooth and small corrections are possible if I am careful with the stick and rudder pedals. The Sky Spot operator sees this unusual degree of flying precision on his display and starts giving commands in half-degree increments of compass heading.

"Come right one-half. Hold. Right another half. Good heading."

We are close to the release point. The operator, who is located somewhere north of Da Nang in South Vietnam, advises,

"Stand by for pickle on my mark. Ready, ready, pickle!"

I have trained Jack (that didn't take too many bananas) to hit his pickle button in the rear cockpit on the radio command, even as I do the same in the front seat. Hopefully this helps eliminate some of my reaction time and serves as a backup if my button is inoperative. Jack says the real reason is when the war crimes trials are conducted, he will be in the dock along with me.

No matter which one of us releases the ordnance, we feel a short, staccato series of jolts as the bombs are ejected to fall invisibly into the thin night air below. I roll the aircraft into a left bank and start a turn back toward Laos; beyond it lays the sanctuary of our home base. The Sky Spot operator confirms we have made a good bomb run and thanks us for making his Christmas Eve a special one.

I can't help but look below, down to the DMZ. The Vietnamese monsoon blows from the southeast, out of the South China Sea, this time of year. The wind sweeps heavy clouds and rain from over the ocean and piles the rotten weather up against the low lying Anan Mountains of the panhandle. A thick layer of ragged gray fluff. covers the DMZ like dirty sea foam blown onto the shore. I see it illuminated by the milky moon shining from over Thailand far to the west.

'We won't be able to see the bomb detonation flashes through this murk beneath us. Six thousand pounds of cast steel and high explosive have disappeared into the dirty fog of war below.

Tonight, we used a nuclear weapon scoring system to deliver conventional bombs in an unconventional war hopefully blowing the living shit out of a lucrative military target hiding in a demilitarized zone. We need irony bombs, not iron ones.

I wonder where those twelve bombs actually hit. The chances are good that we snuffed dozens of sleeping jungle monkeys instead of (or maybe in addition to) a few North Vietnamese military truck drivers. Coldly, I feel more pity for the unsuspecting simians than I do for the sentient humans. The apes didn't sign up for the war. Presumably the North Vietnamese people accepted the risk of death when they started this conflict back in the 1940s. Oh well, I'm sure the monkeys will be happy in primate heaven.

Yikes!

Better make that monkey heaven. I still might have a slight mathematical chance of reaching Valhalla myself. If the Elysian Fields are open to all primates, I would hate to run into a very pissed-off troop of monkeys. They might just be interested in meeting the human being who violently terminated their rainy season slumber. On the other hand, I feel confident that there is little danger of contacting any North Vietnamese troops in any blessed hereafter. It's not that I feel the North Vietnamese are godless Communists (although that's what they profess to be) and are thus ineligible for the Kingdom of God. Rather, I have bought into the relentless mental conditioning telling me they are unworthy of the pity and sympathy afforded to the humans who are not on our side in this ineptly fought war.

For most of this century, the enemy of the moment has been dehumanized by caricatures and insulting nicknames. We fought the Krauts, the Huns, the Bosche, the Jerries, the Nips, the Japs, the Chinks, and the Gooks. The list goes on and on, today and tonight. Maybe those Huns or Zips of yesteryear had mothers and wives that loved them as well. The North Vietnamese have feelings and relatives too, but that doesn't matter this time either. Pinning a demeaning label across the enemy's face facilitates remorseless killing. The image I have in my head of the "Bad Guys" allows me to sleep soundly at night. Or, as is the more usual case, in the daytime after a night mission.

Intellectually, I know the other side is populated with real people. But I also know that they care not a bit that I have loving parents, upstanding brothers, and easy girlfriends, nor that I hope to have a wife and kids someday. They would cheerfully kill me, then pick up their rice bowls and chopsticks and dig in with nary second thought. I wonder what racially motivated nickname they use for us Americans?

Another useful rationalization for the carnage I hope we caused tonight is the apparent lack of regard the government of North Vietnam has for its own citizens. Why should I fret about killing large numbers of Vietnamese when the regime in Hanoi doesn't seem to care either? Does that make me as evil as they are?

"Uncle" Ho Chi Minh is reputed to have said, "You will kill ten of our men, and we will kill one of yours, and in the end it will be you who tires of it first. Then we will win." Uncle Ho's carefully polished avuncular image is somewhat tarnished by his willingness to sacrifice his countrymen in large numbers for the sake of his geopolitical goals.

It seems that the rulers of the North themselves equate ten Vietnamese lives with one American's existence. By all accounts, the North Vietnamese and Vietcong ground troops are dedicated and brave to the point of foolhardiness. They seem to have accepted their role as political cannon fodder. Perhaps they have no choice, no way to opt out. There are no Vietnamese draft dodgers in Hanoi, Stockholm, or Vancouver.

The generals of the North seem to be willing to burn up legions of their own soldiers, throwing them recklessly against the combined firepower of the United States of America. I have heard the phrase, "Life is cheap in Asia." The wasteful military tactics the North are willing to use seems to validate that concept. They lost tens of thousands of regular North

Vietnamese troops in the futile siege of Khe Sanh, an insignificant valley valued only as a killing ground. It was truly as the Bard said, "A tale told by an idiot, full of sound and fury signifying nothing."

Maybe the problem isn't with Asian culture, but with absolutist governments and dictatorships. Globally, the mind masters and the unchallenged demigods of brutal regimes have been responsible for some of the century's most useless massacres. The Somme, Iwo Jima, Stalingrad, Hamburger Hill, Khe Sanh, the list is long of human sea attacks ordered by despots which resulted in crashing waves of the dead. At Stalingrad, two brutal, uncaring dictatorships strove to out kill each other. That WWII battle was fought between the Bad Guys and the Even Worse Guys.

Somehow, against all data and logic, I believe history justifies us being here. We have to stop the madness. It's why Jack and I tonight wakened the Phantom beast to life and flight, then we unleashed its iron bomb fury on the heads of hapless peasant soldiers. Is there any cause on Earth worth defiling a Christmas Eve in this obscene manner? Yes, there is. We have to end the modern era of evil dictators. We have to purge them from the globe, be they Vietnamese Communists, Japanese Imperialists, Russian Marxists, or Nazis. They are the ones who live in their bombproof bunkers. They who control their people with naked force, or brutal ideology, or bogus religion must be stopped. We have to make it impossible for psychopaths to send their citizens into hopeless, winless battles, writing them off in their millions.

Back home in the good ol' USA, things are a mess, with draft riots, protests, and wholesale civil disobedience. Guys are burning their draft cards chanting, "Not me, not this time." No one says that in Hanoi, no one said that in Tokyo, Berlin, Peking, or Moscow. Those pitiful North Vietnamese troopers have no option but to go and to be brave in the face of a messy death.

We are fighting for the right of free men and women to say no, to tell their rulers to get fucked, to suffer the consequences of protest, and yet keep on living. Maybe, just maybe, if we can do our job here in Southeast Asia and elsewhere, others will understand the benefits of a free society. With our actions, we can make possible a world where more people can change their rulers' minds and/or they can change their rulers.

If this nirvana happens, I will be able to afford the mental luxury of considering the current Bad Guys as the humans they have been all along and not as faceless ciphers whose deaths aren't allowed to trouble my sleep. But there are miles to go before I sleep, as some poet once said.

I point the nose of the aircraft west across Laos and toward Thailand while I tidy up the cockpit. Once we re-cross the Mekong, I flip the last missile switch to the "safe" position.

Jack has been even quieter than usual throughout tonight's flight. Before he can check out with Alley Cat, I ask,

"What would you say to us finding a tanker, getting some gas, and looking for Santa Claus?"

Jack replies, "OK by me; what else do we have to do tonight?"

I know exactly what he means by that comment and he knows I made my suggestion for the same reason. This is a night to stay airborne for sentimental reasons if for none other.

The navigator calls the indomitable Bruce in Alley Cat and reports a successful, if less than exciting, Sky Spot drop and asks if there is any extra gas available tonight. There is only one possible reason we would want some extra fuel at this time of night with all our ordnance expended and the weather good. The snarky tone of Bruce's reply in my earphones strongly indicates he knows the rest of tonight's mission includes some serious goofing off. Despite what he thinks of our misuse of the taxpayer's expensive fuel, Bruce finds us a tanker and relays to Jack its call sign, position, and radio frequency.

In short order Jack contacts the orbiting KC-135, finds the tanker on his trusty radar set, and gives me vectors to steer for an intercept.

The tanker crew knows Satan Flight isn't on the official schedule to offload fuel tonight. But, hell, what do they care? As soon as they have passed away all their gas, they get to go home to their base in far southern Thailand. It is rumored the Sultans of SAC have decreed that a pleasure dome be built beside the Gulf of Siam.

The magnificent SAC Officers' Club will have laid on a splendiferous Christmas party, no doubt. They'll probably have a bountiful buffet, live music, Thai dancing girls in costume, and a decorated evergreen tree flown in from the States on a relief tanker. If the tanker crew hurries, they might get to their home away from home in time to partake of some Christmas cheer.

As I carefully slide my jet under the tail of the KC-135 to make contact, I see the crew hasn't forgotten us lowly fighter pilots on this joyous occasion. The darkened boom operator's window in the aft belly of the tanker is outlined with red-and-green Christmas lights. I have seen Playboy pinups, current football scores (received in real time on the tanker's shortwave radio from Omaha), and various obscene messages in the Boomer's window, but this yuletide decoration is a first. I'm truly touched.

We take on 5,000 pounds of JP-4 in midair without incident and the boom operator retracts the boom from the receptacle on the spine of our Phantom, breaking contact. As I edge both throttles back to drift out from under the KC-135, I glance down at my heading indicator. We are pointed directly at the tanker's base; they are headed for home.

While the tanker quickly recedes off into the night sky, the copilot comes on the radio with a parting shot.

"Satan, you-all be careful now, you hear? Don't go be shooting down ol' Santa. You'll be in a heap of trouble, boy."

Great. A tanker crew from the Alabama Air National Guard.

I push my mike button before Jack does and reply.

"Pinch a few girls on the ass for us tonight at the bar. We'll be up here defending freedom."

That gets a double click on the radio and a "Roger. Wilco, Satan" as the Confederate Air Force tanker changes frequencies.

Without a real plan other than to stay airborne, I turn the Phantom back to the northwest and establish the jet at 20,000 feet and 350 knots. With no clouds and few reference points on the ground, the speed is invisible.

Back in the States, even in the most rural areas, a clear night like tonight showcases a ground network of brightly lit towns shining in the dark like luminescent spider webs. Each glowing pattern of streets is linked to its neighbors by roads marked by the red and white lights of moving vehicles. The whole web system shines with points of multicolored electricity resembling dew droplets on a web catching light from an invisible nighttime sun. America at night is incredibly beautiful from the air.

Northeast Thailand is very different, with only scattered lights clumped together here and there indicating the locations of small towns. There is no sense of visible organization, only the unlinked glow of isolated bare electric bulbs and solitary propane lanterns. Yet Thailand is densely populated; we are flying over crowds of people living in the farms and villages below. Tonight, the Thai Buddhists are asleep in the dark; most are unaware and uncaring that it is Christmas Eve for two lonely aviators passing silently overhead at 20,000 feet.

Back at our base, Christmas is barely acknowledged by officialdom. The "'Wolf Pack" wing flies combat softies around the clock every day of the year. National or religious holidays don't fit into this schedule. The Chaplain has a midnight service for the observant few, the chow halls will serve turkey dinners with all the trimmings tomorrow and there will be a few homemade Christmas trees displayed in the living quarters and barracks, but that's about it. The policy seems to be, "If we don't make too much of Christmas, the guys won't miss it too much."

But, they do. The Officers' Club will be jammed tonight with a river of booze flowing like water in the Mekong. The scene will be one of war stories, slightly forced laughter, endless kidding, and passes made at the barmaids. The subject of Christmas won't be mentioned much. But it will be at the back of everyone's mind as they attempt to suppress the memories of what and whom they miss. If you can't be with the ones you miss, make do with the ones you're with. No female, Thai or Round Eye, will sleep by herself tonight unless she really wants to be alone.

Drinking in good company is one of life's great pleasures, but not tonight, not on this night. The wee hour darkness envelops our Phantom like a comfort blanket. Jack and I are each lost in our own private thoughts as we wander aimlessly high above dark, somnolent Thailand.

Our Phantom, which was so beastlike on the ground, has changed its spots. Fresh from delivering death and destruction, the jet is now a benign and agile time machine. It moves us over the sleeping land like a wraith, drifting in the night and for a time, stopping the clock.

I keep the instrument lights turned up, creating a reassuring environment. During most combat missions, I extinguish the glowing red lights, blacking out the cockpit to preserve my night vision. Tonight I need the light. With its pointed nose and swept-back wings, none of the structure of the F-4 is easily visible from inside the cockpit at night. This gives me the eerie sensation of being a disembodied spirit floating over the battlefield, as if I were flying effortlessly in the dark without an aircraft.

The feeling is completely different now with red-glowing instruments and backlit control panels on both sides and in front of me. The former invisible beast is now a willing servant, enveloping and protecting. A jet's cockpit at night is one of the coolest places I can imagine to inhabit. I remember being thrilled by the experience for the first time learning to fly over west Texas. Then, and now, a cockpit magically generates a feeling of isolation from the world. As long as there is fuel in the jet, I can't be bothered by the mundane things that happen on the ground.

Too soon our contraband gas is exhausted. It is time to go back to what passes for home these days. Jack hasn't said one word since we left the tanker. Some things don't need speech to be understood and shared.

I tell my navigator, "Secure your map case and hang on."

Hopefully he won't think I've lost control of the jet, only my senses. I push both throttles forward to their first stop and the airspeed begins to build. Slight back pressure on the control stick raises the nose to ten degrees above the hazy horizon. Stopping the nose at ten degrees, I lean the stick far left, feeding in right rudder when the jet begins to roll. As the wings approach ninety degrees of left bank, I add more right, or top, rudder and start relaxing the back pressure on the stick. Continuing to roll, I bleed off the rudder input and start the stick forward, taking the Gs off the airplane.

As we float up out of our seats, I continue the roll until we are inverted. The scattered lights of rural Thailand have traded places with the stars and now appear to be over us, suspended over the top of the canopy.

I keep the stick leftward and as the roll nears the 270 degree point, I bring the back pressure back in, settling our butts gently back onto our ejection seats. At the same time I add left rudder, which is now top rudder. At the ninety-degree point, I blend out the left rudder and bring the stick back toward the cruise position. With the wings back to level, the nose is still on the distant horizon marking the line between the dark ground and the darker sky.

A slight touch of right stick stops the roll and I center the stick, retarding the throttles back to cruise power. The stars are now once more visible straight up and the scattered lights on the ground are back below us.

The classic slow roll appears easy and lazy, but it is difficult to perform smoothly and correctly. During stateside air shows done by the USAF air demonstration team, the "Thunderbirds" or their US Navy counterparts, the "Blue Angels" the solo pilot always does a slow roll directly in front of the crowd. The general public thinks the elegant roll is a throwaway line, a time killer until something more exciting happens in the air show. However, a successful performance of such a difficult maneuver always blows away the pilots in the crowd. They know how the stick and rudder must be coordinated with precision lest the roll gets sloppy. Manhandle the flight controls and a slow roll can result in a loss of control. It is seldom done at night.

Night aerobatics are such an obviously bad idea the USAF brass hasn't bothered to forbid the practice. It is all too easy to lose track of which way is up, which are the stars and which are the lights on the ground. Avoiding vertigo at night requires one's ass to be firmly in the seat at all times, not hanging from the seat belts, as we were just doing. Stupid? Yes. Fun? Also yes. A night slow roll is my Christmas present to myself.

I turn the F-4 toward Ubon Air Base and start to let down. Jack comes on the intercom and says some of the few words he has uttered all night

"Merry Christmas, Eddie."

I reply, "Merry Christmas, Jack," and contact approach control.

STEVE CANYON AND ME

The Plain of Jars is a hauntingly eerie landscape from another world. Comprised of a roughly circular patch of gently rolling grassland, it sits at an elevation of 2,000 feet, measuring about thirty miles by forty miles in the middle of the northern region of Laos. From the air, it resembles no other place as much as it does a small section of Kansas plunked down into the Southeast Asia rain forest. Surrounding the plain are rolling mountains covered with a dense green jungle canopy in contrast to the tall grass prairies of the plain.

The area got its western name from early French colonizers who must have found it to be even weirder than I do, the French not being familiar with the plains with the American Midwest. To me, it looks a lot like Kansas or Iowa in miniature. To them, it must have looked like nothing in "La Belle France." The French found the plain sprinkled with hundreds, maybe thousands, of immense stone pots. These pots are five to ten feet high and four or five feet in diameter. The "jars" are carved from a type of stone found only hundreds of miles from the plain. Who built the jars and transported them to the plain is not known. There is no cultural memory as to their use among the local people. Not being willing to call the area "Kansas" or "Iowa," the French named the place "Le Plain Des Jares" or The Plain of Jars. We still refer to it by the French acronym as the "PDJ."

Only two roads, an east-west dirt road and another north-south unpaved track traverse the PDJ. The roads meet and cross near the geographic center. There are no substantial villages or towns on the PDJ, just a few scattered hamlets along with the encampments of competing armies and a bumpy dirt airstrip or two.

The hills surrounding the plain are controlled for the most part by Hmong tribesmen. The Hmong are ethnically, culturally, linguistically, and temperamentally distinct from the lowland Laotians. The Hmong are fiercely independent, fiercely proud, and just plain fierce. They are on our side in the war, which is a good thing for us if not for them. The Hmong have little use for their Laotian countrymen and have even less tolerance for Vietnamese people, from either the North or the South.

The North Vietnamese know that if they are to subjugate Laos and threaten Thailand from the north, they must control the northern regions, the hill country. This means occupying the PDJ and establishing a presence there in order to operate in the hills immediately nearby and to block traffic from crossing the plain. The Hmong are being encouraged by the United States not to permit this to happen, not that they need much encouragement to make war on the Vietnamese. Neither side is very mechanized; this is a war fought mostly on foot, although the Vietnamese have trucks and a few light tanks. The Vietnamese find themselves in an ironic role reversal. In Laos. They are the foreign occupiers, supplied from abroad, organized into formal military forces trying to occupy and hold land. The Hmong are the guerrillas, fighting from their hills using hit-and-run tactics.

America is also in an even more ironic mission inversion. We are helping the guerrillas, who are not part of, and would rather not be included in, the internationally recognized government of their homeland. This time the Good Guys are the ones fighting the unconventional war.

The weird topography of the PDJ evidently has the magical power to warp the thinking of all those who deal with the plain and maybe even those who fly over it. Neither our politicians nor the US Army can get their minds around this secret Laotian war. It is both a mirror image and a subset of the current unpleasantness under way in Vietnam itself. Our aim is to help the Hmong tie up as many Vietnamese troops as possible and thus to form a military buffer between North Vietnam and our staunch ally to the south, Thailand. Our support for the Hmong is supplied and controlled by the Central Intelligence Agency using the services of Americans of unknown military lineage and of undisclosed origins.

War in northern Laos and on the PDJ follows the seasons, of which there are two; rainy and dry. During the rainy season, men, ammunition, supplies, and food cannot be moved easily from North Vietnam over the rugged terrain into Laos. When the rains fall, the Hmong are able to push the invaders back north into the mountainous border regions. The Hmong need few supplies themselves to beat the Vietnamese in the hills, only guns, bullets, and whetstones for their knives. Ho Chi Minh's self-acclaimed masters of guerrilla warfare are commonly outfought in the rain by tribesmen just back from the stone age. However, during the dry season the Vietnamese can operate more successfully as conventional mechanized forces. They are able to push back south, toward Thailand, often venturing out onto the open PDJ itself.

The pivot point for this annual ebb-and-flow occupation of northern Laos is the PDJ. It is during their annual march south across the PDJ, bringing along their supplies, that the Vietnamese are vulnerable to air attack. That is when my squadron mates and I spring into the action. The irony is not lost on us. In northern Laos, we are using USAF air power to support guerrillas against conventional forces. In South Vietnam, our Air Force buddies are doing just the opposite, trying (un-successfully) to defeat guerrillas and to support a conventional army, namely ours.

This is why I am orbiting the PDJ at 17,000 feet late on a dry-season afternoon. I am flying as "Satan Four" the last aircraft in a four-ship formation, with twelve 500 pound bombs hanging on bomb racks beneath the jet. The mission of our flight is to bomb North Vietnamese troop concentrations and supply dumps hidden on the otherworldly PDJ.

We can't spot the enemy from 17,000 feet; we can barely see the PDJ itself down through the haze generated by burning rice fields. A Forward Air Controller, a FAC, will find our targets and direct us to them. The FAC, whose call sign is "Raven," is an American Air Force pilot and we all are proud that he is. Raven FACs are on my short list of heroes. They usually fly a military version of the propeller-driven Cessna 180, a tiny, slow, vulnerable airplane. At 130 miles per hour and 1,000 or 2,000 feet over the ground, the Raven is a sitting duck for determined ground fire. His job is to find a concentration of North Vietnamese troops, who are typically not pleased to be considered as targets and will resist being so designated. So, while we orbit at 17,000 feet and four hundred fifty miles an hour in our fearsome war machines, the Raven is down amongst them, unarmed, flying a bug smasher.

The Raven's best hope of survival is the enemy's knowledge that he can summon instant death from the skies. That would be us. Hopefully the North Vietnamese know that if they shoot at the FAC, the Raven can and will bring down tons of bombs on their positions, which they have just revealed by shooting at him. These Raven guys must have big brass balls to go out day after day and offer themselves up as bait.

They live and fly out of an austere forward operating base in Laos, a third world stink hole called Long Tieng. Long Tieng is in the third world because there is no fourth world classification. The primitive air base is due north of the Mekong among the land of the Hmong they support and far from any formal USAF recognition or control. What a deal. Ravens have the worst of several worlds. They have CIA secrecy and non-accountability, Hmong living conditions, and miserly USAF pay. If they are going to go to war for the Agency, they should at least live a James Bond-type lifestyle. I have seen some of these guys in Bangkok on R and R (Rest and Recreation). They are easily recognizable with their long, nonmilitary haircuts, colorful civilian clothes, and a wild look in their eyes that comes from living constantly on the edge. In fact, Ravens define the edge. They are at the edge of civilization, the edge of formal U.S. government supervision, and the edge of declared war. With a casualty rate of over 30 percent they are on the edge of life itself. It is an honor to fly with such men.

My flight leader has made radio contact with the Raven far below and I have listened to the transmitted target briefing along with the other Phantom flyers; the crews of Satans One through Three. Our targeted objective is a company of North Vietnamese regulars concealed in the tall grass of the PDJ. We will not see them at all; the Raven must visibly designate the target area for Satan Flight. His only armament is a pod of unguided white-phosphorous-tipped rockets. Each rocket is 2.75 inches in diameter and 4 feet long. On impact, the rocket's white phosphorous warhead, called "WP" or "'Willie Pete," will bloom with a dense cloud of brilliant white smoke. The Raven will shoot a rocket into the area occupied by the unfortunate troops and it will be our job to bomb the area surrounding the smoke, which we should be able to see from our exalted altitude.

My twelve bombs will be delivered to the target area via the time-honored technique of manual dive bombing. I will replicate the maneuvers used by fighter pilots since WWII using no computers, no laser guidance, no smart bombs, just good old-fashioned Tennessee marksmanship. I have turned on my gun sight, it's projected on the front windscreen as a red dot. A circle of red light surrounds the "pipper." My job will be to achieve precisely 45 degrees of dive, 450 knots indicated airspeed (about 500 mph), .707 Gs, and have all this happen with the pipper on the target at 7,200 feet above the ground. If all this gets done as planned, and the surface winds aren't too strong, the bombs will impact in the general vicinity of the target. If the airspeed varies by 10 to 20 knots, the dive angle by a degree, the release altitude by a few hundred feet, or if the gun sight isn't on the target with .707 Gs on the airplane, the bombs will miss wildly. It is a very hard thing to do well and the probabilities of errors occurring are likely enough that manual dive bombing is a rather blunt instrument. However, with unseen troops being dug in who knows where, all that is required of us is that some of Satan Flight's forty-eight bombs get close. The fragmentation pattern of a 500 pound bomb will make up for all but the worst aiming errors.

Our flight has set up a counterclockwise "daisy chain," a circular orbit around the target area with one aircraft approximately at each cardinal point of the compass at all times. We will make our dive bomb runs in numerical order. Before I can deliver my ordnance, I must have the target in sight, the FAC in view (if he is still in the area), know the position of each of my flight mates, and have positioned my jet so as to accomplish the desired delivery parameters. For a dedicated Sewer Doer, this daytime flying is harder than I remember. It is late in the day and the sun is low on the western horizon, a dull red orb lighting up the ever-present haze. The Hmong practice slash-and-burn agriculture. During the dry season, they are in the burn mode. Smoke is adding to the low-level obscuration. Visibility is rotten and it gets worse the lower the sun gets. At lower altitudes it is really shitty. Already the light brown surface of the PDJ is growing darker with the coming dusk.

The Raven comes on the air.

"Satan Flight, Raven's in to mark the target."

I can barely discern a tiny gray cross far below that is the top outline of the Raven's piddling aircraft. I strain my eyes to pick out a white puff of Willie Pete smoke against the brown-going-to-dark PDJ.

Raven says, "Satan, that's a good mark, hit my smoke. I'll be holding south."

The Raven is no fool; he wants to be well clear of the area when four mighty Phantom jets and forty-eight free-falling iron bombs start filling the air above the target. The intended targets can see the Willie Pete smoke on the ground better than we can. They know what is coming and that there is now no downside to shooting at the FAC. For them, there is only the chance of preemptive revenge. I don't have time to contemplate the fear that must be gripping the North

Vietnamese troops below. I have to confirm that I have selected all the proper switches in the cockpit to release and arm the bombs. I must visually find each of my teammates in the murky sky; a midair collision will ruin everyone's day. Satan Lead, Satan Two, and Satan Three make their runs and pull off as I watch from above, trying to keep track of each jet's position in the dusty afternoon sky. We Sewer Doers aren't used to all this daytime action in the visible realm.

Satan One, the flight lead, reports seeing ground fire aimed at him during his bomb run. He must have seen the angry fireflies of tracer bullets passing near his canopy. Satan Three confirms the twinkle of muzzle flashes against the dusky ground during his run. I see the sharp red impacts of the bomb explosions and feel my adrenaline start to flow. I make one last look inside the cockpit and discover that my fuel gauge is almost below "Bingo" state. Bingo fuel is the minimum amount needed to get back to base or to a tanker. It signifies that it is time to leave the target area and head home. I am supposed to announce "Bingo" to the flight lead, but I think I'll wait until after I get rid of the 6,000 pounds of iron and explosives hanging on the jet.

The other guys have done their thing and it is my turn. I'm on the east side of the daisy chain circle with the target and the sun to my left, westward. This is not the best place to be; if I start my bomb run from here l will be looking into the sun. We night flyers are not used to coping with this sort of problem. Good tactics would suggest a run from west to east. With the sun at my back, I would be using its rays to penetrate the haze instead of having to look into the glare to see the target. Also, coming in from out of the sun would force the Bad Guys to shoot at me looking into the setting sun. However if I wait until I fly around the circle to the west, I will be below Bingo fuel state. So, what the shit, let's do it now and get the hell out of Dodge City.

I look back outside, over the left canopy rail, and reacquire the target. Unexpectedly, I think I can still see the white puffs of Willie Pete floating in place; I thought the other guys' bombs would have erased it. They must have missed completely. Well, I'm not going to miss. Assigned as Number Four in the formation, I am by definition the least experienced pilot in the flight. I desperately want to make my mark in the squadron, to present my credentials as a fighter pilot, and to gain the respect of my peers. Putting bombs on target is the best, quickest way to make a name for myself.

I roll the jet left, almost over on its back and pull the nose down to below the target area. Relaxing the stick, I feel myself get light in the seat with near zero G on the airplane. With no Gs on, I can roll back right side up without changing my flight path. We dive deeper and faster into the gathering haze and smoke. As we do, I spot the pipper projected on the ground short of the target, just where it should be. I quickly check the airspeed; it's building nicely toward 450 knots as we accelerate downhill in the dive.

My navigator's job is to watch the altitude unwind and call out when it is time to press the pickle button. He is also alert to my mental status and if I get fixated on the target, he will call for a pull out.

He announces, "Ready. Pickle," in a tightly controlled voice.

The gun sight is superimposed exactly over the white spot marking what I think is the target; I am pleased about this. I hit the pickle button on the control stick and the jet leaps upward as the heavy bomb load is ejected. I keep the stick coming back and the load builds to five Gs until the nose is above the horizon and we are on our way back up, out of the worst of the haze. I'm not supposed to look back under Gs; it is disorienting, but I can't help but bank left and admire my work. A quick glance over my left shoulder as I start a left turn to rejoin the flight confirms that the white-marked target has disappeared in a cloud of dirty brown bomb smoke. Not bad work for a Sewer Doer caught out in the daytime.

I push the mike button while composing my voice to appear calm, even bored.

"Satan Four is off target and I'm Bingo fuel. Got the formation in sight."

I can see three black dots on the horizon, trailing sooty jet smoke. That is the flight heading south, toward home.

The Raven calls from below, "Thanks for the work, Satan Flight, I'll call the BDA (Bomb Damage Assessment) in on the landlines."

Later on that evening, my first stop after parking the jet and debriefing the maintenance troops on the status of the aircraft is the Squadron Operations Center. I have to sign in before heading down to the Intelligence Shop to recap today's mission for the records. As I walk in, the junior officer manning the duty desk takes one look at me, hurriedly picks up the phone, and whispers into it. I find this rather odd, but I ignore the feeling and turn to complete the sign-in sheet. In seconds, my Squadron Commander emerges on the double from the inner sanctum of his office. He utters a few words which are guaranteed to strike cold fear in the hearts of fighter pilots everywhere,

"The Old Man wants to see you, now."

I have an urgent audience scheduled with the Wing Commander in his lair at Wing Headquarters. As a rule, Wing Commanders almost never require your immediate presence in their offices to tell you what a good job you are doing.

The Squadron Commander volunteers to walk with me to the HQ and fill me in on what has happened between the time Satan Flight pulled off target in northern Laos, the Raven called in the BDA, and my return to our base in Thailand.

Bizarrely, he begins with a history lesson. During one of their periodic, and often in vain, attempts to make friends and influence people in Laos, the Chinese Communists funded and built a Chinese cultural center near the crossroads in the middle of the Plain of Jars. Their idea was to impress the Laotians, both the lowland peoples and the Hmong, with the depth, breath, and superiority of. Chinese culture. The Laotians didn't buy the story, having been sufficiently acquainted with Chinese culture during the numerous invasions suffered by Laos at the hands of successive Chinese dynasties. The Chinese cultural center was poorly attended and probably abandoned, but none of that matters now as it doesn't exist anymore.

When the Raven returned just before dark to the target area, he found three sets of bomb craters in close proximity to the Vietnamese troops, many of whom had just joined their honored ancestors in the hereafter. However, there was one set of impact craters exactly where the aforementioned Chinese cultural center used to be. It seems that Satan Four misidentified the whitewashed, domed building of the cultural center, confusing it with a round cloud of white Willie Pete smoke, and explosively erased the installation from the map. The same maps clearly show the ex-location of the center and the area is clearly marked as a neutral, no bomb area. The compound which used to contain a run-down building full of Chinese propaganda has acquired enough bomb craters to resemble the surface of the moon.

As trusted employees of the ClA, Raven FACs are usually comfortable with keeping their mouths shut about things better left unsaid and undisclosed. However, this screw-up is too big and too politically hot to write off against the fortunes of war as an honest mistake. The Raven called the Agency in Bangkok, who spread the word. The U.S. Ambassadors to Thailand and Laos are in the loop and boy, are they pissed. The Seventh/Thirteenth Air Force Headquarters in Saigon who owns and controls all USAF tactical assets in Southeast Asia is energized. The Commander of Seventh./Thirteenth is definitely not amused. The State Department wants answers. Phone lines are buzzing. When the top brass in the Pentagon come to work in the morning they will want answers as well. This mess could go all the way to the White House.

The worst case scenario for the Vietnam War has always included the nightmare fear of an overt entrance by the People's Republic of China, the Communist Chinese, the PRC, into the conflict. Everyone remembers how a winnable police action in Korea turned into a lethal quagmire when the PRC marched south across the Yalu River. Is the PRC looking for an excuse to enter the war on the side of North Vietnam? Would

Americans trashing a Chinese cultural center provide that excuse? The United States has never publicly admitted to bombing anywhere in Laos, much less in the northern regions far from South Vietnam. Our involvement with the Hmong, the whole CIA supply system, the Raven FACs, all have been closely-held secrets undiscovered by our own left-wing press. The entangled countries of Thailand, Laos, and Vietnam, including the PRC, all know what is going on in Laos, but no one is talking. Will the impact of twelve 500 hundred-pound bombs, precisely delivered if I do say so myself, change all that? What are the political ramifications for our entire war effort?

No one knows the answers to any of this. No one knows what to do. No one knows how to write the after-action report for transmittal to Washington. The only concept the interested parties agree on is that they all want on a platter the head of the junior USAF captain who committed this outrage. That would be me.

We enter the outer office of Wing HQ and announce our presence to the secretary. I wish I had a haircut and that my flight suit wasn't so ragged. While we wait, I think this day has morphed from a triumph aerial dexterity into of into one of the worst in my life. Getting reamed a new asshole by the Wing Commander is bad enough, but getting chewed out by this particular Colonel is even worse. The Wing Commander's alter ego has been one of my heroes ever since I was a small boy.

As far back as I can remember the daily and Sunday comic pages of my hometown Tennessee newspaper carried the syndicated adventures of Steve Canyon, drawn and written by Milton Caniff. Caniff began drawing the strip during the Korean War chronicling the idealized life of an imaginary USAF fighter pilot named Steve Canyon. Caniff's comic hero fought in Korea, flew in the cold war, and generally roamed the globe getting into and out of exciting adventures. These fictional episodes usually involved airplanes, spies, evildoers, and beautiful women, not necessarily in that order. Caniff had his creation progress up the military promotion ladder in the comic strip and Steve Canyon is now a full Colonel.

I didn't miss a single episode while I was growing up, eagerly scanning the comic pages every day to see what Steve Canyon was up to. The life he led, the airplanes he flew, and yes, the women he hung around with, cemented my desire to be an USAF fighter pilot. I always wanted to fly, and in particular, to fly fighters in combat. I really didn't need any comic strip inspiration, but the mythical life of Steve Canyon was another attractive lure for the teen-aged me.

It is common knowledge around the base that the current Wing Commander is a life-long friend of Milton Caniff and that the famous cartoonist used the likeness, attitude, and demeanor of the "Old Man" as the conceptual model for Steve Canyon. It is easier to draw someone you know than to cut a new person from whole cloth. When the real guy got promoted, the comic strip alter ego did as well. To see our Commander in person is to visualize a real-life embodiment of a well-known fictional character; the physical resemblance is uncanny.

So, not only am I about to get my head handed to me by a real Wing Commander, I am going to be grounded, fired, and probably have my career ended by the guy who I faithfully followed in the comic strips for all those years. It isn't just anyone who gets to be busted by his boyhood hero.

The secretary announces that the Wing Commander will see me, alone, now. My squadron boss looks relieved, like a guy who can't stand to see the sight of fresh blood and who doesn't want any of the blood (or the blame) sticking to him.

My mind has been racing, trying to come up with my story. How could I have destroyed a cultural center by mistake, brought shame on the 8th Tactical Fighter Wing, angered two ambassadors, embarrassed a covey of generals, and brought the People's Republic of China's Red Army flooding into the Vietnam War? Failing to devise a really, really good excuse, I decide to play it straight up, explain what happened, and take my lumps. The sun got into my eyes, it was very hazy and almost dark, I was about out of gas, and the Bad Guys were shooting at me. These reasons might just be believable and have the added advantage of. being the truth.

I knock once and hear "Come in, Captain" in return.

I open the door, walk in, and shut it behind me. I salute the Colonel behind the desk and stand at attention in front of it. I try to speak in as firm a voice as a walking dead man can muster:

"Captain Cobleigh, reporting as ordered, sir."

The Colonel raises his head, slowly looks up at me and it is Steve Canyon in the flesh. I recognize the wide shoulders, the six- foot, two-inch frame, and the square jaw. I know the shock of blond hair, parted on the right, and the chest full of medals. I wince at the impact of the steely blue eyes, fixed like twin laser beams on my miserable carcass. I have seen this man wreak daily havoc on the enemies of democracy around the world in black and white during the week and in color on Sunday. Now, I am about to get strafed by my own hero.

Instantly, my carefully prepared story evaporates in my brain. My resolve to present a set of reasons for my error of aerial mis-identification is burned into cranial smoke that is probably coming visibly out of my ears. All I can think of as a reply to the coming barrage will be, "No excuse, sir."

The Old Man looks at me even harder and says, "I'm very disappointed in you. Promise me that you won't let anything like this happen again and I'll take care of it. Dismissed."

I manage to get "Yes, sir" out of my dry mouth, do an about-face, and leave the room, carefully shutting the door behind me. The Squadron Commander is nowhere to be seen and the secretary has suddenly found that tomorrow's calendar requires her undivided attention. I am never so glad to leave a building in my life.

The Old Man's words have cut me like a Randall knife. I was prepared to be chewed out, cussed at, yelled at, and dressed down. That would have been a cleansing catharsis. I could have written the incident off to bad judgment and gone to the Officers' Club for a drink or two. Having the Wing Commander/Steve Canyon speak softly only of his disappointment in me was crushing. I have no answer, and I feel to the core of my being that I have let my mates and superiors down. My only response is to vow never to make such a mistake twice, to not violate the trust, not ever again.

I find out later that the Wing Commander told higher headquarters that disciplining his troops is his job, not theirs. He has told the US Embassy in Bangkok to butt out and has thanked the Raven FAC for his honesty. He has ignored informal inquiries from Washington and has instructed the intelligence officers to remove my name from the after-action report. I suspect he has told the Squadron Commander to forget the whole thing, that the matter is settled, but to see that I get more practice in daylight operations.

The Wing Commander's actions stick. The State Department and the USAF can't very well formally demand retribution for a mistaken action taken in a war that doesn't officially exist. What about the report by a Raven FAC that the Chinese cultural center on the PDJ has been totally trashed? What Raven? There are no Ravens in northern Laos, nor any bombing missions. The CIA is likewise not talking, but they never do.

Meanwhile, I decide that the Steve Canyon comic strip doesn't do the Wing Commander justice. His meeting with me was a masterpiece of motivation. His response to various outraged officials was pure leadership. I have decided that I will fly into Hell itself for this man.

I guess all's well that ends well. Months later, when my combat tour is over, the Wing Commander says a few words at my going-away ceremony. After the party, at the bar, he gives me the name and phone number of a lady friend of his who lives near my new stateside base and suggests I call her and use him as a reference. I wonder, is it the sexy redhead who seems to wear nothing but a trench coat and high heels? Is it the beautiful Oriental spy in the slinky-tight Chinese dress slit to her bare hip, the legendary "Dragon Lady"? Is it the curvy, blond USAF flight nurse with the mini-skirted, nonstandard uniform? I can visualize clearly in graphic detail every one of these famous *femme fatales* from the comic strip. As it turns out, the Old Man's lead connects me with a girl who was never drawn by Milton Caniff, but that is another story.

THE WILD BLUE YONDER

I have dreamed about this flight all my life. I am on daytime MiG CAP mission, looking for enemy aircraft to shoot down. This classic assignment distills to its essence the act of being a fighter pilot; this is what it is all about. Five years of intensive training and a lifetime of mental preparation have brought me to this point in space/time. I am Satan Three in a flight of four, leading the second element comprised of two Phantoms. The Squadron Commander, the Boss, is leading the four jets of Satan Flight. My wingman, Satan Four, whose personal call sign is "Hostile Man" is a hundred yards off my right wing as the other member of my element. When you are going forth to hassle to the death with the MiGs, you want your wingman's nickname to be "Hostile Man."

I am flying in reference to Satan Lead 300 yards to my left as our jets float and move in and out, up and down in loose formation. The four-ship formation we are flying is called a "finger four" as the four Phantoms' positions correspond to the four fingertips of a right hand. This formation was developed by the U.S. Army Air Corps "Wolf Pack" wing in the European Theater of WWII. Then the Wolf Pack flew P-47 Thunderbolts, piston-engined, propeller-driven fighters. The formation was further perfected by the USAF's F-86 SabreJet pilots during the Korean War, who called it a "fluid four." Our wing, which has inherited the "Wolf Pack" nickname, uses this formation exclusively; it is in our tactical doctrine. It isn't clear to me why a formation designed to engage propeller-driven Messerschmitts at 250 miles per hour is the right one for jet speeds and distances. But, as the Boss seems to know what he is doing, I keep my doubts to myself.

We are flying at 450 knots indicated airspeed, about 500 miles per hour, and 27,000 feet high, heading northeast, crossing the invisible border from Laos into North Vietnam. Normally, the objective of a combat mission is to get into the target area, accomplish your task, which usually means bombing the living shit out of. a target, and then get out. Hopefully, this can be accomplished with a minimum of danger and excitement. On a MiG CAP mission the motivation reverses completely. We are looking for trouble and we hope it comes our way. The ultimate goal of every fighter pilot is to shoot down an enemy airplane, or two, or five to become an ace. To do this, you have to first find and then engage the enemy, not avoid him. Our hope for today is that the MiGs will come up to play. Of course, the Bad Guy fighter pilots have exactly the same ambition concerning us; that's what makes life interesting.

My jet has three large, expendable fuel tanks carried underneath it; these will be jettisoned at the first sign of trouble and/or opportunity, Now the three tapered tanks of jet fuel are feeding the greedy engines, sustaining our 450 knots. I also have on board four AIM-7 Sparrow radar-guided missiles, four AIM-9 heat-seeking Sidewinder missiles and an electronic countermeasures pod to jam enemy radars.

Satan Flight's job this fine morning is to serve as top cover, or MiG CAP, for a strike force of twelve other Phantoms who will be doing the actual bombing. The Wing Commander, the Old Man, is leading the bombers and is the overall Mission Commander. In addition to our four Phantoms, the strike force is supported by two four-ship formations of F-105 Thunderchief fighter-bombers, whose call sign is "Wild Weasel." The Wild Weasels' mission is to suppress the enemy's defenses by defeating their Surface-to-Air Missile (SAM) sites. Four Weasels will sweep the egress route and target area shortly before the strike force arrives and four more will follow the bombers out to prevent SAM attacks from the rear. The eight Weasels and four MiG CAP jets are there to make sure the strike force Phantoms get to the target area and get out without suffering losses to either SAMs or MiGs.

Unseen, somewhere up ahead of this strike force armada is a RF-4 Phantom carrying no armament, only cameras in its tapered nose. The Photo Phantom will take "before" pictures of the target. An hour or so after the bombs detonate and the smoke clears, another RF-4 will take more "after" black-and-white pictures of the same target area. The pre-strike photos will be compared to the post-strike snaps to see if the strike force did its lethal job.

What is the job of this airborne armada? We are to attack a suspected enemy truck park and supply depot. It is supposedly hidden under the jungle canopy covering the eastern hills running down the panhandle of North Vietnam. If launching twenty-six USAF jets to destroy a truck park that may or not be there seems excessive, that's because it is.

Air strikes against North Vietnam are conducted under the code name "Operation Rolling Thunder." Strikes on southern Laos are known by the name "Steel Tiger" and northern Laos gets hit under "Barrel Roll." The noted peacenik, marginal musician, and irritatingly nasal folk singer Bob Dylan calls his backup band the "Rolling Thunder Review." Did he name his musicians after the bombing missions or did the Pentagon mock the Troubadour Kid by naming our missions after his band? It is hard to imagine the insular mandarins of the Pentagon having the wit to mimic Dylan or even to know who he is. This juxtaposition is probably just one of the many ironies of war. Right now, I don't really care.

A USAF effort of this magnitude would normally be dedicated to a heavily defended and valuable target near Hanoi, the capital of the North. With this much firepower airborne, we should be headed "downtown." However, we aren't bombing the key areas of North Vietnam just now. The farsighted visionaries running the war from their swivel chairs in Washington, D.C. have announced yet another bombing pause. The idea seems to be; if we stop doing nasty things to

North Vietnam, they will gladly reciprocate and abandon the war they have been fighting for a quarter century to unify their country. Next, ever so grateful to the United States for not bombing them, Hanoi's Communist fanatics would then allow the people of South Vietnam to enjoy the fruits of an independent, democratic peace. I guess I just don't understand international politics.

However, we aren't calling a halt to bombing the entire north, just the areas most dangerous and difficult to bomb. These forbidden regions also contain the most valuable and lucrative targets. Instead of really hurting the Bad Guys, we pull our punches. To show that we aren't kidding; we are periodically ordered to raid selected areas such as today's target, the well-hidden truck park somewhere in the rain forest. Evidently, blowing the shit out of lesser-known parts of North Vietnam won't compromise the goodwill we are generating by sparing the capital. Also, there are no Russian or Red Chinese TV cameramen this far south. They won't be able to document the fact that we are being beastly to their socialist brethren.

The absurdity gets even weirder. We are allowed to bomb carefully selected, politically non-sensitive targets in the North Vietnamese hinterlands only if we pretend we are going downtown. We must seize this opportunity to practice the skills needed to fly and fight against the defenses around Hanoi and the port city of Haiphong. Those defenses, already the stiffest seen in the history of aerial warfare, are undoubtedly being strengthened while we are not attacking them. Today's mission is a giant training exercise to keep us sharp enough to someday attack targets and defeat defenses that are growing stronger because we aren't attacking them. If this situation didn't involve life and death, it would be ludicrous. Instead, it's tragic. The whole wacky concept makes my head hurt, but none of it will matter one iota if the MiGs come up and fight.

The skills needed to pull off a raid of this size are indeed formidable and we certainly do need the practice. The Wing

Commander is leading this vast, or half-vast, fleet of fighters and we are all proud of him for doing so.

Being a USAF fighter Wing Commander is a unique job, maybe the most unusual in our military's history. The Old Man is a full colonel. In the US Army, colonels command brigades of about 2,400 troops. In the US Navy, a captain (the naval equivalent of a colonel) is in charge of an aircraft carrier battle group or a flotilla of destroyers. Those other American armed services require their senior officers to command, period. An army colonel doesn't lead bayonet charges, his troopers do. A navy captain doesn't steer the ship; a lowly seaman does that. In the United States Air Force, the Wing Commander is expected to fly the same fighter jet on the same missions, to run the same risks, and to fight as hard as the lowest-ranking officer in his unit.

Maybe the best analogy to this modern requirement references olden times when the Scottish chieftain was expected to command the clan in battle as well as swing a claymore sword himself. The Old Man flies the same type jet as I do, goes to the same targets, takes the same risks, and is expected to achieve the same results, if not better. This is equivalent to the risk of an army colonel taking his turn walking point on jungle patrols, or of a US Navy captain personally driving a submarine, manning the dive planes and helm all the while peering out the periscope.

I have served under Wing Commanders who didn't fly and wouldn't fight. They only took the easy missions, the milk runs. They still had to fly the jet, but they made sure the missions they assigned themselves to were easy and relatively safe. We despised these frauds as incompetent commanders at best and at worst, cowards. But, no one questions an US Army colonel's bravery if he doesn't go out on night jungle patrols.

Not only does the Wing Commander have to perform individually as well as the greenest pilot; he has to lead the strike force at the same time. This means he has to be able to fly his jet, set up the switches, navigate, dive bomb, and do all those difficult things by instinct. All his conscious thoughts will be focused on leading the extended formation and on commanding the complex, fast-paced action.

Just turning a formation of this size is difficult. If the leader turns too sharply, the planes on the inside of the turn radius will slow down too much and the ones on the outside will be forced to use extra fuel to keep up. The leader also has to make tactical decisions on which men's lives depend. It is a big job and to do it well takes unshakable confidence, instant decision making capability, the utmost in skill, and practice. Most of us in the wing believe we have the first three qualities in abundance; all we need is the last.

The Old Man is leading this huge flight today but the strike force could have been led by anyone who is just as capable. In the USAF the best leader gets to lead at times, regardless of rank. As a junior captain, I have led twelve-ship formations into North Vietnam. Rank has no place in aerial combat. I have had full colonels fly on my wing and in my backseat. They did as they were told and went where I led them. I have heard of a first lieutenant who lead F-105 strike missions. That is impressive. Naturally, the higher-ranking Air Force pilots tend to be the best due to greater experience, but it doesn't have to be that way; talent also matters.

The tradition-bound and overly rank-conscious US Navy can have two leaders in each flight; the tactical leader who flies the lead aircraft and the military leader who is the highest-ranking member of the flight. The military leader could in theory be in the backseat of the fourth airplane. One guy makes tactical decisions and another guy makes military decisions, all at the same time. How that works is beyond me.

What is in front of me is the border of North Vietnam. As the four Phantoms of Satan Flight cross the arbitrary geographic line, I reach down without looking and flip the missile arm switch up to "arm." The radar-guided Sparrows are tuned and ready, each heat-seeking Sidewinder's aural growl in my earphones has been judged to be sufficiently aggressive. The missiles are hot and so am I, at least mentally. I am incredibly stoked; my adrenaline dose is approaching toxic levels.

I wonder if three of the six Earp brothers and Doc Holliday felt this way in 1881 when they stepped onto the dusty main street of Tombstone, Arizona on their way to the OK Corral? Did they flip off the leather safety straps holding their Colt revolvers down in their holsters with the same studied determination that I toggled the missile arm switch on? Did Wyatt Earp nervously loosen his gun in his holster the same way that I adjusted the brightness of my gun sight? Was Doc's double-barreled shotgun as carefully prepared as my Sidewinders? Did the four lawmen have dry mouths the way I do, or it is the pure oxygen I am breathing through my mask?

Satan Lead has pushed the airspeed up to 500 knots and we are weaving back and forth behind the strike force's twelve jets. The enemy MiG aircraft have guns and perhaps heat-seeking missiles that can only be used from behind the intended target. If an attack comes, it will be from behind. That cone-shaped zone of moving airspace where we want to be in relation to the strike force, to head off the attack or to absorb the first punch and then engage the MiGs.

Now that we are over North Vietnam, Satan Flight's formation is edgy with aircraft jockeying around, visually displaying the nervousness of their pilots. All the aircraft in any formation are constantly in motion with respect to each other. What looks from the ground like one welded together entity is really a mix of never-ending movement. At an air show, the USAF Thunderbirds appear to be in perfect formation at all times. However, they too are continually making corrections. Their jets move in and out, up and down, forward and back unceasingly. The Thunderbirds' relative movement is measured in inches. In normal peacetime formations, the jets move in feet. A combat formation in fluid four changes by hundreds of feet. The object is not to look good from the ground but to be ready to fight.

I am sweating bullets, flying formation on Satan Lead, looking all around for bogeys (unidentified aircraft), scanning above and below the horizon for the Bad Guys, while keeping track of the aerial positions of Satan One, Two, and Four. The control stick stirs, the throttles move up and back, the jet responds accordingly.

In addition to keeping my eyes on my leader, Satan Lead, I also constantly check the position of Satan Four, a.k.a. Hostile Man. His job is to watch the airspace behind my jet for enemy fighters. Hostile Man is supposed to keep me from getting shot down while I am shooting down the Bad Guys in front of me. I sure hope he succeeds. I am trying hard to follow one of the basic instructions in air combat: keeping my head on a swivel. I take a look at the aerial position of Satan Lead; then I take a swift glance to my right, locating Satan Four, then scan the hazy horizon.

I have to believe the Earps and Doc also stole sideways glances at each other as they strode four abreast up that desert street into the history books.

I am definitely in the mental state I call the "zone." When I am in the zone, my perception of time both speeds up and slows down simultaneously. Actions that would take minutes can be done in seconds; seconds-long tasks are completed in fractions of seconds. I am flying my jet, operating its systems, doing the routine tasks of aviation without conscious effort. It feels as if my central nervous system is plugged directly into the Phantom's flight controls. In normal time, if I want to climb or turn, I manipulate the stick, rudder, and throttle to accomplish the desired maneuver. In the zone, I need only to think about where the jet and I need to be and we go there. My gloved hands on the throttles and stick need no commands; my brain's inputs go straight to the engines and control surfaces. The jet and I are one living organism with a single purpose, to fly, to fight, and to win.

While time is speeding up in the physical world, it is slowing down in the mental realm when I am in the zone. Relieved of the requirement to think about flying the jet, my mind is free to contemplate the tactical situation at its leisure. I am mentally processing information about the spatial relationships between all the friendly aircraft, our location, the fuel state, and where we are in the world. I am planning actions based on when and where I think the MiGs will appear. I need to be ready for anything and I have the mental time to prepare for everything I can think of.

This is the scenario with all its alternatives that I ran and re-ran in my head last night when I was supposed to be sleeping. The night before a big mission such as today's is a waste of time for sleep. I laid awake for hours visualizing the mission and every conceivable option and preparing for every eventuality, I hope.

I can only prepare for what I can imagine and I can anticipate only those situations that I can conceive. Unfortunately, I can't clearly visualize a dogfight with a MiG because I have never even seen one and I have never fought in training with any aircraft that performs anything remotely like a MiG. In fact, in my years of training, in the constant practicing of my craft, I have only flown against other F-4s. I am very good at defeating poorly flown F-4s; I've done it frequently. If the North Vietnamese Air Force would only fly Phantoms I would know just what to do to defeat them.

For some reason unknown to anyone below the rank of general, we are not allowed to practice dogfighting with any type aircraft other than our own. Combat training with other flavors of jets is strictly forbidden. The outlawed concept is called "dissimilar air combat maneuvering." Only the USAF would give a bureaucratic label to a proscribed action. The officially stated reason is that training with dissimilar aircraft is unsafe. Why it is unsafe has never been fully explained to anyone. I guess it is safer to learn how to fight MiGs by fighting MiGs to the death than it is to learn when the stakes are far lower. I believe when you can't figure out why something apparently illogical is the way it is, follow the money. That is probably the real reason behind the prohibition of dissimilar air combat. When F-4s fight other F-4s in training, both sides of the engagement get trained, a double dip in the training pool. If F-4s were to fly against F-5s, which the USAF doesn't use in combat, only half the cost of the flight is applicable for the war. Twice as many softies need to be generated and paid for. Evidently, the cost of aircraft shot down due to ineffective pilot training, not to mention men's lives lost, is acceptable. On-the-job training is way cheaper than quality education, unless you are the one paying for the lack of training with your life.

All this complaining would be moot if the MiGs were similar in performance to my Phantom, but the two aircraft are wildly dissimilar. The Phantom is a large, heavy jet that accelerates well, goes really fast, and depends on good long-range missiles. It does not turn tightly, particularly at low speeds. At 420 knots and above, it handles well. Below that airspeed, it can be a handful to fly. Only a few Phantoms have internal guns for close-in dogfighting.

The MiGs, on the other hand, are anti-Phantoms. They are lighter, smaller, slower, and they turn extremely tightly. They handle well at low speeds, less well at higher velocities. They have short-range missiles and guns, lots of guns. At least this is what I understand from reading the classified "Secret" books about the adversaries trying to kill me.

Taking the long view, this mismatch of hardware is not unusual for the United States. Our P-47 Thunderbolts and P-38 Lightnings of WWII were less maneuverable than their German opponents, the FW-190 and Me-109 fighters. It wasn't until we introduced the P-51 Mustang midway through the war that we turned the tide. But by then, most of the good German jocks were dead. Our agile Mustangs cleaned up against the inexperienced schoolboys flying for the Luftwaffe late in the European conflict.

In the Pacific, the Japanese Zeros flew rings, literally, around our P-40 Warhawks and F4F Wildcats early in the war. Only when we introduced the F4U Corsair, the P-51, and the F6F Hellcat and when we learned how not to bet the other man's tricks that we started to win.

The F-86 Sabres of the USAF and the MiG-15s of North Korea were fairly evenly matched, but the superior training and experience, gained the hard way in WWII, of our guys allowed us to beat them like a drum. The seven-to-one kill ratio that we boasted of in Korea shows what good training deployed against an inept opponent can produce, even if the respective hardware is comparable. However, superior training and experience is not evident in our flight today. We have practiced some air combat, mostly in the States, and I know all of the set-piece moves. I know that when your opponent does this, you do that. When he commits thus, you counter with your own move. I have never tried any of this with a MiG-type opponent. The differences in characteristics between our Phantoms and their MiGs are as if they will try to play racquetball while we prefer tennis.

Air combat training in the western United States is done over and in Death Valley, California. The gods of war must be splitting their togas with laughter. Whatever deadly game we are playing, it is apt to be a quick one. The average MiG engagement in this war lasts forty-five seconds. Forty-five seconds to determine who lives and who dies. At the end of those forty-five seconds, one guy will go home a hero and one or two will float down in bloody little pieces from the sky. I don't know what happens in North Vietnam, but I suspect their dynamic is the same as ours. In the USAF, killing a MiG marks you for recognition the rest of your career. Everyone knows who the MiG killers are and how many MiGs they bested in aerial duels. Some guys sew a little red star for each MiG kill on the sleeve of their flight suits or paint a bigger star on their helmets, but most do not. Did Wyatt Earp notch the walnut handle of his Colt peacemaker? I bet he did.

My squadron commander is one of those well-known guys. He learned his craft on P-47s at the end of WWII and perfected it in Korea, earning the honorary title of "Ace" by downing five MiGs over North Korea. Besides P-47 and F-86, he flew the F-100 Super Sabre and F-105 Thunderchief before strapping on the F-4. If there is any guy in this war that knows what he is doing, it is the Boss. I am trying very hard to keep his plane in sight.

Regardless of the actions of the other members of Satan Flight, aerial combat always comes down to one versus one. Can I in my jet defeat the other guy in his? Sadly, the training we have done over Death Valley has been unrealistic in the extreme. Early in our training cycle, we usually started each practice session with our F-4 opponent in sight and on parallel paths. Then we progressed to meeting our pretend adversaries head-on. It was a little like being a medieval knight. You shouldered your lance, slammed your visor down, and entered the lists in, say, Crouton, France. Without the invisible lists in the air to keep the contestants on parallel paths, will we know what to do against a bandit (confirmed enemy aircraft) that appears unexpectedly in some other part of the sky?

The scripted scenarios we practiced in the States provided cheap and safe training, but did nothing to prepare us for the swirling real world of air combat. Eighty percent of the guys who are shot down never even see the Bad Guys who shoot them down. This is another reason I'm keeping my head on a swivel. Or course, I will gleefully shoot down any MiG whose pilot doesn't see me. Instead of using the analogy of a face-off with outlaws on the main street of Tombstone, maybe I should be thinking about shooting a guy in the back in the Crystal Palace Saloon.

We are approaching the target area and so far no MiGs have been sighted. The navigators in the backseats of the Phantoms are devoting half their time to their radarscopes, but have not been able to illuminate a single bogey with their searching electronic beams.

At least there have been no SAMs sighted either. The Wild Weasels are doing their job well. It is one thing to take on a living, thinking human pilot flying a MiG aircraft, but quite another to try to avoid a SAM. SAMs are mindless robots the size of telephone poles. There is no glory, only terror, in outwitting an automatic missile guidance computer which is answering the commands of an operator safely located on the ground. SAMs are also not intimidated. If you can get another pilot to believe that he is at a disadvantage by your display of aggressive actions, you are halfway to winning the engagement. Staring down a guy in the street before you draw your gun works. Likewise, pointing the nose of your jet at a bandit gets his attention. The only thing you can do with a SAM is to dodge it.

In the Middle Ages, knights found no honor in warring against the vassals who were under the rule of a rival king. Honor came from defeating other knights, however inept. SAMs, like varlets, only obey their master's bidding. There is no honor in dodging SAMs, only fear, and where is the honor in that?

So far everything has gone smoothly. The strike formation is coherent, our MiG CAP flight is where we should be, and the Wild Weasels have swept the area around the target. We are ready to rain death and destruction on the unsuspecting truck parking lot. There appears to be one small glitch. Someone forgot to brief the weatherman on our plan. As far as I can see, there is nothing but a flat, solid deck of low white clouds far beneath us. North Vietnam is socked in with low-lying monsoon rain clouds.

The monsoon in Southeast Asia is very predictable; you can forecast the weather with an almanac. The mountain spine running the length of the peninsula interrupts the prevailing wind patterns and splits the monsoon. It rains steadily for four months on each side of the mountains, but at different times. When the clouds dump on one side, the other side is clear. That is why we had gorgeous weather for our takeoff, facilitating the join up of sixteen jets in gin-clear air. It wouldn't have taken a genius to predict this low deck of clouds, but the mission was probably planned too far in advance and no one thought to check the Old Rice Farmer's Almanac.

So now, what do we do? There are no MiGs to fight, no SAMs to dodge, and no targets to hit. The ground crews back at the base are really going to be pissed. The mission order arrived on base around 8 p.m. last night and was classified "Secret" as usual. However, word gets around. The ground crews, the ordnance troops, and the flight operations types always know when there is a big mission going and they dig it. They love to believe that they, and we, are winning the war. Nothing enhances morale like preparing for a major strike on the north.

The enlisted guys normally work in two shifts, twelve hours on and twelve hours off, six days a week. When the aircraft began to be loaded for today's strike shortly after midnight last night, both shifts showed up for work. The guys scheduled to be on duty on the nighttime flight line were there as well as the guys who had just worked twelve hours in the hot, humid Thai sunlight. Confusion reigned for a time until the Chief of Maintenance, a full colonel, laid down the law. He decreed that only the guys actually on duty could work. The others could only help, if asked. Those heroes are going to be really disappointed if we bring all these bombs and missiles back home.

The Old Man sees the target area is completely but not unexpectedly covered in cloud. He deliberately and slowly turns the formation southward. We are most vulnerable in a banked turn. The ECM pod loses its coverage of the SAM radars and we are belly-up and blind to any lurking MiGs. We roll out headed south, everyone thinking hard about what to do next.

Due to the politically motivated bombing pause, we are prevented from striking any other target. It says so in the great red book titled "Rules of Engagement" in Wing HQ back at the base. Hitting a non-approved target in North Vietnam, regardless of how effectively such an action might affect our war effort, is a court-martial offense. The strike flight continues southward down the panhandle of North Vietnam with the Wild Weasels and the MiG CAP trying to catch up.

There is one, and only one, ragged hole in the cloud deck ahead. The Mission Commander starts a slow turn around the roughly circular hole, to peer down into the white-walled well. I take a quick glance away from looking for MiGs when Satan Flight is over the hole. I instantly recognize the bend in the river and the karst hills nearby which identify a well-known river crossing, a shallow water ford. I know this target area by heart from my previous flying as a Sewer Doer. Vietnam Highway One crosses a broad muddy river here below us. There is an embarkation point on the north side of the river, a truck park and refueling depot on the south bank. Half a mile down the river there is a huge cave in the side of a karst hill; it looks as if the river flows into the cave, hence the nickname, "the disappearing river." The Bad Guys hide a floating pontoon bridge in the cave to use for crossing the river when the water is too high for trucks to ford. All this is readily apparent to me with one glance straight down as I bank steeply up on my left wing.

The enemy has grown complacent during the bombing pause, enjoying our good will. The monsoon cloud cover is offering them additional ease. Instead of relaxing as Washington hopes, they are taking advantage of our forbearance to move fleets of trucks down Highway One. Each one is loaded with deadly war material for use against U.S. troops in the south. I can spot dozens of trucks on both sides of the ford, several in midstream, and more yet in the dirt parking lot waiting to be refueled.

This is the wrong truck park. Under our flight orders we are only allowed to hit the suspected site farther north. These trucks are off limits and are safe from air attack. Of course, they may be the very same trucks that should be farther north or that were up there yesterday, but let's not split political frog hairs.

We are peering down from on high into the round hole in the cloud deck. The North Vietnamese are also looking up and seeing our sky-darkening armada wheeling overhead. They know there is a bombing pause on, our beloved President told them so on TV. They are probably laughing their little Asian asses off at our impotence and are giving us the Vietnamese version of the finger.

We get lucky. Someone down below on the ground panics and yanks the firing lever on a fifty-seven-millimeter antiaircraft gun, hurling a seven round burst skyward. We all see the dirty gray puffs of smoke as the shells detonate harmlessly at about 15,000 feet. The explosions look like used cotton balls.

That's all we need. The Rules of Engagement clearly state that we have the right to return fire if shot at. The Bad Guys have the right to remain silent with their guns if they so wish. They did not exercise that right. Now we are operating on another page in the ROE book, one we know by heart.

The Old Man doesn't even need to call his shot or to change the plan on the radio. We all know what is coming now. I hear "Lead's in" echoing in my earphones. The four ships in his flight roll in together and take up their respective positions in a forty-five-degree dive. One after another, the other three strike flights of four Phantoms each perform the same maneuver from different points of the compass around the hole in the clouds. I watch their jets change from green/brown to white as their pale bellies are rolled skyward and then back to green, their top color, as they dive steeply toward North Vietnam. Each flight salvos its bombs in the clear air of the hole and pulls off individually through the side cloud wall, joining up again on top. The attack is carried out as planned, only about fifty miles south of the original target. For such intensive airborne action, there are very few radio calls. These guys know what they are doing and they don't need a lot of chat to do it. Each flight leader calls "in" and calls "off" then specifies a compass heading on which to rejoin the formation.

Once the nose of the Mission Commander's jet was pointed toward the earth, the Bad Guys instantly got the picture that they were under attack. The sky opens up with antiaircraft fire, with guns firing wildly in all direction into the gap rent in the clouds. The white puffs of thirty-seven-millimeter fire and the dirty bolls of fifty-seven-millimeter shells are everywhere. Instead of aimed fire, the panicked Vietnamese seem to be trying to put as much iron in the air as possible in hope that someone will run into some of it. Flak explosions sully the flat, clean white top of the cloud deck. The hole in the clouds partially fills with drifting shell-burst smoke.

Our MiG CAP flight has the best seats in the house as we continue to circle the scene of the action. No MiGs are to be seen. They would have to be stupid to fly into that flak; they might get shot down. I estimate that at least 1,000 rounds of large caliber bullets are shot at the strike flights.

There is bloody carnage below. Burning trucks litter both sides of the river with several turned over in the middle of the ford. Brown and white geysers of muddy water erupt in the river as bombs go astray. The refueling depot is aflame with the thick black smoke of burning petroleum. Secondary explosions triggered by the bombs sparkle on the ground as flammable truck loads are torched off. The flames from the burning trucks and the fuel dump mingle with the AAA muzzle smoke and with the bomb splashes.

The few folks left alive on the ground are probably wondering, "'What the hell happened? The Yankee Air Pirates (that's what Hanoi Jane, the heavily accented voice on the Hanoi propaganda radio station, calls us) aren't supposed to do that. One little fifty-seven millimeter squirt and they bomb us all to hell."

The strike package forms up and heads southwest, toward our base in Thailand. It wasn't pretty; it was war.

Did we destroy the fifty-seven millimeter gun that started it all and allowed us the excuse to "return fire"? We must have; we scattered bombs hither, thither, and yon around the ford area, one of them surely must have damaged the offending gun, wherever it is, or was. If our bombs didn't take out the hotheaded gunner, I'm sure his commander summarily shot him, for bringing the steel shit storm down from the skies.

I didn't shoot down any MiGs today but no MiGs shot me down either. The experience was great, today's flight fueled my adrenaline addiction big-time. The intensity started during the preflight intelligence briefing at 0430 hours; the atmosphere in the room was electric. Usually, the guys are trying to stay awake, or are laughing and joshing. Today we knew we were going north and it showed on our faces.

We hung on every word the Boss uttered as he briefed the flight; after all, he has been there before. The ride out to the flight line in the blue USAF bread-van truck was silent and tense, no kidding allowed.

The ground crew was all business today as I pre-flighted the jet. As usual, the crew chief climbed up the ladder to the cockpit and helped me strap in, managing the parachute/shoulder harnesses for me. He handed me my helmet, today he said, "Good luck, sir." That meant a lot to me.

I have never felt as proud of my country as I did today while flying formation on the aerial refueling tanker in the predawn twilight. There was nothing to do then but fly formation and think while the other guys got their gas. Dawn was breaking over the Plain of Jars; the tankers had permission to go further north than usual. On routine missions they drop us off at the Thai border. As the sky lightened and the stars faded, I could see tankers all around me, each with its four ship of Phantoms or Thunderchiefs close behind. The sight was awesome; the Wolf Pack was going north.

As we cross the fence, the Mekong River, on our way home and enter Thai air space and into relative peace, I reach down and deactivate the missiles, flipping the missile arm switch to "safe."

The Boss leads us back for landing and I get to practice my close formation flying skills. On our initial approach to the field, we fly down the runway with all four jets aligned on Satan Lead's left wing in echelon formation. I tuck in tightly, leaving only three to five feet between my canopy and the wingtip of Satan Two. I am sweating, trying to fly good formation on Satan Two, but at the same time, I can't bounce around too much. Hostile Man, as Satan Four, has to line up the other three jets of Satan Flight and tuck into the ever-moving line. His is the hardest job, averaging out the movements of Satan Lead, Two, and Three. If he can't, the formation will look crappy from the ground.

'We want to look good for the waiting enlisted guys on the ground. They are the ones who busted their humps to put us in the air. We want them to know that we care as much about how we fly as they care about their essential but unglamorous and uncomfortable jobs. As we pass over the ramp, they'll see that the bombs are all gone; that will be well received. Once we land, they'll note that we brought all the missiles back; that will be a bummer. No MiG kills today, no red stars to paint on the sides of the jets below the canopies.

Later, I plan to meet Wyatt and Doc at the bar. I hope they don't ask how many kills we recorded today.

WAR FOR THE HELL OF IT

It is two o'clock in the morning; sadly I'm not flying. Instead of committing aviation, I'm sitting, drinking, and watching it rain and rain hard. Sleep is out of the question, my internal diurnal clock is programmed to deliver massive jolts of adrenaline at this time of day; I am as wide-awake as a tree full of owls. I have flown combat missions for the last thirty-three days or nights without a break and my Squadron Commander has taken me off the flying schedule. He says he's worried about me being affected by combat fatigue, that I need a rest. I'm more worried about incipient boredom. This rank inequality of personal priorities, not to mention the inequality of military ranks has gotten me temporarily grounded. I have been ordered to travel down south to Bangkok on official leave. When I told the commander I'd rather not go to Bangkok, his reply indicated that this was not a offer I could refuse. I fly out in the morning on the C-130 shuttle run, call sign "Klong." The Klong will take me to Bangkok and return with me plus a load of mail in three days.

Oh well, maybe it will be fun to see the exotic sights of Bangkok once again and eat some food that hasn't been (over) cooked by someone whose call sign is "Cookie." Maybe I'll meet a lonely, round-eyed airline stewardess over on a trip from the States who wants to slip out of her uniform. Maybe we'll spend a romantic weekend together in Bangkok. Maybe the Chicago Cubs will win the World Series. Perhaps my new love and I can catch the games on TV in our luxurious hotel room at the Bangkok Officers' Club. Yeah, right. But as long as I'm wishing for the moon, why not go for the whole impossible dream?

In the meantime, while I'm dreaming of getting lucky in Bangkok, the rain is still pouring down in torrents here in Ubon. Hailing from the temperate climate that predominates in the southeastern United States, I have never seen the like of Thai rain. East Tennessee has basically two types of rain. The first type leaks, drips actually, from flat layers of stratoform clouds. This rain falls softly and lightly, interspersed with periods of drizzle. It can go on for a few days at a time and usually occurs during cool or cold weather. The second type is generated by summer heat giving rise to cumulus clouds and thunderstorms. This rain falls heavily and quickly for half an hour followed by the sun breaking through after the thunderstorm moves on. Thailand has managed to combine these two flavors of rain into a monsoon storm. It has been raining harder than anyone has ever seen in Tennessee and it has been doing it constantly for four days. All the while, the temperature has not budged from 85 degrees. It's as if the gods of rain have something to prove or else Thailand needs a thorough cleansing. We have tropical thunderstorms embedded in warm stratoform clouds. This weather would be amazing if it wasn't so miserable.

Everything and everybody is soaked. I haven't been really dry since the monsoon started a week ago and I won't be dry again until it ends in about two months. I get soaked walking to the squadron. I get drenched doing the preflight inspection of my airplane. When I open the canopy, there is a puddle in the middle of the seat cushion a quarter-inch deep. By the time I strap in, I am even wetter. During the climb out to cruising altitude, the Phantom's air conditioner spits cold, visible white condensation and ice chunks at me as it dries itself out. By the time I get to the tanker, I am both soaked and freezing. Hours later when I return to land, the dry air at altitude has desiccated me somewhat, but when I park the jet and open the canopy in the rain, the process starts all over again.

I could wear my official USAF hooded poncho while on the ground but that would generate uncountable jokes about walking around in a giant prophylactic. I would rather be wet than be the subject of crummy humor. I can't wear a poncho around the jet anyway, too many sharp edges to catch it on. So, for a few months I'll be wet. Being sodden hasn't improved my mood. Being grounded and wet is just the pits. I won't be able tonight to clear my head by flying, to hide in the air. The rain is impinging on my mind as well as my body.

If I could only get airborne my mood would improve. When the mountains of Laos stop the monsoon clouds from blowing farther east, Thailand is covered with a wet blanket of vigorous precipitation. It is clear over North Vietnam now and there is aerial work to be done there. Only I'm not doing it right now and no one else in the squadron is either. We are observing another bombing pause dictated by our fearless leaders in Washington, confining us to only flying over Laos, which is socked in, inaccessible.

Flying combat missions can be as repetitious as any other regular activity. More dangerous certainly than punching in at the office, but just as routine in schedule. While I'm sitting here on my damp butt watching the rain come down, my inner self thinks I ought to be over North Vietnam getting shot at. I have broken my nightly routine and I haven't had my adrenaline fix tonight.

What I have had is lots of Bourbon, not the free rotgut stuff in the squadron fridge, but the real thing from Lynchburg, Tennessee, with Jack Daniel's name on the label. Of course, I know that Jack Daniel's isn't really Bourbon, it's better. However, at two o'clock in the morning in northeast Thailand with the monsoon in drenching progress, the exact distinction between true Bourbon and Tennessee Sour Mash Whiskey escapes me; it has something to do with charcoal filtering. I am on my second (or is it my third?) ice-tea glass of Bourbon and water, as if I needed more water just now. I started earlier at the Officers' Club, but adjourned to my quarters to sit, think, and drink. Not necessarily in that order.

I am sitting on a U.S. government-issue folding chair on the porch of my Officers' Quarter, better known as the "hooch" for reasons long lost to history. The hooch is built like a cheap

1950s motel, with six two-man rooms in a row, three on each side of a central day room, latrine, and shower. Each room has an outside door that opens onto a covered porch running the length of the hooch. A wooden railing, the current resting place of my wet-booted feet, fronts the porch. The Officers' Club is almost deserted now with only drunks at the bar. "Who wants to talk to drunks anyway?" I ask myself as I take yet another sip. The cute and curvy Thai barmaids went off duty at midnight, replaced by their male counterparts. The Thai guys are friendly enough, but not much to look at compared to the alternatives. The nightly poker game broke up around one o'clock and I drifted over to the hooch porch to ruminate and drink undisturbed.

Unbothered by others, I am deluged by my own thoughts as they come flooding into my head, the rain continuing to pour down. There is no one else around to interrupt my contemplation.

Two rows of hooches face each other, separated by a courtyard of muddy, patchy grass and by cascading water. There is no one on the porch of the facing hooch; I am very much alone with my glass and my thoughts. No rice paddy in South Vietnam has more water in it than the bare area between the hooches; still the night's hard rain falls on, splashing in the shallow pond in front of me.

Thinking of South Vietnam, that miserable country is the reason I'm sitting here watching falling sheets of water. What am I doing here? Why are we fighting this so-called war? It isn't a real war, of course. You fight real wars to win and we aren't doing that. When we start winning, when we get the North Vietnamese on the ropes, our politicians in Washington call a bombing halt to allow the Bad Guys the opportunity to stop what they are doing. Naturally, they regroup and re-arm and we fly back north once again to get shot at some more. A few more empty stools at the bar. A Sergeant comes and packs up some missing pilot's belongings to mail home. Another mother or wife gets a knock on the door from three USAF officers in full blue uniform; the Duty Officer, a Flight Surgeon, and a

Chaplain. Someone loses a son or husband, more kids grow up fatherless. We call another bombing halt and the futile cycle continues.

This war is not turning out as I was led to believe when I signed up to attend it. I was told, and I believed, that we were fighting for freedom and independence for South Vietnam, to allow those good folks to live in a Jeffersonian democracy. I've been to Saigon; that was an eye-opener. We are fighting for crooked politicians, profiteers, pimps, prostitutes, and drug pushers. We are fighting for peasants that are on our side during the day and are Vietcong at night. The capital of South Vietnam is awash in Saigon Cowboys; these street hustlers are everywhere, like shoals of sharks. Each young Vietnamese stud seems to have a fake Rolex and a motor scooter with a longhaired girlfriend in a high-slit skirt perched crossways on the back.

Maybe I should look on the idealistic side. We are fighting for a guy's democratic right to be a draft dodger as well as a Saigon Cowboy. However, all those draft dodgers are in the United States. South Vietnam doesn't have compulsory service. Saigon Cowboys have no draft to dodge. We are drafting our young men to fight for a country that won't draft its own. The idea of fighting for South Vietnam doesn't hold water, of which I have plenty in front of me.

If a free and democratic South Vietnam isn't worth spilling our blood over, what about the concept of keeping the worldwide Communist menace at bay? This isn't a war, it's a game of regional dominos and we are trying to keep another one from falling. Saigon today, Laos tomorrow, then Cambodia, Thailand after that, and soon the Commies land in Honolulu. That rationale only holds up if we are trying to win, to prevent the next domino from toppling, which we clearly aren't. That is where I got into this endless logic loop.

The latest background intelligence briefing I paid any attention to indicated to me that we were barely holding our own in South Vietnam. Actually, we are substituting for the inept South Vietnamese army; it's their own we're holding, not ours. We seem to be better at fighting for their country than they are.

The sole reason I paid any attention at all to the intelligence briefing is because the new female intelligence officer has a great pair of shapely legs that lead to a firm, round bottom. On the elevated presentation platform in the wing briefing room she displayed her pert figure in a tight, USAF dark blue skirt that was clearly cut a good deal shorter than official regulation length. Her minimum version of a uniform skirt made we want to see a lot more of her and a lot less of the intelligence briefing. The unfortunate lady lieutenant had obviously been victimized by a sadistic supply sergeant who issued her a skirt one or two sizes too small. Someone should report that guy, but I won't.

How the hell did that carnal image intrude itself into my head? I was having a serious political debate with myself here. In the process of thinking about the rationale for the war, if any, this salacious scene swells up. Maybe there is something about not having had a date in months that generates random prurient thoughts. I'm sure Bourbon had a role in that daydream as well. But, back to mental work.

If I can't fathom why our country is expending so many resources, or why it is wasting some of its citizens' lives, and why it is warping many more, perhaps I can deduce why I am here, personally. After much thought, I decide my involvement can be separated into three overlapping phases. At first, I bought the story about saving South Vietnam from the North. Or was that saving it from itself? Is there any difference between North and South? Anyway, it was my patriotic duty, and duty is what I signed up for when I joined the US Air Force. That motivation lasted about two months, until my first trip to Saigon. Now, I couldn't care less if South Vietnam is washed away by the Communist red tide.

Thailand is another case entirely. Despite its propensity to flood annually; it is a hell of a nice country. The people are relaxed, friendly, attractive (as evidenced by the aforementioned barmaids), and honest by Southeast Asian standards, which isn't saying much. The Thais seem to sincerely like Americans instead of considering them only as a resource to exploit. I'd gladly fight a war for Thailand if called. If we don't win the one we're in now, I may get that opportunity in the future as the dominos fall.

By the six-month mark, the war had become personal. I wanted revenge for my friends and buddies that weren't coming home anytime soon, and their numbers were growing. Once, I chalked the names of all my lost mates on a 2,000-pound bomb and dropped it on the north. I only included the guys I used to call by their first names. The olive-colored bomb was dusted white with scrawled writing when it left the airplane. I wanted revenge for what North Vietnam is doing to my country, the way America is being torn apart by the war. If I want revenge for the discord, maybe I should bomb Washington instead of Hanoi. Hanoi knows what it is doing; Washington doesn't, and that is the root cause of the nation-wide protests. The revenge phase of my motivation lasted a few more months and then leaked slowly away. I found that revenge doesn't satisfy if it doesn't end by winning the war. The longer I tried to avenge my dead and captured friends, the more friends I was obligated to avenge.

Finally, I sunk to my bedrock motivation. That's the level I am operating at now. Fueled by primal needs, the man I have become scares me. Another sip of Bourbon and rain water clears up the murky thoughts in my head. All my life, ever since I can remember, I have wanted to fly, to be a fighter pilot for the USAF. That was my goal throughout school, college, and pilot training. I read all the books, I saw all the movies, and I knew the history of fighter aviation, and of famous fighter pilots. I never wanted to be a fireman, or a cowboy or a doctor, or anything else. I risked everything to get where I am now, to learn the skills, to get those silver wings pinned on my chest.

But why am I here at this bogus war? There are fighter squadrons in Germany, the Philippines, Korea, the UK, and all over the USA itself. I could fly instead at one of those safer peacetime places. Indeed, many of my squadron mates have come from those other bases and units, none of which is at war with anyone. I'm sure many of them would rather be there, or anywhere but here. Before the Vietnam War lurched into being, it was possible to contemplate a twenty-year career as a USAF fighter jock and to look forward to never firing a shot in anger much less for revenge. It is still possible to spend your active flying years sitting on alert status in Germany or training pilots in west Texas.

West Texas, that reminds me of a pretty blond girl I know there, her with the big hair and the high, smooth-as-silk ass. She has a liking for thin, skintight slacks and an aversion to wearing panties under them. Wait a minute, how did that thought break the surface? I'm trying to concentrate here and these kinds of images keep welling up in my head. Why do I keep getting diverted? Is it my dammed-up hormones or the Bourbon? I suspect the reason for these mental sidetracks is I know where this conversation with myself is going and I'm not sure I want to go there. Fantasy sex offers an appealing side channel for my mental efforts. I could easily sit here and watch it rain, sipping my self-medication, and letting my mind do the breast stroke in imaginary warm lakes of lust.

But no, I have to work this out. This question cannot be denied. The rain is coming down even harder, which I thought was impossible, but there it is splashing into my glass. I'm getting bursts of wind, which occasionally blow pelting rain under the overhanging tin roof of the porch. The monsoon is trying to change me from damp to wet. My glass is almost empty, but there is plenty more where that came from in my hooch room.

So, why am I here, when I could be somewhere else? I can rule out patriotism and the obligations of duty. I've already flown more than enough missions to fill that square. Judging by the effects the war is having on America, I'm not so sure that it is patriotic for me to be so aggressively prosecuting it anyway. I have to admit that the revenge motivation has proved to be a dead end, literally. Is it the flying? What about my boyhood dreams? No, I could fly many other places than here.

I drain my drink, which is getting more diluted, and slowly swallow the last of the Bourbon and rainwater. The fiery, smoky, sweet liquid dissolves the last of my internal defenses as the storm tries to blow away the hooch. If it were light enough to see my reflection in the growing pond in front of the porch, I wouldn't be able to cope with the hard-eyed visage I would see staring back.

Down deep, I'm here because I like it. I enjoy the lifestyle; all I have to do is fly, drink, eat, play poker, and sleep, with the occasional sexual fantasy thrown in. Life in a fighter squadron is highly emotionally rewarding; there is something about trusting other guys with your life that builds deep comradeship. I know that I'll never be tighter with a group as I am now. Yes, what the Aussies call "being with your mates" is a big plus. Are we tight with each other because of the shared danger? Undoubtedly, but what's the harm in that?

Another large factor is my need for adrenaline. Jolts of adrenaline are very addictive and I'm hooked deep. Flying fighters is dangerous enough in peacetime. If I fly for twenty years, with no time out for staff jobs, the numbers say that I will have one chance in five of busting my ass. Combat takes that danger to a new level. Dedicated people try to kill me every time I fly outside of Thailand. Being shot at and missed is supremely exciting and really gets the craved adrenaline flowing. Flying combat is the ultimate in flying. Being a fighter pilot in the peacetime air force would be like practicing with the baseball team and never going to a game. The war had already started when I got my orders to pilot training and I knew that my flight path would lead to it, if not precisely to this wet porch. I can still remember tearing open those orders to active duty while still at college in Atlanta.

Atlanta, that's where I met the vivacious redhead whose hourglass figure bounces and jiggles, stretching her amazingly clinging knitted dresses to the breaking point. No! I have to see this through. My resolve to persevere in hard thinking is met by a yet stronger burst of wind and rain. It seems that the storm is reaching some sort of meteorological climax. I don't have to fly tonight to get strafed; horizontal rain is an acceptable substitute.

My job, my avocation, requires a physical exam 98 percent of the population can't pass. I have spent years in training to do what I do and have seen many others fail to make the grade. Every night I lay my life on the line, betting that my skill and capricious luck will prevail long enough to let me return the next night to test it and myself again. It isn't the patriotic duty, it isn't the lost buddies, it isn't the career, it's all about me and what I live to do. Forget fighting for some vague geopolitical goal or for some abstract altruistic patriotism, that's all bull shit; I fly and fight for me.

Is it immoral to enjoy a war by personalizing it? Is it egocentric to dig the danger, the status, and the friendships of a fighter squadron? Does feeding off the action and taking pride in doing what most men can't do make me a war criminal, or a hero? The differences in the two labels are small and depend on whether this is a "just and legal" war. Is it? Who the hell knows? I do know that in the future, I will look back on the years I spent flying and fighting as the most exciting ones of my life. Is it corroding my soul to take pride in dispensing violence and in doing it very well indeed?

I care not for the Vietnamese that I kill. Given the chance, they would gleefully kill me just as coldly. Failing that, they would relish throwing me into the Hanoi Hilton prison camp and letting me rot away with my ex-roommate. No, exchanging death efforts with the North Vietnamese excludes sympathy; quarter neither given nor asked for. After getting shot at without effect, I am capable of exhibiting reptilian detachment while killing the people doing the shooting and sleeping like a log the next day. This is the aspect of what I have become that is the most scary to me.

Fear is part of the equation. If there is no fear, my adrenaline fix wouldn't flow. But what I fear is not the fear of a more rational person. Deep down, I don't really fear death. I believe that it can't happen to me. I have to believe that or I would be dysfunctional. The fear that spurs me on is of failure, of humiliation in front of my peers. I am tighter with the guys I fly with than I am with my own brothers. What keeps me awake at night is the fear, not of death nor of the Hanoi Hilton, but of failing to perform well, of letting my squadron mates down. On the upside, there is no feeling like the one that follows a successful, particularly dangerous and difficult mission.

Do those my squadron mates feel the same way I do? Who the hell knows? We have our debates over the war, but only at the level of tactics. We endlessly speculate on how to win. Sometimes politics rears its ugly head and we roundly curse the elected hacks that seem intent on getting us all killed for no good reason. Fighter pilots are an articulate and outspoken lot. Most will say what they think at the drop of a shot glass. But on the rare occasions when the subject of personal motivation comes up, you can cut the silence with a Randall knife. Are they here for the same selfish reasons that I am? Do they pride themselves on doing one of the most dangerous jobs in the world and doing it with skill, style, and grace? Have any of them sat on this porch drinking and watching it rain while plumbing the depths of their souls? Do they too fight off a flood of imagery of wanton blonds, mini-skirted intelligence officers, nude redheads, and willing stewardesses to grapple with their own motivations?

My ruminations have uncovered more questions than answers, but the asking of the questions has washed away the façade of self-deception. I know now that I'm doing this because of me, my pride, my adrenaline addiction, and my self-satisfaction at what I do. Very few people in the world can do it and fewer still would enjoy doing it so much. None of my civilian contemporaries will ever have the opportunity to fly fighter planes in combat, to lay it on the line night after night. I would be foolish to pass up the chance, whatever I think of the geopolitical underpinnings of this bull shit war. The war and the underlying rationale are not inherently evil, wrong, or even illegal. The war can't be won under the present rules and with the present allies in the south. I can't affect the dim-bulb military bureaucrats or the amoral politicians (isn't that redundant?) who are criminally mismanaging the war; all I can do is fight in it. If it is ego that drives me, then so be it. I'll live with that as I can't live without it. I'll have to deal with this, but right now it looks like an acceptable trade-off. I get to fly and fight if I don't get too upset about the futility and frustration of it all.

Frustration, that characterizes my relationship with the cute brunette in North Carolina, she with the laughing dark eyes and the raven hair. "Geographic separation-induced futility" is the name of that game. I haven't gotten enough of her or her long, shapely legs displayed bare in black four-inch stiletto heels with nothing else on but the radio. Why do my thoughts of the girls I know revolve around their bodies? Now I've done it, the bug-eyed monster is out from under the bed and I have to deal with it.

Do I appreciate women only for their bodies or is my brain thoroughly marinated in months of dammed-up hormones? My physical longing is as real as the rain that continues to pour down, but is that all there is? Is that all there should be? It is easy to be cavalier about the opposite sex, too easy in fact. But the drenching I am receiving and the Bourbon I am drinking makes it hard to be dishonest with myself. Digging deep, I have to admit that having a girl-type friend and lover would be very, very rewarding. I'd love to go out for dinner in exotic Bangkok, to conduct a whirlwind romance, to see the sights with some feminine companionship for a change. It would be fun to flirt and talk about things other than airplanes. To commune with a woman, to understand a woman's view of the world. To get to know someone I don't know now. Such a relationship sounds ideal about now as long as the sexual aspect and fulfillment isn't neglected.

I have read that for women, friendship and intimacy lead to sex. While for men, sex leads to intimacy. If that natural, reciprocal fit is true, there is hope for me yet. Something along those lines could play out yet. Just maybe, my current mental preoccupation with attractive female bodies is due to the fact that my fingertips haven't touched a woman's soft skin in an eon.

I feel good about my last conclusion on the preferred treatment of women. I'm not an exploiter after all. However, I remain profoundly uneasy about my seduction by the siren bitch of war. I enjoy my violent job too much. Psychologically, all you can hope for is to break even. The old baseball adage is spot-on, "Win some, lose some, some are rained out, and the rest are fixed."

It's three o'clock in the middle of the night in the midst of the monsoon. Or at least the monsoon was doing its thing up until now. Amazingly enough, the storm seems to be abating, the rain has slacked off to what could be called a hard drizzle. There are so many unanswered questions left, but I do know two things. First, I had better get some sleep before I get on the Klong tomorrow. Those C-130 Klong drivers will fly in almost any weather and the pause in the monsoon makes it certain that they will leave at dawn. I would hate to meet my mythical, friendly stewardess hung over and sleepy. Secondly, I know people like me should never be involved in making decisions as to when and where to fly and fight. If it comes to war, my type is indispensable if you want to win, but you don't want us to vote on accepting the engagement. Last, I know my longing for women has more than a horizontal dimension. I'm tempted to see how far I can throw my now empty glass into the dying storm, but I just set it gently down on the wet porch railing and go off to bed.

THE KING OF VENICE

The sprawling Thai capital, Bangkok, personifies chaos and I love it that way. The swampy, people-crammed city is the antithesis of my normal habitat, a USAF base. Even in exotic Thailand, an Air Force base has its well-tended grass cut to the regulation length, its neat, standard-issue buildings are painted the same color in neat rows, the roads are all smoothly paved, everything is in order and every detail is squared away. In Bangkok, nothing is squared away. There's probably not a true right angle in the whole city outside the many immaculate Buddhist temples. There is no grass of any length and the buildings are a mishmash of make-it-up-on-the-spot designs scattered around among algae-covered canals and dirt roads.

Bangkok exhibits the freedom of total chaos, rampant disorganization, a complete lack of order, and endless possibilities for interesting situations. The tolerant, lassiez-faire attitude of the inhabitants is a welcome antidote to overwhelming, suffocating militarization, to regimentation, and to effective central planning.

You can find anything you want in Bangkok and you can also find lots of stuff that you don't want. That's not quite right, you can find anything but bad manners. The only shortage in Bangkok is of rude people. The Thais frequently tell me that theirs is "The Land of Smiles" and I believe it. Genuine friendliness, courtesy, tolerance, and good humor seem to be universal national characteristics. Everyone I rub against seems to have a smile for me and in a city as overcrowded as Bangkok, a lot of rubbing goes on. The Thais' politeness isn't reserved just for us "farangs" or western foreigners. To my round eyes, they seem to interact among themselves with equal respect and good manners.

Only bus passengers in Bangkok never seem to smile. Beat-up bus after beat-up bus crammed full of Thais going to and from work passes me by on the crowded street. The dimly seen faces in the dusty bus windows have the same weary, exhausted expressions as they do in any large city in the world. Does taking a bus to work beat you down or does the ride free you to express your exhaustion? Is your true self on display when surrounded by other commuters who will forever remain strangers? In any case, bus riders everywhere have the same hangdog expression; it is both universal and sad. Yet in Bangkok these same forlorn riders will step down from their crummy bus and greet you with a radiant smile.

There are various ways to get around in Bangkok, but none of them seem to work very well. The city is stacked to overflowing with people, beyond even normal Asian crowding. The jammed streets seem to generate pervasive, but polite, chaos, which then spreads outward into the rest of the city. Just as the monsoon rains overfill the many canals and then flood the streets; the street traffic floods the city with its liquid chaos.

I have been sightseeing, alone alas, as my mythical, lonely airline stewardess failed to materialize. To see the sights, and there are many worth seeing, I have to choose my preferred mode of dysfunctional transportation.

I can take a taxi, which will invariably be a compact Japanese sedan with more dents in it than the outfield wall in Yankee Stadium. However, the interior will be spotlessly clean and tidy. All taxis have a pungent air freshener hanging from the rearview mirror; often the freshener is aided by a lei of fresh flowers. Perhaps to promote survival in the cut-and-thrust traffic, each cab has good luck incantations finger-painted in Thai on the headliner just aft of the windshield. In a Bangkok taxi, I have plenty of time to enjoy the attention the ever-smiling driver lavishes on the interior of his cab. Most daytime rides take quite a time to complete in the choking traffic. I like to measure our progress by watching individual people walking on the sidewalk to see if we are logging blocks faster than they are. Usually the pedestrians win the unannounced race, but bicyclists blow us away with superior speed.

Another, more sporting, transportation alternative is the "tuk-tuk." These are motorized samlors named after the coughing sound their smoky two-stroke engines make. Holding tight to the handlebars, the driver sits in front of the underpowered tricycle. The passengers sit between the rear wheels and over the putting engine. Tuk-tuks are scarcely faster than taxis and more exposed to the smoke and exhaust of the street. Alas, I never, ever, have had a desire to ride a tricycle in Bangkok traffic.

Rickety buses are everywhere, dirty and crowded. They are cheap, but their route schedules are unfathomable, as the Thais insist on labeling everything in their own Thai language. Who knows where any given bus is headed? Besides, I am in too good a mood to join the sourpusses on the buses.

For the seriously suicidal, there are motorcycle taxis beyond counting. These dart and swim in the river of street traffic, avoiding immobilized buses like shoals of fish swimming through rocky rapids. For a few baht, you tell the driver where you want to go. Then you hop on the back of his tiny Japanese motorbike and hang on for dear life. You can actually get around town fairly quickly on the back of a motorcycle taxi, if you live through the ride. However, these bikes work better if the terrified passenger is a 100-pound Thai than they do with a 175-pound American embarked. I see Thai girls in their traditional ankle-length, tight silk skirts perched crosswise like colorful oriental mermaids on the backs of fifty-cc motorbikes as they head to their jobs as waitresses or hostesses. I wonder how on earth they survive the commute.

Walking the crowded sidewalks of busy Pat Pong district, I spot a particularly curvy hostess in a shimmering silk dress and spike heels sliding off the back of a motorbike taxi. She is obviously reporting to work the lunch hour in a small Thai restaurant where the bike has let her off. That reminds me how hungry sightseeing has made me. Hungry for food, that is.

I leave the hot, sunny street and enter the cool restaurant, my eyes wide open in the dim light. This place must be an upscale eatery; it is air-conditioned and all the chairs match each other. Another tip-off is the large, gilt-framed portrait of the King of Thailand hung with reverence on the back wall. The luscious hostess I followed in flashes a radiant smile and greets me with well-spoken English. She shows me to a table with a vinyl tablecloth and softly hands me a leather-bound menu. As her high heels click-clack her away, I peruse the fare. They must get a lot of farangs in here as the dishes are listed in both Thai and English. The heat outside has wilted my appetite somewhat. I just want a simple lunch.

Ah, there's the ticket, something light. The dish called "Thai pepper beef salad" sounds refreshing and healthy. A smiling waitress arrives and seems surprised when I order the salad with iced tea. Maybe she was expecting me to include a beer.

In what seems like no time at all the salad arrives on an oblong platter. The white china platter holds a bed of lettuce hosting a sprinkling of onions, tomatoes, cucumbers, and strips of thin-sliced, rare roast beef. The salad is moistened with a clear dressing and garnished with bits of red, yellow, and green peppers. I can't wait to dig in.

The pretty teenaged waitress sets the salad and tea down, then asks in broken English,

"You like?"

I reply that it looks very good, but she doesn't walk away as I expect. She remains standing beside my table, wearing a dark blue waitress uniform that she must have borrowed from her little sister or from her Barbie doll. Her dress is so short and so tight, I don't see how she got into it and if she ever has to bend over very far, she'll be out of it. I smile my best lecher's smile, but still she remains. I think she wants to watch me eat this salad. Oh well, while she is observing me, I'll enjoy watching her stretch her mini-dress to the breaking point. A little provocative floor show during lunch won't be too hard to take.

The first forkful of salad tells me I have made a serious, perhaps fatal, mistake. What did they use for dressing on this salad, napalm? This stuff is like eating a green veggie welding torch. The tender parts of my mouth are being cauterized, my tongue is melting, I am dying of chili overload. I have never eaten anything this hot in my entire life. I choke down the first bite and grab a gulp of cold ice tea. The tea affects the flame in my mouth like pissing on an oil well fire. In my agony, I steal a look at the waitress still hovering nearby.

She smiles and repeats, "You like?"

I managed to gasp, "Yes, it's very good."

What this salad is good at is an incendiary assault on my taste buds. I take another bite and things only get worse. My vision is going blurry. I am breaking out in a fever, my upper lip is dripping with sweat and curling with pain. I can feel my heart pounding in protest to the abuse I'm shoving down my throat. Passing out is not out of the question. Another swig of tea helps a wee bit, enough for me to notice that the slinky hostess has joined my pert waitress to enjoy the show of a farang dying a fiery death by Thai salad.

Discretion dictates that I give up this spicy torture and order something else, perhaps a quart of green tea ice cream and yes, there is such a dish. But I am not going to give up that easily with the flowers of Bangkok womanhood watching. I force an anguished smile and press on eating as another dark-haired girl joins the gallery.

At last, with the help of four glasses of ice tea, I finish every bit of the 400-degree salad. By now, all five mini-skirted waitress and the hostess in her long silk sheath are watching from close by as I push away my now empty platter.

My waitress reaches for the implements of torture and asks once again, "You like?"

All I can do is nod affirmatively. It is a bold-faced, or rather a red-faced lie.

She smiles and goes on, "I never see American man eat this before."

That is really comforting. If I could talk, I'd thank her.

She finds one lone bit of red chili left on the empty platter and points to it.

"Not even Thai eat that."

Evidently I was supposed to push the offending chilies aside and chow down on the salad itself.

I don't know whether to swagger or to slink out of the restaurant. Did I show them how tough us farangs are or how stupid? In any case, my original plan was to use a hoary line on the beautiful hostesses, "Hostess honey, what time do you get off?" has gone up in oral flames. I open the door and reenter the shoals of sweltering people on the sidewalk, sadder but probably no smarter.

After the cool and quiet restaurant, the street seems even more chaotic than it was thirty minutes ago.

The streets of Bangkok are like great, dusty rivers of traffic. Dirty buses, smoking tuk-tuks, darting motorcycles, and battered taxis jostle in the flow as the traffic stream sluggishly makes its way between its curbed banks.

The real river in Bangkok, the Chao Phraya, flows much faster than the streets do. The river is the lifeblood of the city, bringing its commerce, transporting its citizens, housing some of its people, and carrying away its waste. The river is brown-green with mud and decaying vegetation, its waves churned to dirty froth by squadrons of boats. It is so polluted you could develop film in it, yet little naked Thai kids swim in it like miniature brown dolphins with no apparent ill effects.

Even the boats in Bangkok are exotic and strange. Long and slender, the typical wooden boats range in size from a dug-out canoe, full of fresh fruit for sale, to "long-tailed boats" thirty and forty feet in length. The long-tailed boats are maybe four feet wide and are powered by converted car engines mounted on swivels on the sterns. A slanting propeller shaft extends ten or fifteen feet behind each boat like a watery stinger. These long-tailed boats skim across the turbulent river like snarling dragonflies.

Bangkok boats are long and narrow to navigate the hundreds of canals or "klongs" that earned the city the title of

"The Venice of the Orient." Even given the Italian propensity for exuberant living, the chaos of Bangkok must make Venice, Italy look as tame as Sunday morning in St. Mark's Square.

The street-born chaos extends to the sidewalks awash in people. Polite and friendly people, but people in their millions. Pushcarts are everywhere, selling food I mostly recognize, but with some I don't. The streets of Bangkok are lined with mom-and-pop stores, each fifteen or twenty feet wide and twice as deep. The owner's families live on the second floors and business is done from breakfast until late at night. Bangkok has never heard of zoning; that would be way too organized. So, a welding shop is next to a restaurant, which is next to a dress shop, which adjoins a spice shop, which abuts a shop selling furniture. Somehow it all works and people find what they need and keep their good humor in doing so.

After a hot, tiring day of sightseeing, I'm waiting in the bar of the Bangkok USAF Officers' Club for some guys I just met. We have dinner reservations tonight at the best Hungarian restaurant in Bangkok.

I'm reading the Bangkok Post, Bangkok's daily newspaper for English-speaking expatriates. The front page tells me unbridled chaos isn't limited to Bangkok, Thailand. The antiwar movement back in the States is gathering size like a ball of wet manure rolling down a barn aisle. There have been violent riots and angry street demonstrations in most cities on the West Coast, in Chicago, and in the northeastern parts of the United States. Civil disobedience is spreading, arrests are numerous, and bonfires are being lit with draft cards. College ROTC offices are being firebombed. What the hell is going on back there? Shocked, I read on.

The paper tells me the latest tactic of antiwar movement is the protest march. The objective seems to be to gather everyone with a beard and a bitch about the war. Then the assembled mob attempts to disrupt as many public functions as they can while marching. The thought of a protest march on paved city streets reminds me that my feet hurt.

I have been jogging barefooted again. The intelligence troops tell us the first thing the Bad Guys do to a captured American is to take away his boots. They know all Americans have been shod since infancy and thus have tender feet. If a downed airman attempts to escape his captors, a mile or so of running on jungle rocks and underbrush will cut his soft feet to ribbons. Further flight is then impossible. As all wounds suffered in the jungle are septic, his cut feet will become masses of infection in a day or two, making even normal walking too painful to endure. Gangrene isn't unknown. So, I'm jogging barefooted to toughen up the soles of my feet in case I have to make a run for it. Meanwhile, some misguided folks back home are marching in sandals to protest my dedicated efforts.

From the paper, it seems the protestors have just discovered that the Vietnam War is unjust and an outrage. That's funny, just a couple of years ago, the very same war was righteous and good. Recently, the war was popular. Col. Robbie Risner, a famous F-105 Thunderchief fighter pilot, was on the cover of Time magazine. "Ballad of the Green Berets" was a hit song. The press was full of praise for our military efforts and for the guys doing the fighting. What happened? The aims of the war didn't change. Our so-called allies in South Vietnam didn't get any less lovable (that would be impossible). The war is no more unwinnable now than it was back then. So why the sudden interest in massive, out-of-control antiwar protests?

From my remote location, actually at said war, the answer seems to lie in the military draft. The key to my admittedly self-serving analysis is the fact that the burgeoning antiwar movement is based on college campuses. When only professionals like Robbie Risner and me were fighting the war, it was OK, even heroic.

That's rich, placing Colonel Risner and me in the same category. That's like saying that Mickey Mantle and I both played baseball.

Anyway, the war was publicly supported when only three demographic groups were fighting in it; professional soldiers like fighter pilots and the U.S. Army's Green Berets, white southerners, and urban blacks. Membership in the U.S. armed services has traditionally been heavily weighted toward these three distinct sub-cultures.

The stateside trouble started with the rapid buildup of U.S. forces in South Vietnam. The services' usual three manpower pools could not provide the sheer number of troops required. For the first time since the Korean War, white, middle-class guys were being drafted off college campuses. Sons from California, Massachusetts, and Chicago started coming home in body bags.

College freshman everywhere suddenly had to contemplate the awful possibility of giving up their guitars for M-16 rifles. Night jungle patrols aren't nearly as much fun as rock concerts. What's more, protesting the war is way more fun than actually fighting in it. An ambitious student leader could become an instant campus hero by leading a protest march for a few hours and let others less fortunate (and braver) lead the bayonet charges. Of course, saving the world is much more satisfying than more mundane activities, like studying or taking exams.

Suddenly the war became inherently wrong when the wrong guys were called to participate. Does the political justification for a war change with a rise in the social class of those called to fight in it?

As I read about the street chaos back home, I wonder why the Thais passing by outside the Officers' Club in Bangkok aren't protesting. The Communists have taken over all of North Vietnam, half of the south, a third of Laos, and a quarter of Cambodia. For Thailand, the war is a few hundred miles away, not on the other side of the earth. Perhaps because of this proximity the Thais don't protest the war; they support it with troops in Vietnam and bases in Thailand to stage our air attacks.

The protestors and I agree on one thing; the war is unwinnable as it is being fought. Could we win it if we tried? I don't know. I don't know if South Vietnam is worth winning. What I do know is that we could, if we wanted, convince the North that they lost. All that would take would be firepower finally unleashed.

Meanwhile, the political chaos continues back home and the garden variety of chaos reigns delightfully in Bangkok. I guess I shouldn't read the Bangkok Post while drinking.

After joining up with the three guys I met last night, we hop in a taxi to the restaurant. These guys are F-105 pilots, based at Korat Royal Thai Air Force Base in central Thailand. There is a definite pecking order among USAF fighter pilots. At the top of the pyramid are pilots who fly single-engine, single-seat jets like the F-105 "Thud." Those airmen who fly two-seat fighters, like my F-4 Phantom, occupy one small step down. Just this once, the F-105 jocks have condescended to dine with the likes of me. Maybe they wanted to fill up a table of four.

I would have preferred to go another round with Thai food, but these guys are intent on visiting a joint called "Nick's Number One."

The taxi deposits us outside a run-down, colonial-style building with a red tile roof and a covered entranceway. A small, unlit sign is the only indication that this is the famous place. The restaurant looks ready to fall down, with jungle weeds growing against the peeling, plastered wall. A tarnished brass plaque outside announces that a past King of Thailand built this decrepit relic in the late 1800s for one of his mistresses. Given the vast number of pretty girls in Thailand serving at the pleasure of the King, it is a wonder he didn't construct his own subdivision.

We enter the darkened entranceway and we are greeted by a courtly older gentleman sitting at a dimly lit wooden desk just inside. His upper class, faintly European accent marks our elderly host as Nick himself. The restaurant is dark with circles of cream-colored light cast by hanging lanterns. Still, we can see that the walls are covered with zillions of business cards, stuck up in substitution for wallpaper or paint. Curious, I strike up a conversation with Nick and he is only too willing to tell me the tale of the best Hungarian joint in Bangkok.

I learn that Nick was a war protestor himself in his younger days. In the early 1930s, Nick saw the dark clouds of war gathering once again over his native Hungary. He missed the first European War of the Century, WWI, and he was unenthusiastic about his personal participation in any new conflict, righteous or not.

Nick cashed in his chips in Budapest and protested with his feet, leaving Europe to burn once again with the fires of conflict. He selected a spot on the globe which seemed to offer an exotic, languid lifestyle and was as far away from the Hitler war as he could get.

Young Nick arrived in Bangkok about a year prior to the successful Japanese invasion of what was then called the country of Siam. Despite his protesting flight to avoid it, World War II came to Nick. Leon Trotsky was right, "You may not be interested in war, but war is interested in you."

Somehow, he lived through the awful Japanese occupation of Siam/Thailand, and after Liberation Day opened his restaurant to serve the legions of westerners flocking in to help reconstruct the country. His business prospered, but not to the extent of being able to afford building maintenance. His patrons got into the habit of covering bits of the flaking walls with their business cards and the unconventional decoration scheme caught on. Now the cards are four deep in some places. At our rough-hewn wooden table, we read down through the layers of cards stuck on the nearby wall. It is like peeling back layers of recent history, each layer of cards reaching further back into the past .

Nick's verbal saga (isn't that redundant, aren't all sagas verbal?) starts us four pilots discussing our favorite obsession, the current war. OK, make that our second-favorite obsession, after girls.

One of the Thud drivers tells the rest of us there is a senior USAF sergeant at Korat who joined the US Army Air Corps as a lad and was stationed in Hanoi, then part of French Indochina.

His unit flew bombing raids on Japanese forces stationed at Korat, in the Kingdom of Siam. Now his present unit flies missions from Korat, Thailand, to bomb Hanoi, North Vietnam while. U.S. bases in Japan support the war effort. You can't tell the current geopolitical players without a scorecard.

I wonder if any of the peaceniks marching back home have any appreciation at all for the political complexity of this war. Probably not; all they know is that war is icky and dangerous and not in their personal plans, thus, it must be wrong and unjust.

Over our aperitifs, we agree that once the earnest members of the antiwar left decided the current chapter of the continuing war in Southeast Asia was wrong, they had to dream up a moral rationalization for its wrongness beyond the potential for their own personal inconvenience. I guess being unwinnable, as it is being fought, wasn't enough justification to oppose it. What I can't fathom is why the guys who are fighting it and who know it to be a lost cause aren't opposed to it as much as the folks who only have a mathematical lottery chance of participating. Maybe it has to do with concepts like duty, honor, and courage. On this, the Thud drivers and I agree.

Thud drivers aren't known for their sophisticated thinking. In fact, most of them have one eyebrow that goes all the way across at the base of their cranial ridge. But these three guys are smarter than most. We wonder aloud how our country could have gotten into such a quagmire, given Gen. Douglas MacArthur's public warning not to get involved in a major land war on the continent of Asia. How did we get led astray? What herd mentality in Washington took over? Who couldn't see the waiting, sucking quagmire?

The server comes to take our dinner orders. He is male, much to our mutual disappointment. One of us could still get lucky tonight if a comely Thai girl delivers our drinks.

The Thud jocks all order steaks of various types. I want to try one of Nick's Hungarian specialties, like goulash, but I go along with the crowd and decide on a steak as well. The menu lists in English, "Steak Tartare." That sounds interesting; I enjoy tangy tartar sauce on fried fish. But, I've never had tartar sauce on beefsteak, so I order it. The Thai waiter looks at me in surprise, as if to say, "Why are you doing that?" but I ignore his expression of doubt, the second time today I have failed to read the culinary warning signs. Strangely, he asked the other three guys how they wanted their steaks prepared, but not me. I guess Steak Tartare only comes one way.

The cocktail waiter who delivers our drinks also turns out to be of the male persuasion, so we return to our second-favorite interest, the war. We ask each other why, if we can't figure out how we got into the war, can we deduce why we can't get out of it? Once it became obvious to the political/military brain trust in Washington that the war is unwinnable under the present rules and with the current regime in South Vietnam, why didn't they change the game? Why not just cut our losses and leave? What makes a politician never admit an error? Why doesn't our military leadership strenuously object to pouring men's lives down a muddy jungle rat hole? What machismo forces are in play here? Why is it so hard to quit something that we are screwing up?

Our dinner arrives before we get drunk enough to come up with all the answers. The other three steaks look conventional and well prepared.

The nervous waiter sets my meal in front of me. I am looking down at a large wooden platter. In the center is what looks to be over a pound of raw, chopped beef. Not medium well, not medium rare, not plain rare, but totally raw. The fresh meat is piled into a red mound with a depression in the center, like a bloody bird's nest. In the center of the nest, the chef has thoughtfully cracked a raw egg. Across the top of the platter are helpings of condiments; raw chopped onions, capers, fresh parsley, and a bottle of dark Worcestershire sauce, also raw I assume. The waiter retires to the shadows, but doesn't leave; he wants to see what I will do with my Steak Tartare. The three Thud drivers' jaws drop as one.

One of my dinner buddies asks, "Did you know what that was when you ordered it?"

I reply, "Of course, I have this all the time. It's one of my favorites, but it's hard to find good Steak Tartare up-country in Ubon. "

After completely blowing my dinner order through gross ignorance, there is no way I am going to admit that I had no idea what I was getting. If I were alone, I might send this raw meat back, but not with three F-105 pilots watching and ready to laugh their asses off at my expense the rest of the evening. I am going to choke this stuff down if it is the last thing I ever do. Given the well-known Thai cavalier attitude toward food hygiene, consuming raw meat in the tropics isn't the wisest. But, I season the chopped pile of fresh flesh with a liberal dose of Worcestershire, sprinkle on some onions, add a few capers, along with salt and black pepper. I can't add anything else without giving away my attempt at covering up the fresh meat's flavor. The other three start to chow down on their (cooked) steaks, watching me out of the corners of their eyes. The Thai waiter peers from a darkened recess just outside the table's circle of light. Even Nick looks over from his nearby desk.

I lift a fork half full and with great trepidation, dump the load on my tongue. One gulp and it goes down without chewing. I don't gag and the bite stays down. The residual flavor in my mouth is of rare meat, onions, pickled capers, and sauce. I take another portion and risk a few quick chews this time before swallowing. To my great surprise, the sensation isn't yucky at all.

I chew my third bite properly and find the mixed flavor to be not bad, in fact, it's pretty good. By bite number four, I'm enjoying my Steak Tartare immensely. I finish my platter clean, raw egg and all. After a final sip of my Bourbon and water, I ask the amazed waiter to summon Nick. The old man quietly materializes into view by the light over the table and asks us how we liked our dinners.

I tell Nick and the waiter, "Nick, that is the best Steak Tartare I have ever had" which is certainly true.

My dinnertime friends pretend to take no notice and compliment Nick on their charred, blackened steaks as well.

Over coffee, we resume our discussion of the war. We rehash how our country got into it, unaware of the possible consequences. We ask again why our so-called leadership can't seem to back out. We finally admit that those of us fighting the war have learned to enjoy our mission enough not to complain about it. It is amazing what you can put up with, if you have to or want to. That's as far as we get; the overall situation remains a mystery, and we can't even get to an answer one bite at a time.

The F-105 jocks want to go back to the O Club and drink. They think there might be a few flight nurses or USAF female officers at the bar. I'm not up for that plan, as I can see a long, drunken, horny evening ahead for them.

I have heard of a Bangkok Dixieland jazz bar supposedly frequented by airline stewardesses, but I'm not about to tell my newfound friends that. Who needs the competition? We part company outside Nick's and I catch a waiting taxi to a joint named "The Balcony" across town.

The bouncer admits me to a jammed and smoky two-story club. The open main floor has a bar in the middle and a low stage at one end. Sure enough, a balcony outlined with wrought-iron lacework circles the room at the second-floor level. Cigarette smoke hovers near the ceiling like an indoor stratus cloud. It is enough to get me all misty for New Orleans, my birthplace.

The clientele consists of trendy young Thais of both genders, fresh-scrubbed American servicemen, and older male civilian westerners in faded leisure suits. The latter are sitting alone, observing with weary eyes which have seen it all and are nursing their drinks. These guys are probably "old China hands," businessmen who have been in the Orient too long. Or maybe they're CIA spooks undercover. Perhaps, they might be wartime hustlers. Maybe, they're all three at the same time.

The jazz is pure Dixieland and it is surprisingly good. The all-Thai band does their best imitation of the "Firehouse Five

Plus Two" or "The Dukes of Dixieland" and they don't miss a hot lick. Their instrumentals are superb, but their verbal introductions in English to each number are not as successful. There isn't a Thai tongue in Bangkok that can wrap itself around the r's in the song titles "Muskrat Ramble" or "South Rampart Street Parade."

I am so homesick I order a mint julep, almost shouting over the din. It comes to me just right, in a frosty mug, sweet and strong. I'm not so lucky in my quest for female companionship. There are no single round-eyed women in sight and all the Thai girls have attentive escorts. Oh well, I have good jazz to listen to and a good libation to sip; two out of three isn't bad.

During the band's second set, an additional musician slips from out of the dark wings onto the stage and joins in the fun. The newcomer Thai jams expertly with the group on a tenor saxophone, weaving his riffs into the mix with considerable skill. I ordinarily wouldn't notice just another guy in the band, but this cat looks familiar. Racking my booze-sodden brain, I ask myself where I could have seen this late-arriving member of the band before tonight.

Suddenly, it hits me like a laser-guided bomb right between the eyes. Of course, I've seen this guy before; his picture is all over Thailand.

Today on my sightseeing rounds, I gawked at the Temple of the Emerald Buddha. The eighteen-inch-tall Buddha isn't really an emerald, but something called "greenstone." Anyway, the temple is spectacular, all gold and white with bright red tile on a steeply pitched roof. As part of his religious duties, the King of Thailand changes the tiny garments clothing the emerald Buddha with each change of the seasons in a solemn ceremony. Through pure dumb luck, I happened to be at the temple today for the show. It was magnificent, with suitable pomp and circumstance, Thai style.

I saw the King from afar as he entered the temple. He is a solemn-looking, slightly built man with large, black-rimmed glasses. As he is always pictured, today he had an earnest expression, indicative of him taking his role in Thai society very seriously. He is greatly revered throughout Thailand and well respected by every ethnic Thai I have ever met. Indeed, he is considered to be the human embodiment of Thai culture and history; he is the living symbol of Thailand.

Even from my distance and over the heads of the adoring crowd, I could see that the king looks just like his portraits that hang in every significant Thai building, whether governmental, public, or private. He also looks just like the sax player in the band on the dimly-lit stage at the Balcony.

I hail the Thai manager of the club, being careful to use the proper gesture: hand held horizontal, fingers dangling down and waving. In Thailand, an up-crooked finger is used only to call dogs.

I ask the manager, "Is that new sax player who I think he is? I can't believe it, if he is."

The manager looks at me as if I just fell off a turnip truck. Even his innate Thai courtesy can't prevent his face from showing considerable alarm.

He replies, "Sir, is this your first time at my place?"

I tell him that it is, and that I like it a lot.

That seems to mollify him some and he tells me. "You know who he is. We all know who he is. He knows who he is. So we don't make a fuss about it. No one loses face."

Now I get it. This is Asia. If no one acknowledges a fact, then it doesn't exist. Heavy-duty royal courtesies would be necessary if anyone lets on that they know what everyone else knows; then, the principle of maintaining face would have to be honored. This willful ignorance allows their beloved king to relax with the jazz band, without any of the required protocol getting in the way. The denizens of the Balcony are cool with this. They allow the King some well-deserved recreation by ignoring his royal presence and the band gets another jamming sideman with his wailing sax for free.

Despite me being all by my lonesome, this evening looks to be almost a winner, perfect mint juleps, superb Steak Tartare, and good Dixieland jazz, royally done.

★★★

I'm sitting on the porch in front of Wing Headquarters back at my home base in Ubon. It is late, almost midnight, and I'm waiting for the USAF blue shuttle bus to take me to the BOQ area and my hooch. Ordinarily I would walk, but I'm hung over from a few too many mint juleps last night. The ride up from Bangkok in the back of a noisy C-130 didn't help my aching head any.

On the plane, I read in the latest Bangkok Post that the protest demonstrations have escalated even more back home. Now, the President of the United States of America rarely appears in public anymore. When he ventures out, violent, hairy, profanity-spewing protestors (if not crazed assassins) usually confront him. The leader of the free world is a prisoner in the White House. Maybe he should take up the saxophone.

After my hectic three days in chaotic Bangkok, I could really use some quality sack time. Sleep beckons to me as I wait on the bus and I start to drift off where I sit. Even now, I can't get the news of the antiwar movement out of my thoughts. As I doze slumped on the wooden bench waiting for the bus, I remember reading the rallying cry screamed by the members of the antiwar protestors back in the States is "Hell no, we won't go!"

The engine noise of the approaching shuttle, a converted school bus, rudely jolts me awake. I am startled to find I am now not alone on the dimly lit porch. Five or six heavily armed, silent men have materialized out of nowhere in the night. Three are on my right and two or three more are semi-hidden in the damp darkness on my left. The quiet group has spoken no words and no man has made a sound of any kind.

Glancing furtively left and right, I can see each of these night ghost soldiers is dressed in jungle camouflage from head to foot and each man is toting a black M-16 rifle. Long, crossed bandoliers of bullets decorate each skinny chest. I don't see how they can handle the weight of all that lead, as none of the mute troops is over five foot five and 130 pounds. Besides his personal weapon and ammo, each of the unspeaking men has a large green pack nearby almost as big as he is.

The five have managed to gain the porch, deposit their heavy packs, and squat down, ignoring the wooden benches, without making a noise loud enough to wake me, and I was barely dozing. These are men long practiced at not announcing their presence. They are either Hmong tribesmen or Laotians; it is too dark to tell the difference. The Laotians tend to be taller. I'm sure none of them are Americans. But, I know who they are, why they are there, and where they are going.

Waiting patiently, silently, on each side of me are the members of a Laotian road watch team. Sometime later tonight, a helicopter without navigation lights and no national insignia will touch down without warning on the concrete ramp in front of this headquarters building. The blacked-out chopper will not have a flight plan on file and tonight's sortie will appear nowhere on the wing's official flying schedule. Americans will be flying the chopper. Americans without uniforms, with long hair, and with no name tags. The CIA covert air transport network, "Air America," at your service.

The road watch team will rapidly board the helo while its engines are running, piling all their gear and weapons inside with practiced haste. The helo will lift off without further ado and disappear into the warm night, headed northeast toward the border of Thailand and Laos. Just before dawn, the chopper will touch down briefly on a ridge top deep in the area of the Laotian panhandle controlled by the North Vietnamese. In a scant few seconds, the road watch team will jump off with their gear and disappear quickly like brown wraiths into the dense jungle. They will covertly monitor enemy truck traffic along the winding Ho Chi Minh Trail and radio what they see back to a CIA operations center in Thailand located on the west bank of the Mekong River. The road watch team's mission will be to collect and transmit as much intelligence data as they can without being detected. Any slip, any noise, any wrong move at any time will reveal their presence. If the Bad Guys suspect the team is watching, even while hidden by the dense jungle, they will go all out to capture or kill my nighttime companions. If captured, immediate execution will be the best outcome. Torture for information and recreation is much more likely.

These unconventional native troops, volunteers all, lead a hard life. Each probably has a wife or two in a thatched log shelter near the Plain of Jars. A few naked kids and scrawny dogs will complete the family homestead. They get paid fifty dollars a month, maybe, when the agency gets around to it. Their only other possessions are in their backpacks. Their medical benefits consist of first aid administered by a buddy. There is no retirement plan.

In a week or so when the team's supplies are exhausted, the same covert helicopter will furtively hover over another ridge top just after dusk. The members of the team who are still alive will clamber back on and the chopper will depart at high speed to the west and the safety of the Thai border.

In this insane world, there are soft children of plenty and privilege who have much to fight for, but would rather not be bothered. They chant "Hell no, we won't go"' In other parts of the same world there are hard warriors who possess nothing beyond but their honor and their dreams for a country of their own. These real men thirst for their time in hell.

LASER PILOT AND THE COSMIC GIB

I am in the pit and I'm not too damn happy about it. No pilot likes to fly in the rear cockpit. The back cockpit of the F-4 Phantom is unaffectionately called the "pit" and for good reason. Slotted between two massive air intakes for the jet engines, the canopy rails on each side of the pit are high, about chin level. The canopy itself is small, one-third the size of the Plexiglas unit covering the front cockpit. To the rear is a bulkhead, behind the ejection seat. The front of the pit is filled by an instrument panel, with only a limited sight line forward. Visibility to the outside is also constrained. Standing on the left air intake and looking down into the rear cockpit gives me the definite impression I am about to descend into a confining aluminum pit lined with switches, gauges, controls, handles, dials, levers, and circuit breakers. The denizen of the Phantom's rear cockpit is known as the GIB, or Guy In Back.

The term "cockpit" itself was first applied to a pilot's work space during the early years of aviation, coming into general usage during World War I. The open biplanes of that era carried their intrepid aviators in round holes in the fuselage with only their heads sticking out into the breeze. These Spartan accommodations reminded folks of the small circular pits used for staging chicken fights, with roosters, hence the term "cockpit." Provisions for those early aircrew members were primitive to say the least in the stick, fabric, and wire age of aviation. Things improved as aircraft became faster. Fighter cockpits during World War II were much more comfortable with great visibility outward. First, large green house type canopies were fitted, and then the modern bubble canopy was invented. The jet era marked a return to cramped, almost hidden cockpits due to the needs to reduce aerodynamic drag caused by the bubble canopies and to save space to cram as much fuel inside the airframe as possible. With the F-4 back seat, cockpits have come full circle. WWI ace Frank Luke would not feel claustrophobic if he were to lower himself into the Phantom's pit instead of his Nieuport 28 biplane..

At least I have access to a full set of flight controls in the pit. The rear cockpit of the F-4D comes fully equipped with a control stick, rudder pedals, a pair of throttles, and flight instruments due to the largess of the U. S. Air Force. The U.S. Navy Phantoms have none of this good stuff. I can take off, fly, and land the USAF Phantom from the rear cockpit. It is even quite amusing to perform aerial refueling from the rear seat. With dual controls, it is common to have a pilot in the pit as well as in the front seat. The Navy guys always carry a navigator in the back of their F-4Bs, as a pilot can't fly their jet from the rear. There are those of us who feel that the USN has enough trouble flying the F-4 from the front seat. Those guys are good at one thing though; landing jets on boats.

While I should be counting my blessings in the rear cockpit, I am not. Today's mission is a radical experiment in the evolution of tactical aviation. We are out to determine if the laser-guided bomb is a good idea for combat. The bombs go by the official code name "Paveway," but we have already started calling them "smart bombs." Smart bombs are supposed to know where the target is and go there by guiding themselves. Dumb bombs are the kind we usually drop. They know only where the ground is and they don't care where they hit it. We have had all the technical briefings, talked to the civilian representatives from the manufacturer, and discussed in depth the procedures and tactics to be used. We have run the mission over and over in our respective heads, trying to foresee all the likely possibilities. It is now time to see if we are going to revolutionize tactical air-to-ground warfare or not.

Service planners recognized the need for guided bombs as early as WWI. Dumb bombs always have been and always will be limited by the fundamental laws of physics and aerodynamics. It is extremely difficult to hit a small ground target with a dumb bomb dropped from a fast moving airplane. Even small errors in achieving the planned delivery parameters, such as dive angle, airspeed, and altitude, produce large errors on impact. Even if I manage to nail all the things I have control over when manually dive bombing, other factors can plant the bomb far afield; wind, altimeter setting, target elevation, aerodynamic turbulence, and manufacturing tolerances all conspire against even the best fighter pilot.

There are two possible solutions to this lack of precision in dropping dumb bombs. I can drop the dumb bombs from a lower altitude and at a slower airspeed to reduce the effects of the inevitable errors. This isn't a very popular technique as it also reduces the errors of the guys on the ground who are trying to shoot me down. Speed and altitude are life. Dueling with the defenses while low and slow is death. The other solution is to drop lots of bombs and hope that one happens to hit the target. This plan is inefficient and costly. Fighters don't carry many bombs compared to large bomber type aircraft. Putting many bombs in the air requires many fighter planes, which puts that many more guys in harm's way.

Dumb bombs, with their inherent tendency to go astray, have another drawback. When they miss the target, which is the usual case, what do they hit instead? The aim of tactical air power is to explosively take out the enemy's tank factory, not the orphanage across the street. As the Good Guys in this war, we are concerned with what is euphemistically called "collateral damage." We don't want to take out that nearby orphanage. The Bad Guys know this and they locate their most lucrative targets in close proximity to things that we are known to be loath to destroy. I have seen military targets parked in schoolyards and on flood-control dikes. We need a way to surgically take out these targets without fear of damaging the things that would be politically embarrassing and morally troubling to blow up.

Is Paveway the answer? There have been many past attempts at developing smart bombs to avoid the glaring limitations of unguided ordnance. Way back in WWI, the Brits developed an unmanned, gyro-controlled Sopwith Camel, intended to crash on the heads of the Germans. It didn't work. Human pilots found the Camel notoriously tricky to fly and hard to hold steady. There was no way a mechanical gyroscope could follow a predictable flight path. The Germans and the US Army Air Corps both tried radio-controlled gliding bombs and kamikaze drone aircraft during WWII without notable success. The vacuum tube electronics of the day weren't up to the task and the bombs were more often stupid than smart.

Eschewing electronics altogether, the U.S. Navy tried pigeon guidance in the Pacific Theater. A pigeon (one hopes it wasn't a homing pigeon) was placed in a compartment on the front of the bomb. In front of the pigeon was a glass screen on which was projected the image of the target, say, a Japanese battleship. A lens in the nose of the weapon produced the image. The bird was trained to peck at the image with a wire cemented to his beak. The contact point of the wired beak and the screen gave the bomb its guidance commands. As long as the pigeon kept pecking at the image during his one-way trip, the bomb would steer toward the targeted ship. Unfortunately this plan had a fatal flaw. In free-fall flight while riding the bomb down, the pigeon would get airsick. Like some aviators, birds tend to get airsick when they are not doing the actual flying themselves. The poor barfing bird would soon lose interest in pecking on the screen and the bomb would go stupid.

Not to be outdone in the loony idea sweepstakes, the US Army Air Corps tired dropping canisters of bats on Japanese cities. Each bat carried a miniature incendiary charge in a tiny backpack. The plan was for the bats to roost in the eaves of the wood and paper Japanese-style houses where the time-delayed fire bomb would detonate. Alas, the mammalian suicide bombers proved to be no more reliable than the USN's avian aviators, looking for caves to roost in, not houses. We resorted to mass raids on Japan by B-29's dropping uncounted tons of fire bombs which did the trick.

In the 1950s the USAF developed a command-guided missile, the Bullpup. It was launched with its own rocket motor from a fighter and was steered by a fighter pilot through the magic of radio control. A tiny joystick was installed next to the launch jet's throttles to command the missile. The hapless pilot had to fly his own jet with his right hand on the big aircraft control stick and simultaneously fly the rapidly departing missile with the small control stick in his left hand.

This was akin to rubbing your head while patting your stomach. Eighty-seven percent of pilots are right-handed, flying anything with a left hand is tough. Needless to say, this feat of manual dexterity was beyond the skill level of most jocks.

Naturally, knowing this history of berserk biplanes, barfing birds, homesick bats, and left-handed rockets, the guys in the squadron are profoundly skeptical of Paveway and its laser guidance scheme. Rumors and scuttlebutt emanating from the States have fueled our skepticism. The laser-guided bomb program has been very hush-hush and tightly classified, but still the word gets around. We heard in whispered terms about the development of the system while it was still in the government weapons laboratories. Like all scuttlebutt, the real facts get garbled and sensationalized with each successive transmission.

We heard the Paveway system was invented in some guy's garage (where else?). Rumor has it the initial tests involved hand-throwing scale models of the bombs out the window of a Cessna bug smasher flying over the weapons test ranges in Florida. While this tale of technical derring-do didn't exactly inspire confidence in the combat potential of Paveway, someone must have been impressed. The Cessna hand-launched tests were followed by a full-scale, hurry-up development program, the output of which is now hanging under the wings of the two jets of Satan Flight.

The Squadron Crew Room has been abuzz lately with sketchy third-hand accounts of the stateside test program, giving rise to the legend of the Laser Pilot and the Cosmic GIB. No one has ever met these individuals, but we are all convinced that they exist. How else to explain the hush-hush success of Paveway?

The Laser Pilot has skills and knowledge that us mere squadron jocks can only dream about. He flies in a silver space suit, similar to those worn by the crews of the SR-71 Blackbird, to protect him from deadly laser radiation. Flying laser-guided bomb test missions is his only duty and he is the only one that flies such demanding sorties. No one knows the name of the Laser Pilot and no one is permitted to have that knowledge. His shining flight suit has no insignia, no name tag, and he never takes his helmet off in public.

The Cosmic GIB is similarly attired and equally anonymous. He was selected from a wide pool of candidates, none of who knew they were being evaluated for the top secret job. The Cosmic GIB has the reflexes of a gunfighter and the steady hands of a brain surgeon, as it is he who aims the deadly laser.

The Laser Pilot and the Cosmic GIB live in special quarters on the ocean beach bordering the test range in Florida, but no one knows exactly where. Their private residence is guarded night and day by Security Police personnel and by black attack dogs. To ensure optimum performance, they work out on purpose-built equipment, sleep on cooled waterbeds, and eat a special diet prepared by dedicated USAF cooks. They probably even have exotic girlfriends with special talents, also provided by Uncle Sam. Is the legend of the Laser Pilot and the Cosmic GIB based on fact or military fantasy? No one knows. What we do know is that something weird was developed stateside and we have it and we intend to use it.

Now, we know what the Laser Pilot and the Cosmic GIB have. wrought. Paveway has been sent to our squadron for its initial combat test. When the munitions crews opened the sealed shipping containers, they found hardware of a decidedly pedestrian, maybe even agricultural, nature. Paveway is a kit that is bolted onto a standard dumb bomb.

The front end of the kit is comprised of a laser seeker, called the "birdie." This isn't a reference to the heroic pigeon pilots of WWII, but is suggested by a strong resemblance to a metal badminton birdie. The birdie is gimbal-mounted to a control section that sports four steering fins. A thermal battery powers the unit. The control section with its attached birdie and fins screws on to the front of the dumb bomb. A set of wings stamped cheaply from sheet metal bolts to the rear of the bomb casing. That's it. This set of simple parts painted dull olive drab is what the Laser Pilot and the Cosmic GIB have sent us. This add-on kit is supposed to change the nature of air warfare for all time.

The other higher tech component of the Paveway system, the laser, is in the pit with me. On the left side of the cockpit, inside the canopy rail, is a mirror box and optical eyepiece. Down under the left canopy rail is a laser beam generator and a small joystick. A red-guarded off/on switch completes the installation. The operation is simple in the extreme. The laser beam is generated and captured in the mirror box. The mirror set is movable and is steered by the joystick. The laser beam shines out the left side of the aircraft through the canopy and is aimed by looking through the 4X eyepiece.

The laser beam propagates in the infrared portion of the electromagnetic spectrum; it is invisible to the human eye. But the spot generated on the ground is easily seen by the seeker mounted on the birdie riding on the front of the bomb. In fact, the laser spot is the only thing the bomb can see. To a Paveway the whole universe is pitch black except for one tiny infrared spot reflecting from and designating the location of the target. After release from the aircraft, the bomb steers itself with its movable fins to the laser spot on the ground. If the spot is superimposed on the intended target, bad things will happen there when the fully armed bomb arrives from the sky.

The tricky part is getting the laser spot shining on the target. It is impossible to laser illuminate for a bomb you drop yourself; a buddy system is essential. The pilot of the illuminator aircraft must fly a very smooth, even circle in a left turn around the target. During this orbit, the GIB, that would be me, aims the unseen laser beam. The second aircraft in the flight, Satan Two, will dive, dropping his smart bomb inside the circle being flown around the target by Satan Lead. If all goes as planned, Satan Two's bomb will see the laser spot being generated by Saran Lead and it will guide unerringly to the desired impact point.

The best aspect of this tightly choreographed series of maneuvers is that the whole process can be done at higher altitudes than normal dumb bombing. Indeed, the higher the better, as a longer drop time gives the Paveway bomb more opportunity to see, and guide to, the laser spot. For the human members of the Paveway team, this is great as we can fly with impunity above the guns defending the target. The Bad Guys' flak won't be able to reach us at 12,000 feet. If this all works, I won't mind nearly as much flying in the pit. If it doesn't, I guess we can always go back to dumb bombing and put off the revolution in aerial warfare until the next war.

In the front seat of my jet is another squadron member, known to be a steady hand on the control stick. He gets to fly while I aim the laser. Floating in formation 100 yards off our right wing is Satan Two, like us equipped with two 2,000-pound laser-guided bombs and a Paveway laser illuminator in the rear cockpit.

We are across the fence, the Mekong River, and into southern Laos, looking for our FAC. Over southern Laos, unlike up north around the Plain Des Jars, the Forward Air Controllers are real USAF serving officers, with real military haircuts and official uniforms. They are not tarred with the CIA brush like those scruffy Ravens up north on the PDJ. Their call sign is "Nail," and they are based at Nakom Phanom, a Royal Thai Air Force base on the west bank of the Mekong. Nail FACs also have better aircraft than the Ravens; they fly the OV-10 "Bronco" a twin turboprop craft designed for just this mission. However, they still have to fly low enough to spot the targets and the OV-10's top speed of 220 miles per hour won't outrun many bullets or missiles.

Satan Two spots the FAC far below as we reach the designated target area in the foothills near the Ho chi Minh Trail network. The terrain here is mostly covered with rain forest, but there are a few scattered cleared fields. We have been tasked against this particular target, whose nature we know not, by the daytime counterpart of Alley Cat, another C-130 command ship whose call sign is "Cricket." When the airborne controller in Cricket gave us the target coordinates, he didn't and wouldn't tell us what it was. He referred us to the Nail FAC to get the exact description. The controller's voice on the radio was serious and somber, as if he knows something we don't. I wish Bruce were on duty in the daytime; he would have spilled the beans.

The Nail come up on the radio and tells us,

"Satan Flight, your target today is an antiaircraft gun complex, six pits with thirty-seven-millimeter guns. Some reports list it as a flak trap."

He goes on with the weather, the altimeter setting, the target elevation and such like, but Nail has already gotten our undivided attention, big-time.

The North Vietnamese have increasingly moved large caliber antiaircraft guns down the trail from the north, towing them behind trucks at night. The guns are carefully dug into pits, with high sandbag piles surrounding the installation. Each gun has a dedicated crew whose dream in life is to shoot down an American aircraft The towable thirty-seven millimeter guns are dangerous enough for fast movers like the F-4, but they are lethal to slow aircraft such as the OV-10 and the C-130. I can understand the desire of the Nail to take out these guns before they take him out. But it gives one cause for thought attacking an installation whose sole mission is to shoot you down.

Normally, attacking a well-protected AAA gun installation with dumb bombs is nonproductive. The guns are set into pits about forty feet in diameter with six-foot walls of sandbags ringing the site on top of the ground protecting the crews from near misses. It is almost impossible to place a dumb bomb inside the sheltering pit without flying very low and diving at a very shallow angle. This gives the gun crew the edge in the engagement and allows the other guns to help protect the one under attack. Bombing from a higher altitude guarantees at best an ineffective near miss. A close miss gets the gun crews' ears ringing, then they return to their duties with renewed vigor. This is why attacking gun sites is not anywhere on the top ten list of the most popular missions with us.

The Nail further describes the target as a chain of gun pits dug into a tree line on the border of a small field. From our altitude of 20,000 feet, all we can see are several scattered, irregularly shaped fields, each a lighter green than the darker jungle, any one of which could border the targets.

Nail tells us that he will put in a Willie Pete smoke rocket to mark the correct field. The impact of the marker rocket will also tell the gunners that an attack is imminent and to man their guns. Once he has stirred up the Bad Guys, the Nail will hold off safely several miles to the west.

Satan Lead tells the Nail on the radio;

"Roger that, Nail. We have you in sight. You can remain in the target area, as we will be well above you at all times."

Satan Lead's transmission tells the Nail that we won't drop bombs on him or run into him with our planes. I can hear the biting sarcasm in the Nail's voice as he answers;

"Roger, Satan, very well."

I can almost hear him think through the radio;

"These Phantom-driving pussies are going to drop bombs from the stratosphere, scatter their ordnance across southern Laos and then go home to the bar. Meanwhile, I'll still be down here with some very annoyed and very motivated gunners."

'We drop down to 15,000 feet to illuminate with the laser. From here we can see the target better, but we remain out of easy reach of the guns. My pilot in front rolls the jet into a gentle left-hand orbit as the Nail shoots his marking rocket. Satan Two has remained at 20,000 feet and trails us as we circle.

Out the left side of the canopy, I see a white puff of smoke blossom in one of the fields. The northern tree line of that field looks scalloped, more irregular than the others.

The Nail comes back with,

"That's a good mark, Satan; the guns are in the tree line to the north, and they're shooting."

It is a sunny, cloudless day over Laos, but suddenly a dozen small, dirty gray clouds magically, instantly appear, like used cotton balls. The thirty-seven millimeter shells self-destruct with an explosion of shrapnel and smoke when they miss. The gunners now know they are under attack and there is no reason to not shoot at the FAC. Fired at our intrepid FAC, the shells reached 12,000 feet, just below us, and then detonated. I can understand Nail's concern; he is down there among them, while we are relatively safe at altitude. One thirty-seven millimeter explosive shell can turn an OV-10 into confetti and the Nail pilot along with it.

Now that I have the correct field visually identified, I retract my tinted helmet visor with my left hand and put my right eye directly against the four-power scope of the laser illuminator. My leather-gloved right hand is grasping the laser joystick with two fingers and slewing my field of view through the aiming scope. After a quick search, I pick out the targeted green field with the smoke puff in the center. The laser scope has a crosshair in the middle, just like a telescopic rifle sight. I skew the image to the west and there they are!

The 4X scope shows me a line of dirt gun pits, growing like cancerous tumors on the tree line. I can pick out the brown pits, the recent earth excavations, and the tiny black crosses that are the gun themselves. As we circle, I marvel at the view. I have never seen anti-aircraft gun emplacements this clearly. Whenever I have flown low enough to see them with the naked eye, I have been too busy dodging and weaving to look.

On the hot mike intercom, I tell the guy in front of my plane to instruct Satan Two to aim at the western end of the north tree line. I don't want to take my hand off the laser scope to push my radio mike button.

Satan Two radios back that he has the target area in sight, but he can't see the guns from his altitude. He adds he will be rolling into his dive in ten seconds.

At the promised time, he calls;

"Satan Two is in. FAC in sight."

I reach over and raise the red guard, pushing the toggle switch controlling the laser to the "on" position. In confirmation, I hear a pulsed tone in my earphones, a chirping electronic bell, perhaps the echoes of the sonars of the kamikaze bats of WWII. It signals the laser is firing. It is time to bear down.

With 100 percent of my available concentration, I focus on keeping the thin crosshairs in the laser scope superimposed over the westernmost gun pit. My pilot is flying smoothly, but the task of tracking the target is not easy. The aircraft is traveling at 500 miles per hour, the hot, sunny day in Laos is producing thermals and bumps, and I am nervous.

With no warning, the gun pit displayed in the scope under the cross hairs erupts in a massive explosion of flame, smoke, and red dirt tossed high into the air. A 2,000-pound bomb impacted exactly in the center of the gun pit, vaporizing the gun, the stored ammunition, and the unlucky human gunners. It couldn't have happened to nicer guys. As the smoke and dust drifts, clearing away, all that remains is a much larger, darker hole dug by the bomb. A 2,000-pound bomb has enough explosive force in it to destroy the factory the gun was built in; its effect on the contents of a forty-foot pit must have been devastating. The circular sand-bagged revetment, intended to protect against a near miss, has instead focused the hell from above.

I am amazed. This thing actually works. However, I am the only member of Satan Flight who can see exactly what has happened. I whoop it up a little and tell my pilot,

"Shit hot. A direct hit. Right down the tube."

The Nail goes berserk on the radio.

"Satan, that was a shack (pilot slang for a direct hit), you took out one gun, there's nothing left. That was terrific, one bomb, one gun destroyed. Can you guys do that again?"

It appears Nail hasn't been briefed at all on Project Paveway; he doesn't know what, or who, he is dealing with here. Considering his likelihood of being shot down, captured, tortured, and interrogated, that is probably a good thing for the security of the program.

Satan Lead replies;

"Roger that, Nail. We'll try. Satan Two, go for the eastern most gun this time."

In a minute or so, Satan Two calls, "Rolling in again. FAC in sight."

I aim the crosshairs on the eastern pit and turn on the laser. I am rewarded with a repeat performance, a huge explosion, a smoking crater, and another gun blasted into tiny bits along with its crew.

The Nail is beside himself.

"Satan, that is the best bombing I have ever seen. How are you guys doing that? Can you keep it up?"

Satan Lead laconically answers in the affirmative. The casual tone of his voice implies this is just another day at the office for us Phantom/Paveway jocks. Reversing roles, we climb up to our bombing altitude and Satan Two descends to illumination altitude, still circling the doomed target. We make two dive bomb runs, drop two Paveways, and destroy two more guns with direct hits. It is Satan Two's turn to have some fun. Since the beginning of the war, hell, since the dawn of aviation, antiaircraft gunners have shot at us and our aerial predecessors with impunity. They have always known they had the upper hand. We couldn't touch them in what has been to date an uneven fight. Now, we're the predators. We can pick them off at will and with relative safety. That is a good feeling, knowing the hunter has become the hunted. Let the dispensers of fear now taste panic's drying flavor in their mouths for a change.

Satan Lead calls the Nail;

"Nail. Satan is Winchester (meaning no more bombs) and we're RTB (Returning To Base)."

The Nail is speechless. For days, maybe weeks, he has been skirting the now-destroyed guns, waiting for them to shoot him or someone else down. The gunners have been shooting gleefully at all and sundry and having a grand old time trying to kill Americans. Now four guns are utterly destroyed, four gun crews have been liquidated, and the rest undoubtedly have fled their posts for the surrounding jungle. Nothing like seeing four sets of your buddies blown to smithereens to undermine your resolve to produce American widows and to win the war for Uncle Ho.

Nail comes on the radio with a good-bye as we leave the area and head back to Thailand.

"'Satan, that was the most unbelievable bombing I have ever seen. Come back and work with me anytime. You guys are shit hot."

The Nail knows the surviving gun crews will quickly spread the word that shooting at an OV-10 is a one-way ticket to oblivion. The FAC's job just got safer.

We cross the fence, check out with Cricket, and turn toward our temporary home. Results on the first day of the revolution: four Paveways dropped, four direct hits, four guns obliterated. This has been a good day's work for Laser Pilot and the Cosmic GIB. With nothing to do but wait in the pit until the landing, I'm thinking this laser-guided bomb business might be something good after all. From the backseat, using Paveway is like being God. I point at a target and lightning strikes it. Do I feel sorry for the dozens of human beings I have dispatched today to Commie hell? Not in the least. Those dead guys would have happily killed the Nail, all my buddies, and me. Then they would have awarding themselves medals of the heroic socialist struggle (second class) and celebrated afterward. In fact, the presence of their carefully aimed flak bursts indicated they were trying to do just that.

Late at night when no one is around but me, I usually ask myself moral questions about bombing civilian installations. I take no pleasure from trashing a town. In moments of weakness, I feel some pity for ground troops caught under my falling bombs; that fight is so one-sided. But killing antiaircraft gunners is somehow different. I have lost friends, squadron mates, acquaintances, and fellow airmen to guns. It is gratifying to return the favor, to be able to strike back. Revenge is a dish best served cold by laser light.

A NICKEL ON THE GRASS

My squadron is having a social bash to welcome new members, to say good-bye to guys rotating back home, and to recognize one, maybe two, deaths. It promises to be one hell of a party.

The USAF, for reasons unknown, decided early in the Vietnam War to leave specific fighter squadrons in place in the theater and to rotate members in and out of those squadrons. So, Satan's Angels, my squadron, is permanently located at Ubon Royal Thai Air Force Base as its members check in, serve their tours, and check out. Most guys check out back to the States, but some poor bastards check out in a more permanent manner.

No one can figure out why this constant turnover of personnel is a good idea. But what I do know is all I have to do is fight the war for a year and survive. I'm not charged with managing, or even understanding, USAF personnel policies.

Since the time of the Roman legions, and probably earlier, men have been motivated to perform heroically by the comradeship of their buddies. Soldiers fight, risk death, and sometimes die not for some vague geopolitical objective but for their friends. Fighter pilots are definitely no exception. To a man, we will chance some idiotic aerial risk in combat rather than let our squadron mates down.

I fly with one other guy, a navigator. Usually, we are in some sort of formation made up of several aircraft to support and protect each other. Inside the cockpit, as well to a slightly lesser degree in the formation, teamwork and trust are essential for survival. However, given the current USAF constant rotation policy, I often find myself trusting my life to some guy who I met only yesterday.

In past aerial wars (most of which we won), fighter squadrons trained together as a cohesive unit. This time together allowed essential mutual trust and teamwork to develop and taught the squadron to fly and fight as a unit. As the French say, *esprit de corps* grows out of belonging to a band of brothers, only they say it all in French. Once trained, the squadrons back then rotated to the war as a whole. The squadron would stay in combat until one of three things occurred: (1) the war was won, (2) the squadron was rotated out of the war zone for replacement, or (3) enough guys were lost to destroy the unit's volatile morale. Traditional air forces such as the *Armée de l'Aire Française,* the Royal Air Force, and the U.S. Navy still operate in this way.

Maybe the USAF idea of keeping a squadron in some sort of steady state of flux with guys checking in and out constantly isn't some sort of industrial engineering attempt at an optimum personnel policy. I suspect a more sinister intent. Time-based individual rotation changes more than the makeup of squadron *esprit.* It changes the whole basis of one's risk calculations and tampers with your professional ethics. Perhaps those guys in the bowels of the Pentagon aren't so dumb after all. If you want someone to compromise his professional pride and patriotism, you have to provide a powerful incentive. A better chance for personal survival, even including the approbation of squadron mates you barely know, might do the trick.

In the arcane algebra of war, pilots are always trying to balance chances of survival against the actions necessary to win. Most times, the tasks you need to do to win can reduce your chances of surviving the war. It doesn't matter whether you are trying to win the approval of your peers or to win the war itself.

However, it is abundantly clear to all of us here that the United States of America is not trying to win this stupid war. If winning were a national objective, we would not be going to the enormous lengths we are to avoid winning. If we were trying to win, i.e., to defeat the North Vietnamese, we wouldn't be conducting periodic bombing pauses, or placing key targets off limits, or imposing geographical constraints, or coddling our corrupt and cowardly South Vietnamese allies.

I am beginning to suspect the USAF never-ending rotation policy recognizes the underlying goal of not winning if only in the sub-consciousness of the personnel planners. It would be absurd to send intact squadrons over here for the duration of the war when the war's length isn't defined by a victory or isn't defined at all. No one would willingly fight in such a war without end. There would be wholesale mutinies and resignations. No one is drafted to fly fighters; we are all volunteers. If we realized we had signed up to fight forever in an unwinnable war, we would most probably un-volunteer.

So, as I get dressed to party, I understand the deal on the table. It's a hand dealt by the Devil or the Pentagon. Face up, the cards say "Fight the war for a year, don't ask why, don't question the basic strategy, don't try too hard to win, and you can come home. What's more, you get a sterling career-enhancing line item on your professional résumé." In return for prosecuting an unwinnable war, I get to fly fighter planes in combat and perhaps get promoted. All I have to do is not think too much and not get killed. Unfortunately for two guys in the squadron, the Devil's most recent cards dealt came up aces and eights for them, the legendary dead man's hand.

I zip up my dark green "party flight suit" and I wonder if there is a way to beat the Devil. Instead of enduring the experience, what if I embrace it? If I ignore the futility of it all, am I changing the game? While I am avoiding thinking about the waste and the idiocy, what if I dig the action for its own sake? That would be like playing for the pot of chips on the table instead of trying to come out ahead for the night. Doing nothing but flying fighters in combat for a solid year, it doesn't get much better than that. Fly, Fight, Eat, Sleep, Drink, occasionally get Laid. Such a deal. How does the game change if I enjoy it? If I do, have I beaten the Devil (or the Pentagon) or have I joined him or them? That is a question I don't feel like answering prior to attending a squadron party to welcome players into and out of the game. I don't have time to think about that tonight, I'll think about that tomorrow, Scarlett.

My party suit is modeled after a real USAF flight suit, but is sewn to fit well by a local Thai tailor. Instead of fireproof Nomex, it is cooler cotton, in the squadron color, green. It is festooned with insignia and badges galore. My call sign, "Fast Eddie," USAF pilot's wings, and rank are carefully embroidered on in silver as well. I'm sure that using official emblems on a wildly unofficial party suit violates numerous dress regulations, but no one in the squadron is losing any sleep over the consequences.

The squadron has been taken off tonight's flying schedule and we have reserved a private room at the Officers' Club. I arrive and see the tables are in a horseshoe arrangement with the Squadron Commander's chair reserved at the arch's keystone position with the operations officer on his right. The rest of us grab a seat wherever we can with them lower ranks gravitating to the base of the arch. The tables are festooned with white tablecloths, not the usual bare wood. The food serving staff is splendidly decked out in classic native Thai outfits.

I take my seat with the rest of the guys and the Thai bar waitresses fill our wineglasses with cheap rosé wine from Portugal. This is serious business. I attempt, without much success, to ignore how well the long silk Thai skirts fit the girls who will serve the food. The cocktail waitresses are in their customary miniskirts. That is an American native custom, not a Thai one.

As dictated by ritual, the lowest-ranking lieutenant proposes a toast by standing and announcing;

"Mr. President, a toast."

The "President" of the Officer's Mess, the Boss of the squadron replies,

"Yes, Mr. Vice."

The lieutenant (Mr. Vice) responds, "To the President of the United States" and lifts his glass as we all spring to our feet.

We all echo, "To the President," and take a sip. I remind myself that I am toasting the office of the president and not the crude Texan now defiling it.

Mr. Vice, who doesn't appear to be yet of legal drinking age, continues;

"To the King of Thailand."

We raise our glasses to the King of Thailand, whose name is unpronounceable by western tongues, but by all accounts is a good guy.

Mr. Vice, the President of the Mess, and the assembled squadron finish by toasting the Chief of Staff of the USAF. Oh well, one out of three dignitaries worthy of a toast isn't too bad.

Now for more a somber toast. The Squadron Commander raises his glass and solemnly says;

"To our departed comrades."

By whom he means the two guys shot down this week. One was killed and one is missing.

We all manage to choke out, "To our departed comrades," and drain our glasses.

When their last drops of wine are gone, the Commander and the Operations Officer turn and hurl their glasses against the nearest wall. The glasses shatter into tiny shards, breaking the strained silence in the room. Without a command, I sit down in unison with my remaining comrades and dinner is served. It is many minutes before normal conversation returns.

The ritual we have just observed originated with the Royal Air Force, then called the Royal Flying Corps, during WWI. It has been handed down by generations of fighter pilots who have lost comrades and thrown glasses for half a century around the world. The exact origin of the ceremony has been lost in the obscuring mists of time, but not the obvious symbolism.

Two lives have been lost and two glasses shattered. Also shattered were the lives of those who loved the two men. Back in the States, two new but unaware widows answered their front doors to find three USAF officers standing nervously. Once the ladies saw the men, they knew instantly why they were there. The team of three were the duty Officer of the Day, a chaplain, and a doctor. It was their sad duty to deliver the terrible news and to help the bereaved cope as best they could.

During WWII, the shattering news arrived by telegram, with no one there to take the widow under an official but protecting wing. I can't imagine the shock of opening an impersonal telegram (probably addressed to "Occupant") while alone and learning that your husband or son won't be coming home.

Here on our air base, a well-practiced bureaucratic process has already begun. A senior sergeant has begun to pack up the two flyers' personal effects for shipment to their next of kin.

Undoubtedly he will discover sealed, stamped letters addressed to wives, mothers, and fathers. Usually, there will be a note attached to each that reads, "To be mailed in the event of my death or capture." Sometimes the letters are in a shaving kit; sometimes pinned to a wall; mine are in the top drawer of my clothes chest. Upon finding the letters, the sergeant will stop what he is doing and walk immediately over to the base post office and hand the letters personally to the enlisted postmaster. They will go out on the next flight to Bangkok and from there to Hometown, USA.

I have read that during WWI, there were no provisions for shipping back from the war zone the personal possessions of casualties. After the toasts and the ritual breaking of the wine glasses, the Squadron Commander would auction off the dead pilot's belongings to the members of his squadron and send a check to the widow, another tradition we picked up from the British then. I'm glad we don't do that anymore.

Dinner is allegedly a steak. On my plate is a lump of meat, dark black, approximately the size and shape of a softball but not as tender. The mystery meat is coated with glutinous brown gravy speckled with canned mushrooms. Lumpy mashed potatoes and soggy green peas keep the steak-thing from rolling around on my plate. Dessert is apple pie and ice cream. But the kitchen has run out of vanilla ice cream and is substituting whatever is in the freezer. I get a scoop of chocolate ripple on top of my Dutch apple pie, not too bad. The guy on my right gets lime sherbet on his.

The Officers' Club kitchen is run by a USAF sergeant (always nicknamed "Cookie"), but the staff, including the cooks, is Thai. The Thai cooks and waitresses are eager and try hard to learn the ways if not of Western cuisine, then of USAF chow. However, nuances are often lost in the translation, as evidenced by the wide variety of frozen desserts piled on the apple pie. I'm not even sure "nuances" is the right word when applied to food prepared according to the USAF manuals.

These kitchen outrages are committed in the midst of the culinary heaven surrounding the base. The local Thai food is terrific, a blend of Chinese, Laotian, Vietnamese, Burmese, Indonesian, Indian, and God only knows what else. The gamut of flavors available spans the known food universe. The Thais take pride in the fact that they eat everything in Thailand. Everything that grows, swims, flies, walks, slithers, or creeps in Thailand ends up in a rice bowl. This cornucopia of ingredients is stirred with a variety of spices only a few of which even have Western names. The Thais specialize in melding mutually incompatible flavors; sweet and sour, spicy and cool, salty and fresh, peanuts and meat, it's all there and it's all great. Some Thai chili peppers make Mexican jalapenos taste as mild as the vanilla ice cream I don't have on my pie. They serve hot sauces that make me feel like I am eating a plate of napalm, lit. Eating good Thai food is like having a war go off in your mouth.

All this is lost on the USAF Mess Sergeant, who strives mightily to replicate standard, bland mid-western American food. I'm afraid Thai food is mostly lost on my squadron mates, who seem to prefer green peas instead of say, lemongrass prawn soup. It is no wonder the Thai cooks can't seem to get the hang of American chow. Why should they when it all gets eaten anyway? Nobody's fools, the waitresses always eat in the kitchen where the cooks stir-fry a new Thai delicacy for them every night.

Speaking of waitresses, the one serving drinks to my table seems particularly attentive. I have seen her in the club many times, but we have only exchanged pleasantries to date. She notices that I have given up trying to cut my charred steak and asks me if I like it. I tell her that I would prefer Thai food and that comment gets a big smile on her delicate face. Now my wine glass seems to get refilled more diligently.

The free flow of Portuguese rotgut rosé is having its effect on the squadron. Conversation returns, jokes are exchanged, and the mood improves rapidly. Only the Squadron Commander seems immune to the alcohol-fueled merriment. His face carries a serious demeanor, not frowning, but not happy either. I guess he hasn't written his letters yet and with no flying scheduled, he will be at his desk later tonight.

If not tonight, then in the next few days, the Commander will sit down and hand-write a personal note to the next of kin of both pilots we lost. He will extend sincere condolences and include a few positive vignettes of his impressions of the downed airmen.

Sometimes he includes a brief, unclassified description of the circumstances of their final combat action. If there is any hope that the flyers survived, he stresses that possibility. The hardest letters to write are when parachutes were sighted in the air or when there was contact from the ground on a survival radio, but no one was rescued from the jungle. What do you say in a situation like that? Were the aircrew captured by the Bad Guys and are they now en route to the Hanoi Hilton? Is it better to hold out some hope, however slender, that the loved one will someday return at the end of the war? When will that be? Or is it easier to say that no chutes were seen when it is clear that no one got out of the doomed jet? Being a Squadron Commander is a tough job and writing next-of-kin letters is the hardest part of it. Other routine correspondence can be assigned to a clerk or administration officer and signed when completed. Next-of-kin letters have to be handwritten and heartfelt. I believe it is a skill which comes with practice and lately the Boss has been getting lots of it.

Speaking of practice, the Boss says it is time for choir practice. For some reason still unknown to me, I got handed the job of publishing the squadron songbook. There are dozens of fighter pilot songs; everyone knows a few. The Operations Officer thought it would be a great idea to compile as many of these ditties as I could find. I accomplished this task, asking everyone to scribble down the words to any tunes they thought would fit in such a book. Then, I spent a few weeks editing the result and getting it printed in town with the squadron's emblem on the cover. The Thai printer asked why a green devil was on the cover of a songbook. I told him these were songs to keep away devils. He nodded in knowing agreement.

All the songs that the guys knew seem to originate from WWII. Why is this? Maybe the guys in WWI couldn't sing. Actually they probably didn't get much time to raise their voices in song. The average life span of a fighter pilot on the Western front during the Battle of the Somme was about three weeks. German or British, it didn't matter, three weeks was all you got. The fighter jocks of WWII actually had a chance of living through the war. Staying in the same unit for the duration, they seemed to have time to write a lot of songs. As stereos and tape decks hadn't been invented yet, vocalization was about the only participatory music they had available.

The background of these songs has been lost over the years and no one knows what they mean. One favorite chorus goes:

Hallelujah, Hallelujah,
Throw a nickel on the grass,
Save a fighter pilot's ass,
Hallelujah, Hallelujah,
Throw a nickel on the grass,
And you'll be safe."

Throw a nickel on what grass? Why would that save anyone's ass? Who cares? We sing it anyway. Other songs are understandable, but dated:

Don't give me a P-39,
With an engine that's mounted behind,
You can loop, roll, and spin,

But you'll soon auger in,
Don't give me a P-39.

The P-39 "Aircobra" had its big, heavy, Allison piston engine mounted behind its single-seat cockpit. The spinning propeller shaft ran between the pilot's legs up to the nose. It was one of the least successful fighter aircraft of WWII. They were so bad, we gave them all to the Soviets under the lend-lease program. Why such a turkey of an aircraft is immortalized in song is beyond me, but this history might explain why the Soviet Air Force is helping the North Vietnamese in today's war. They're probably still pissed about getting those P-39s. There is probably a Russian song with lyrics similar to ours.

Some of the songs concern the opposite sex and not in the most respectful of terms either. It seems that a female needed insatiable sexual needs, spectacular attributes, and remarkable physical prowess to make it into a WWII barroom song. As the singing starts, I get a sly smile and wink from our waitress, Judi, as she catches my eye for about the tenth time. I wonder if she is listening to the words to *"Mary Ann Burns, Queen of the Acrobats."* Probably not, or a blush would redden her light brown skin.

Most of the squadron gathers around the room's small bar and lift both their glasses and their voices in bleary song. In this ad hoc choir, enthusiasm counts for more than the ability to carry a tune. In our green party suits, we look like some sort of berserk barbershop singing group, only without any collective musical talent.

We have to sing acappella tonight; one of the shattered glasses was for our only guitar player. He was from rural Louisiana, Lake Charles, and called himself a "coon-ass." I was born in New Orleans, but I never heard the term coon-ass. I guess it applies to genuine Cajuns from the bayou country. He was a back seater, a pilot that flies only in the rear cockpit of the Phantom.

His jet was shot down near the southern mouth of Mu Gia Pass. Mu Gia Pass is a break in the mountains separating North

Vietnam from Laos. It runs northeast to southwest and nearly all the traffic destined for the Ho Chi Minh Trail system in Laos passes through Mu Gia. Consequently, this potential choke point for supplies and men is heavily and constantly bombed. Parts of it look like the world's largest kid's sandbox. All the vegetation and surface features have been pounded into nothing but sand and mud.

After being hit by ground fire, the crippled Phantom managed to make it out of the pass and over the relative safety of the Laotian jungle before coming apart. Both guys ejected and got good parachutes. The pilot came up on the radio first, but then contact was lost. He is listed as MIA, missing in action. No one is likely to know his fate for years; either he was captured, or the Bad Guys killed him on the spot. Another mother will have to wait years to know if her son is coming home. That is one letter that will be tough to write.

The Cajun back-seater also made radio contact, but the North Vietnamese decided to play games with him and the recovery effort. If they know if a pilot is down but alive on the ground, they will use the poor bastard for bait. Instead of taking him prisoner, they will leave him alone, calling for rescue. While the search-and-rescue team; the Sandys, the Jolly Greens, and King are enroute they will surround the survivor with as many antiaircraft guns as they can move into place in hopes of shooting down more of us when we attempt the pickup. They know we will make every effort to save our own. They also know the rescue team and the supporting fighters will lay down a carpet of bombs to suppress the ground fire. If they lose 200 guys to our covering fire and manage to shoot down one or two of the rescue aircraft, that will be a victory for them. The Bad Guys are fighting the war not only in Mu Gia Pass, but also in the pages of the New York Times. The loss in Laos of a Jolly Green Giant helicopter and its five crewmen will make the Times; the deaths of 200 Vietnamese troops won't up north. There isn't an equivalent paper in Hanoi.

This time, the Sandys had a new trick to change the rules; gas. Each propeller-driven A-1 Skyraider carried gas dispensers under both wings. On each pass over the area where our friend was hiding, they laid down cloud after cloud of gas. This gas is designed to incapacitate unprotected troops. It induces nausea, vomiting, diarrhea, disorientation, and panic. The rescue forces call it "give-a-shit" gas. A few good whiffs and the most dedicated Commies are supposed to not give a shit about the war for the rest of the day.

The Geneva Convention strictly prohibits poison gas. This scrap of paper is a treaty signed by the Vietnamese, the United States, and most of the world. It sets down the rules of war. The status of give-a-shit gas is murkier, both literally and legally. Most legalists would argue that this sort of nonlethal gas is also beyond the pale of civilized warfare, whatever that means.

When it comes to rescuing one of my squadron mates, particularly one being used as human bait in some deadly Bad Guy political game, I say, "Screw the Geneva Convention! Use the gas!" The convention definitely concerns prisoners of war as well as the use of gas. However, the North Vietnamese prison camps for captured American pilots are beyond the reach of the convention. God only knows what goes on in the Hanoi Hilton. The Red Cross and the UN are denied private access to the hapless prisoners, access required by the almighty Geneva Convention. What use is a treaty that only one side obeys? When the innkeepers of the Hanoi Hilton follow the rules of war, then so will we.

Evidently, as the Bad Guys were being gassed, they realized that their trap wasn't going to be sprung the way they hoped. Before they collapsed in puddles of their own vomit and shit, they managed to kill the back seater where he was hiding.

The gas mask equipped USAF para-rescue guys descended from the Jolly Green helo, ready to winch up the downed airman, who would have been rendered unconscious from the gas intended for the Bad Guys. They found our friend shot, execution style, and left to die alone in the hot, stinking Laotian jungle. The area was too hotly defended to recover the body. Thus, we have an empty seat at the party, a shattered glass, and no guitar music.

The group singing is getting rowdier and louder, but no closer to being on key. Despite several glasses of cheap wine, I am in no mood to use the songbook I wrote. I know where this evening is headed. Most of the guys will get a snoot full of the adult beverage of their choice and retire back to their quarters. There they will get together and sing the same obscure, profane, and obscene songs again and again. Maybe this is a good way to forget all the reasons for the party. I think I'll pass this time.

I could go back to my room, turn on the stereo, and put on a good album. Something restful and serene sounds about right. *Johnny Cash, Live At Folsom Prison*, cranked up to full volume should do the trick.

I return to my chair from the latrine intending to pick up my song book and then hit the sack. At my place is a folded bit of paper cleverly fashioned into a tiny swan. It is a masterful example of Thai origami. The paper swan, wings and all, easily fits into the palm of my hand. No one else has such a party favor and no one has noticed it waiting for me.

I hold the origami up to the light and try to focus my eyes on it. I see that there was writing on the paper before the swan was crafted. I hate to spoil such a work of folded art, but I have to see what is on the paper. Reluctantly, I unfold the swan and read in English, "You like some Thai food after the party?" It is signed "Judi."

Now this is quite a shock. Judi is one of the most lusted-after waitresses at the club, but she is famously chaste. She is bright with a delightful personality but has always been somewhat aloof and unobtainable. Her attractive package includes a slender, almost thin figure, a pretty face, and a radiant smile. Judi also proudly displays the longest raven-black ponytail and the shortest miniskirt in Thailand.

The behavior of the girls working at the Officers' Club runs the moral spectrum from "happily available" to "no way, don't even think about it." Judi has no known American lovers or boyfriends. She takes the bus home alone every night at midnight.

On the other hand, I have never been in the railroad business (laying Thais) myself. I have always been friendly to the girls at the club, but have seldom seriously flirted, much less made a successful move on one. Maybe Judi and I are meant for each other. I don't know what she has in mind, whether her offer extends past a Thai meal, but it sounds like a better time tonight than listening to the drunken chorus.

I find her alone in a corner of the club and accept her invitation and get the second big grin of the night. She says she thinks I am a real gentleman, which gets a return smile from me. Instead of the name of a local Thai restaurant, she gives me a hand-drawn map to her house in town. Homemade Thai food sounds good, but I wonder what comes after that. Thai food isn't famous for its sweets; maybe dessert is Judi herself. After numerous glasses of wine, the prospect sounds interesting.

At 2330, I excuse myself from the party and catch the "baht bus" outside the club. The local bus fare is one baht in Thai money, equivalent to five American cents. That is reasonable enough but the bad news is that the bus seats are designed for shorter Thai legs. I don't fit. I have to sit sideways on the upright, wooden seats as the rickety bus rattles and chugs its way into town.

At the bus stop, I hop off and hail a waiting samlor. This personal service may cost me all of five baht or twenty-five cents. The samlor is a large tricycle pedaled by a sturdy Thai guy with legs like knotted cords. There is a seat for two Thais or one American between the rear wheels. The driver pedals and steers from the front. The samlor driver speaks no English and my Thai language skills need work and lots of it. With hand signals, I direct him along the streets to Judi's house. A samlor is a relaxed and civilized way to travel if you aren't in a hurry and if you don't mind watching a Thai guy's butt go up and down as he stands on the pedals at close range in front of you.

It is nearly midnight and the side streets of Ubon City are still alive with people. The only paved road in town leads to the air base; the rest of Ubon's thoroughfares are composed of hard-packed red dirt. The dirt tracks are lined with wooden houses, each with its fenced yard. It is still warm tonight, but the night air isn't as humid and oppressive as when the sun beats down.

Nighttime in rural Thailand is a dark dreamland, smoky from cooking fires, with the slightly-built ghosts of Thais drifting in and out of the scattered lights and my view. The silent samlor drifts along the dirt streets like a tiny ship sailing the canals of Venice. We overtake people who barely take note of our passage as they clop-clop along in rubber shower shoes. We meet folks carrying buckets hanging from the ends of tote sticks slung across one shoulder, their pace dictated by the resonate frequency of the bouncing sticks. I hear laughing and soft conversation in Thai, with no voices raised. The scent of Asia is very strong tonight with no wind to dispel it. I have no alternative but to drink in the aroma and wonder why no one seems to notice it but me.

Despite the late hour, there is an electric light, only one, on in each house we pass. People move in and out of the harsh glows, visible from the street. Thai houses feature open spaces, no need for heating, ever. The traditional style houses are mostly windows; even the shacks have very few walls under their tin roofs. The streets are lighted by single fifty-watt naked light bulbs, one suspended on the intersection of every block. Smoke from charcoal fires under woks drifts in and out of the dim circles of light cast by the streetlights. The smoke is mixed with oily steam from the bubbling woks, the burning of incense in tiny spirit houses, and the foul vapors from the open ditches.

The food pushcarts are still out and are still doing business. Each has its own propane lantern lit and its own specialty for sale. One might serve satay; chicken or pork roasted on a bamboo skewer and dipped in a coconut, chili, and peanut butter sauce. The next might have cut fruit, the one after that omelets or steamed jasmine rice. The pungent ones sell dried squid. The hand-sized squids are transparent and flat when dried. They are hung up on strings above the pushcart, ready to be stir-fried and doused in a fiery chili sauce. The smells of charcoal, squid, aromatic rice, and fetid ditches wafts over the samlor as we cruise silently along the dirt road. I wonder what Judi is planning on for our romantic midnight dinner?

Thais eat constantly, they seem to snack every waking hour, hence the popularity of the pushcarts. Yet, they are invariably slender. The people of Ubon have access at all times to some of the best food in the world, yet it is rare to see a fat Thai. People on the streets are making one last raid on the pushcarts before bed. The neighborhood is getting more rural and quieter as I am transported by pedal power in the samlor.

Now we are at Judi's house and it is impressive in a Thai sort of way. I pay the driver and take a good look. The house speaks volumes about the earnings to be made working on the American air base. Few twenty-something girls in Thailand have their own digs. The house has several airy rooms with open windows and wooden walls. It is built on stilts with enough room to walk under it. A ramp leads up to the living quarters on the second and only floor. The underside of the house is smaller than the second story giving it the look of a wooden mushroom with a tin roof. It is also completely dark.

Judi said that she gets off at midnight. She has to check out and catch the baht bus home. I expect her to arrive about 12:30. I find myself speculating on how it is possible for her to sit down in her tiny, tight skirt on the baht bus and still stay modest. Maybe, despite her high heels, she can cross her bare legs while perching on the straight-backed wooden seats. My mental image of Judi sitting on the bouncing baht bus, trying to hold her micro-skirt down with both hands, makes my upper lip break out in beads of sweat.

Across the dirt street from Judi's dark house is a large mangrove tree with expansive roots. The spreading mangrove roots are one to two feet high and will make a good seat. It has been a long day and an intense party and I can stand to take a load off. With only one fifty-watt streetlight every block, it is dark here among the roots of the mangrove tree.

While I wait, I start thinking, which is always dangerous. Is what I am about to do a good idea? Sure, I'm single, but how badly do I need a Thai girlfriend? Judi didn't invite me to her house after midnight just for fried rice. She will be an exciting, exotic lover, but what happens afterward? Can I afford, the emotional involvement while I'm focused on laying my life on the line every night in combat? Can I sleep with someone and not get involved? I doubt it.

Can I afford not to enjoy my life to the fullest now? Who knows how long that life will last? What if I spend some of my future years in the Hanoi Hilton? Will I regret that I laid Judi down tonight or look back on her intimate memory to sustain me? Did the two guys we lost this week die with regrets for chances not taken? The chance of buying the farm could justify a ton of bad behavior, but what if I live through it all?

I could see myself falling for her big-time; she is so pretty and perky. I can already imagine candlelight playing on her shiny ebony hair as her undone ponytail cascades down her nude back spilling over her smooth shoulders like a midnight waterfall. That image makes rational thinking very hard for me tonight. My upper lip was beaded earlier, now I'm sweating bullets and it hasn't gotten any warmer tonight in Ubon City.

Is this a smart thing to do? What if I survive this crummy war? I won't be in Thailand forever. Is my family in Tennessee ready for a Thai daughter-in-law, if it comes to that? But I'm really getting ahead of myself with that line of thought, sitting on a mangrove root in my green party suit. Would I be here if I were sober?

Maybe I should let sobriety and future events take care of themselves and only live for the enjoyment of the moment. Wait a minute! Isn't that the deal I have with the devils in the Pentagon? I'll fly and fight and experience the most exciting time of my life. I just won't think about what it all means too much.

Why not enjoy Judi's exotic favors and let the emotional chips fall where they may for both of us? But I have to admit to myself that taking a hand dealt from the U.S. government devil is very different from me dealing the cards to a nubile twenty-one year old Thai girl. But just how innocent is a mini-skirted barmaid? Particularly one who loves showing off her nude, shapely legs? As the King of Thailand never said, "It is a puzzlement."

★★★

There is a bright light shining through my welded-shut eyes and I can hear several children giggling. What the hell is going on here?

I manage to pry one eye open, only to be blinded. I shade my aching head with my right hand and crack the other eye open. The hot Thai sun is trained directly on me. I am lying between two mangrove roots, neither of which is offering any shade. Three Thai kids, ages six to eight, are looking down on me, they're silhouetted with the sun at their backs and giggling. By the angle of the sun, I judge the time to be about 0800. What's with these kids, haven't they ever seen an American pilot in a green party suit sleeping on the ground between mangrove roots before? I feel terrible. I hope I can find a samlor to take me all the way to the base so I won't have to bounce on the baht bus. As I stumble up the dirt street I leave both Judi and her house un-entered behind me. I have to get back to the war, where I know the rules.

SAILING, SAILING

The flight deck of an aircraft carrier conducting flight operations at night is the most dangerous place on the planet where people are regularly called upon to work. I can say that because I have never been in a deep coal mine. I am, however, on the deck of the USS Hancock and it looks plenty dangerous enough to me here.

Jet aircraft are frequently taking off, aided by massive shots of acceleration delivered by two steam-driven catapults. Most launches involve A-4E Skyhawk attack planes but occasionally an F-8E Crusader fighter taxis on to the catapult and blasts the deck behind with its afterburner plume. The jet blast from the J-57 engine in the F-8 glows white hot, with shock diamonds of flame imbedded in the trail of plasma-colored gasses. Even the A-4s with their much smaller J-52 engines suck and blow furiously, scouring the steel deck with its rubberized coating.

The noise is terrific, even with Mickey Mouse style ear protectors on my head. The A-4s are loud enough to wake the dead, but are nothing compared to the Crusaders. The F-8's engine is so loud, I feel the noise in my gut, rather than through my covered ears.

Crewmen trundle racks of live bombs and missiles close by slow-moving aircraft. Fuel hoses turgid with highly flammable jet fuel snake across the deck. A thirty-knot, ninety-degree Fahrenheit wind blows from the bow down the flight deck at all times as the massive Hancock powers its way across the Gulf of Tonkin. The ship always sails into the prevailing breeze just fast enough to provide thirty knots of hot, humid headwind for flight operations. The huge steel deck is rimmed with horizontal nets to catch unlucky sailors who sometimes get blown off by the wind or swept off by jet blast. Steaming off to one side of the carrier and to the rear, a destroyer cruises in formation with the Hancock across the gulf to rescue anyone who leaves the deck and misses the nets. The USN destroyer's mission also includes the rescue of a pilot from any jet that lands in the drink instead of on the ship or anyone who ejects nearby.

The sea is rough tonight, with dark waves of black water that seem to be fifteen feet from their deep troughs to their foamy tops. The carrier blasts its way through the incoming marching walls of water, pitching up and down with the waves. The shepherding destroyer, a much smaller ship, occasionally takes solid water over its bow. Riding on that boat must be an e-coupon tonight.

Night operations on the flight deck consist of an intense scene of complex, carefully orchestrated action which constantly threatens to degenerate into chaos. The heat, the wind, and the danger sculpt all human movement into a kind of industrial strength ballet. Enlisted crewmen scurry everywhere wearing helmets and earmuffs, scant protection against the incessantly howling noise. Each of their job specialties has its own colored jersey; the fuel guys have purple shirts, the bomb guys red, the catapult team are in yellow, and so forth. They all also have big brass balls for just being here. Despite the obvious danger and omnipresent violence, the deck crewmen have an air of studied indifference and a way of moving indicating there is nothing abnormal about walking past a jet engine screaming in full afterburner. Men are working hard, but are moving deliberately, only walking fast enough to get the job done, apparently without care. Or, has long exposure to the danger numbed their sense of self-preservation?

I am not numb. A U.S. Navy sergeant, I think they call them Chief Petty Officers, has been assigned to show me around. He told me to stick to him like glue while we are out on the flight deck. You couldn't separate me from the Chief with a spatula.

Without his guidance, I wouldn't survive a minute in this horrific environment. There is just too much heavy metal, sucking intakes, and fiery gasses moving around without regard to any human life in the immediate vicinity.

An A-4 loaded with six 500-pound bombs quickly taxis into position on the left-hand catapult track at the bow of the ship. Teams of sailors swarm all over it like multicolored army ants checking everything in sight. One guy hooks the Skyhawk's nose to the catapult shuttle using a braided steel cable fashioned into a bridle for airplanes instead of horses. Another sailor pulls the arming pins with their attached red safety flags from the bomb racks and the fuel drop tanks. This crewman shows the handful of pins to the pilot in the cockpit, who seems remarkably calm in the middle of such a maelstrom of dangerous activity.

The flight deck is dimly lit by red floodlights to preserve the pilots' night vision, lending the aura of a hot, windy hell to the proceedings. Even in this dim light, I can see the pilot look at one of the deck officers, who has some key role in all of this dedicated effort. The catapult officer twirls his right hand high over his head as a signal for the pilot to jam the throttle forward. The noise, even through my acoustic earmuffs, is skull splitting. The pilot checks his cockpit gauges and turns on the jet's navigation lights as a signal that he is ready for flight. The cat officer stops twirling his hand and leans forward dramatically to touch the deck in front of him, toward the bow of the ship.

One instant the Skyhawk is there, the next it isn't. The little jet disappears like the roadrunner in a cartoon in a wisp of smoke (more likely steam from the catapult), leaving a fading visual image in its place as the real jet disappears off the front of the ship. As soon as the first A-4 has been launched into the hot, black night, the sailors begin to minister to the next one. A second A-4 leaves a few seconds later from the right hand catapult and two more Skyhawks taxi into position, ready to be shot off the ship into the void.

This time, I watch the A-4 as it is hurled down the deck and off the bow. As soon as the aircraft's wheels start rolling on thin air, the pilot starts a right bank away from the ship's course, flying at what has to be close to his stalling airspeed. I am told this maneuver allows the ejection seat to save your life if the jet's engine quits on takeoff. If the fire behind you in the aircraft goes out and you have to eject, you don't want the 50,000-ton USS Hancock running over you in the water.

I have never seen such a demonstration of barely controlled mechanical fury. A fully loaded A-4 has to weigh 14,000 or 15,000 pounds, small for a jet aircraft, but still impressive. A seven-ton jet is hurled off the ship like a manned rock from a schoolboy's sling shot and another one is readied before anyone misses the first.

As I watch, an outboard section of the steel deck the size of a tennis court disappears downward. In a minute or so the flight deck elevator reappears, climbing upward, to merge flush again with the flight deck. It carries an A-4 from the hanger deck below, ready to be loaded with bombs, fuel, and an intrepid pilot.

After forty-five minutes of furious action, all the ready aircraft have been launched and the ship slowly turns 180 degrees to run downwind. It sails in a racetrack pattern in order to maintain its position off the coast of North Vietnam. The ship is so huge it feels as if the horizon is swinging around the ship instead of the ship turning. It is marvelous that something as immense as the Hancock can even move across the surface of the sea, much less at thirty knots. I have enjoyed about as much of this as I can stand, so I ask the Chief to escort me to someplace safer and quieter. As a matter of fact, any place would be safer and quieter than here on the flight deck.

I am on the USS Hancock for a few days to instruct the US Navy on how to drop these newfangled laser-guided bombs they have heard so much about. The Hancock is on "Yankee Station" off the coast of North Vietnam to take the war, such that it is, to the enemy. Another aircraft carrier is off South Vietnam on "Dixie Station" to fly in support of U.S. troops in the south. Yankee and Dixie Stations are really two ill-defined orbit points in the South China Sea.

The USAF is having terrific success with our Paveway laser-guided bombs. Some days, my squadron in Thailand alone racks up more targets confirmed destroyed than the rest of the US air effort, including the US Navy. In the world of inter-service rivalry, and there is no other world, this is wholly unacceptable to the admirals. The idea that one upstart USAF F-4D Phantom squadron in Thailand can destroy more targets in a day than the whole US Navy's air arm goes down poorly in Washington. If this very unbalanced success rate continues much longer, some flinty-eyed congresspersons might have the nerve to ask why the American taxpayers are spending so much money on aircraft carriers for such relatively poor results. Even worse, the green eyeshade types in the Congressional Budget Office might divert funds from the supposedly inept US Navy to the wildly successful US Air Force. Oh, the horror!

The US Navy brass, of which there is an overabundance, reminds me of the mafioso Don who was told by a classy dame that he had no couth. The Don immediately dispatched all his hit men to buy up every drop of couth in town. In belated response to the USAF's Paveway success, the Navy has obtained a limited supply of laser guidance kits from the civilian contractor in Texas for immediate installation on USN dumb bombs. The kits were air freighted to Hawaii to meet the good ship Hancock during a port call in the islands on its way westward from the United States to the war. En route from Pearl Harbor to the Subic Bay naval base in the Philippines, the navy guys opened the boxes to check out these new, wonderful "smart bombs." Much to their surprise, they discovered the bombs need a laser to illuminate the target. Paveways are smart bombs, not genius bombs; without help they don't know the target's location. Thus, lasers were hastily procured and flown to Subic Bay for use by the Hancock's bemused flight crews.

During the short sea journey from Subic Bay to Yankee Station the munitions troops learned how to assemble the bomb kits from instruction by the civilian contractor's technical support person on board. He told them how to insert tab A into slot B. But, the pilots are clueless on Paveway flight operations and tactics. Navy pilots tactically clueless, why am I not surprised?

The Commander of the Hancock's air wing swallowed his considerable naval pride in the interests of achieving success with the laser-guided bombs and made an urgent radio call for help to USAF headquarters in Saigon. The request rolled down the chain of command hill to Ubon, Thailand, located at the bottom of that slippery grade. My Squadron Commander, who obviously wishes to see me dead or humiliated or both, tagged me to go sailing with the Navy. So here I am, trying not to get sucked down a jet intake on the hellish flight deck of the USS Hancock. The entire A-4 squadron, VA-212, the "Flying Eagles," tasked to introduce the concept of smart bombs to the fleet was just shot off the front of the boat tonight one by one. They are all flying. So, I have no one to brief and/or educate.

I really wanted to first check out how flight operations are conducted anyway. I have never seen a carrier flight deck in operation and it is a real trip, scary and impressive at the same time. Somehow, the Chief and I manage to traverse the open air mayhem without incident and we start downstairs to the lower decks of the carrier. We descend several sets of stairs; the Chief calls them "ladders." The Chief leads me along a labyrinth of halls ("passageways") and through open watertight doors that periodically interrupt the passageways. I don't want to know why they need watertight doors in the middle of the ship.

The chief shows me to my bunk in the bowels of the Hancock and I throw in my scruffy duffel bag. I ask the Chief to wait while I stow my gear, as there is no chance I could ever find my way back up on deck again by myself. I should have dropped bread crumbs on the way down.

As he waits for me, the Chief asks if I have ever been at sea before. Not wanting to be branded a landlubber, I tell him that I used to be a commercial fisherman. To be honest, I add that I have never been on a naval vessel before tonight and certainly not on any ship of this size. I neglect to mention that my limited time as a commercial fisherman was spent helping my uncle catch channel catfish on the Tennessee River in a fourteen-foot outboard skiff.

The chief briefs me on life on board the Hancock; how to find the latrine (which for some reason he calls a "head") where the chow hall is located (a "galley"), when chow is served, the general layout of the ship, and what to do if there is an emergency. Evidently, the worst thing that can happen at sea is fire. I have to know how to reach the flight deck if there is a fire somewhere on the ship, to know where my life jacket is located, and how to swim away after jumping seventy-five feet down from the flight deck into the shark infested South China Sea. After a cup of coffee and this cheery briefing, the Chief takes me up to the "island," the part of the ship that sticks up from the flat flight deck. It is a good spot from which to watch the squadron return to alight back on board.

The ocean is rough tonight and even a ship the size of the immense Hancock responds to the heavy seas. I am told in "Pri-Fly" (which is the naval equivalent of an airfield control tower) that the landing zone on the deck is pitching up and down by twenty feet or more. I am used to landing strips that stay put, so to me this sounds like quite a challenge for the returning aviators.

A loudspeaker somewhere above in the ceiling (the "overhead") commands, "Prepare to recover aircraft."

The deck crew scrambles to evacuate the landing zone at the rear ("aft") end of the flight deck. There are four steel cables stretched across the deck to snag the tail hooks of the jets as they attempt to land. Off in the pitch-black night behind the ship I see the red and green navigation lights of an A-4 on final approach to the Hancock. In the dense, humid night air, I can't make out the aircraft itself, only the nav and landing lights. The lights get brighter and farther apart as the jet silently approaches the ship on final approach. Only when the

Skyhawk gets within one hundred yards of the back of the ship do the dim deck lights illuminate it. Then, I can discern the outline of the A-4.

The Skyhawk with its landing gear, wing flaps, and tail hook dangling, flies very slowly over the landing zone. The jet is descending at the same time the pitching deck is ascending. The A-4 hits the deck, or is it the deck that comes up and hits the A-4? In either case, there is a terrible impact producing a thud that I can clearly hear all the way up in Pri-Fly. I have no doubt that jet is badly damaged. The spindly looking landing gear on the A-4 is compressed instantly to the stops and the tail hook catches a cable. I'm glad it does, as it would be a bad scene if this totally wrecked aircraft were allowed to go over the side into the ocean with the luckless pilot still strapped in the cockpit. The derelict jet pulls the cable out a hundred feet or so. It is caught slightly sideways in the extended wire.

With its stubby body, short, swept-back wings, tall landing gear, and bulbous cockpit, the A-4 looks like a giant, gray fly snared by a four-strand steel spider web. The desperate pilot obliviously jammed the throttle forward at the last instant in a vain attempt to save the situation. The doomed A-4 is brought up short by the cable, despite its engine screaming at full power.

I am shocked and appalled; the first carrier landing I have ever seen in person results in a terrible crash. No one seems hurt, but I'm certain the jet is a write-off salvage case, despite the fact it appears to be still intact, no pieces have fallen off, yet. As I watch worriedly, a sailor with what looks to be a long crowbar runs to the jet caught in the cable. Is he going to try and extract the injured pilot? I expect the fire, medical, and rescue crews to arrive soon, but they are nowhere to be seen. The sailor pries the arresting cable from off the jet's tail hook and another sailor in front of the A-4 gives the unlucky pilot the same "tail hook up" hand signal we use in the USAF,

To my amazement, the sailor in front of the jet commands the wrecked A-4 to taxi toward the front of the ship, the pilot must not be unconscious. The arresting cable is retracted, snaking across the deck like a skinny steel python. What is left of the Skyhawk somehow taxis forward under its own power and everyone's attention is focused on another set of nav lights approaching the ship on short final approach. The second landing is, if anything, more violent than the first, but again, no one is concerned but me. The second Skyhawk to crash on the aft deck taxis forward on the ship, again as if nothing is amiss. At this rate, the Hancock will soon be out of serviceable aircraft.

I slowly get the picture that these semi-controlled crashes are somehow normal. How can such a thing be? How can a machine built lightly enough to fly sustain the impacts that I am witnessing? How long do these jets last, a week? Skyhawk after Skyhawk arrives back on the Hancock in similarly violent fashion as the first two. Well, if these navy guys think this cruel display of aircraft abuse is normal, who am I to argue?

As I watch, an A-4 misses all four deck wires and continues on off the ship again. The landing zone is canted at an angle of about twenty degrees to the long axis of the ship; this very short runway leads off the left-hand side. The steel tail hook of the Skyhawk skips across the metal deck spraying sparks as the jet takes off again. I see now this is why the pilots ram their throttles home when they touch down. If they miss all the wires, they simply perform a touch-and-go and keep going. If they were to pull the throttles back before catching a cable and then miss them all, they would end up with the fishes before they could get the power back on. I'm used to pulling the power to idle at touchdown or before in my Phantom. I don't know if I could get the hang of this aircraft carrier landing technique or not.

Once the final crash, I mean landing, has been demonstrated, I find my way down below decks by following a returning pilot to the squadron ready room. This is a windowless, low-ceiling room, the shipboard home of the squadron I am supposed to smarten up. It is filled with chairs bolted to the floor ("deck") facing a low-rise briefing platform. The Squadron Operations Officer and the Squadron Duty

Officer each have desks along one wall. The squadron guys filter in after stowing their flight gear and debriefing the intelligence shop on the meager results of tonight's missions. They are swilling soft drinks and coffee. I decide not to tell them about the free mission booze the USAF provides us after every combat sortie.

I am eager to start discussing Paveway laser-guided bombs, but now is not the right time. First, everyone has to watch some television. There is a TV camera buried on the centerline of the flight deck facing back up the glide path. It tapes each landing and identifies each aircraft's tail number (which for some reason is painted on the nose) so each pilot can view his own landing in retrospect on the ship's TV channel. After watching the horrific landing impacts from the island, I am interested to see the deck's eye view of what must be the USN's greatest hits.

On the left ("port") side of the flight deck, near the touchdown zone, there is a perch for a junior officer called the Landing Signals Officer or LSO. The LSO talks to each pilot on the radio during his approach, coaching, encouraging, chiding, and being a general pain in the ass. He also grades each landing and the scores are recorded, superimposed on the TV tape. The LSO platform is located adjacent to the cabled touchdown area for a better view and also to ensure that if something goes dreadfully wrong, the LSO gets wiped out along with the errant pilot. This ensures dedication and concentration on the part of the LSO.

The pilots and the LSO watch all the landings on the VCR and comment on every one. This is serious stuff, with not much joking around. Obviously night carrier landings are a major preoccupation of the squadron's pilots. I keep my mouth shut for once and listen to the chatter in the crew room. I hope to get a feel for the atmosphere in the squadron before I try and communicate with VA-212's members about laser-guided bombs. All I hear are vivid accounts of the night's landings on the boat. There are no discussions of the missions, the bombing, the targets, the defenses, or of anything else but the landings.

I ask one of the A-4 guys, "'What did you hit tonight?"

He replies, "Oh, some night FAC found some trucks in Laos, but I couldn't work the target over. I had to salvo my bombs to get back to the ship with enough gas to make three passes at the deck if I had to."

He then went on to tell me all about his landing and wanted me to see it again on TV.

These warped navy jocks have turned fighter aviation on its head. A landing is merely something you do at the end of the flight. You can take pride in doing it well, but it is only a punctuation mark on the sentence of a combat sortie. In a USAF fighter squadron, no one discusses landings; they are assumed to have occurred safely. The focus is, as it should be, on accomplishing the combat portion of the mission, not on what happens just before you taxi back to the ramp. However, these A-4 drivers seem completely obsessed with their landings. Maybe the fierce deceleration produced by the short arresting cable has bruised their frontal lobes. Yeah, that's it. When their brains impact the forward bulkhead of their skulls, the mental image being processed, i.e., the carrier landing in progress, is implanted into their minds, erasing any combat results.

I decide that I won't bring up the subject of Paveways until I have had a chance to scope things out more. I also want the pilots to get over their obsession with getting back on the boat, so they can pay attention to what I intend to say.

I'm bunking with the XO, the Deputy Squadron Commander (not the brandy classification of the same name, XO); his roommate is on detached duty ashore in Saigon, probably teaching those guys how to land an airplane on a boat. I heard that US Navy ships are dry with no alcohol allowed. The rumors must be true; I haven't seen any booze. How can you debrief a flight without adult verbal lubrication? Surely this regulation left over from the Prohibition era Navy doesn't apply to us USAF types. So I have secreted a quart of Jack Daniel's in my duffel bag. I think I had better tell the XO about it. When I do, he thanks me politely and adds my offered bottle to the locked cupboard full of booze located in our room. We start in on one of the open bottles, drinking and discussing the differences between USAF and USN operations.

After several drinks, I'm feeling no pain and decide to turn in. I rack out in the upper bunk and fall asleep listening to the noises a giant warship makes in the night. About two hours later, the PA system comes on with an emergency notice that wakes me up.

"Fire in the number two paint locker,"' it says.

That sounds serious. Mentally I run through my options. The Chief said that in case of fire, I'm to fetch my life preserver and make my way to the flight deck. I have no idea how to get to the flight deck from where I'm sleeping and I'm not sure I could make it anyway after half a bottle of Jack Daniel's. I say to myself, "I can either die in bed or overboard in my life preserver with the sharks. The sailors are either going to put the fire out or they aren't. Either way, I can't help." So, I turn over and go back to sleep.

★★★

It's the next morning and I'm in Pri-Fly overlooking the huge deck and watching daytime flight operations. The takeoffs and landings are just as scary and violent as they were last night, but under the hazy tropical sky, operations seem less ominous than in the dark. The white foamy wake of the ship is now visible, stretching for miles behind the Hancock. The churned water gives the impression of a visual glide path indicator on the surface of the sea to guide returning aircraft.

The flight deck crews are scurrying around readying jets for launch, fueling them, loading them, and generally giving the impression of a parking lot/service station from Hell.

Suddenly the ever-present PA system barks loudly on the flight deck.

"Prepare to launch the BARCAP!"

The action below me, which was merely busy now becomes frantic. Two fully outfitted pilots sprint from the base of the island. They run toward two F-8 Crusaders parked out of the way, behind the island in the niche left by the angled landing zone.

I ask the guys around me what is going on and in between commands to the crewmen running about below they tell me what the term BARCAP means. There are always two Crusaders on alert duty, with fully loaded internal cannons and two Sidewinder missiles on each. Two pilots are at the ready at all times. If any bogey, or unidentified aircraft, appear to be headed for the ship, the F-8s are quickly launched to identify it and shoot it down if need be. The USN doesn't have enough aircraft to keep a MiG CAP constantly airborne, so they sit what we in the USAF call "strip alert." The Crusader jocks' goal is to be airborne in fifteen minutes or less. This is similar to how the USAF Air Defense Command operates, with interceptors on ten-minute alert status. The acronym stands for Barrier Combat Air Patrol, or BARCAP. The F-8s, once launched, will serve as an airborne barrier to prevent enemy air attack on the ship. I am also on the ship, high in the vulnerable island, so I think the BARCAP is an excellent idea. However, the scene I am watching below has its downside.

I think to myself, "This is just great. The MiGs are airborne and these navy guys are getting launched to intercept them. Meanwhile, I am stuck here on this floating airport hundreds of miles from my Phantom. If these two Crusader weenies come back with a MiG kill, I intend to throw up."

There is only one obstacle between the Crusaders and the MiGs. That is a gaggle of half a dozen ready A-4s on the flight deck blocking the F-8s from reaching the catapults waiting to launch them to possible glory. While the F-8s'engines whine into life, the sailors are working at a feverish pitch to clear a path for the BARCAP flight to taxi to the front of the ship. Yellow tractor tugs are towing jets out of the way, teams of sailors are pushing Skyhawks around by hand, bomb dollies are moved, everyone is turning to and clearing the deck. They are trying to launch the Crusaders immediately; if the F-8s get a kill, the whole ship will rejoice. I fully expect the frenetic crowd below to push several A-4s over the side to make more room, but in the time it takes the Crusader pilots to strap in and crank their engines, a narrow alley is cleared between the A-4s and the taxi path to the catapults is open, but just barely.

The pair of Crusaders is lashed to catapults, the safety pins are pulled off the Sidewinder missile launchers, the flight leader is given hand signals to go to full military power, and then to light his afterburner. However, in haste to get the two jets spotted forward and readied for flight, someone has forgotten to deploy the Jet Blast Deflector. The JBDs are Ping-Pong table-sized sheets of steel that fold up from the flight deck behind each jet on the catapult. Their purpose is to deflect skyward the supersonic blast from the jet engine of the aircraft about to be launched. This prevents the howling jet plume from cleaning off the deck behind the catapult of men, material, and other aircraft. However, the JBD has to retract to allow a plane to taxi over it to get to the catapult. Whoever is supposed to deploy the JBD up after the Crusader has passed over it is asleep at the switch.

Without the deflector up, the Crusader's afterburner torch is pointing directly at the Skyhawk just bumped from the number one position for takeoff. The A-4 is loaded with two drop tanks, six 500pound bombs, and a pilot. It was pushed off at an angle to the catapult, making way for the taxing pair of Crusaders. Once they passed his position, the A-4 pilot started to pull in behind the catapult to resume his mission once the F-8s are launched.

The Crusader's jet blast catches the Skyhawk under its right wing and picks up the smaller jet like a toy. The A-4 almost tips over, but its left wing tip touches the deck. For seconds that seem like hours, the little A-4 is balanced on its left main landing gear, nose gear, and left wing tip with the right wing sticking up in the air and the right main wheel off the deck.

At last, the deck crew notices the impending disaster and gives the Crusader pilot the cut signal, a finger drawn across the throat of the catapult launch officer beside the jet. The Crusader pilot cuts his engine to idle. The Skyhawk, no longer tipped in the air by the jet blast, slams back down on its three wheels.

Sheepishly, the remiss deck crew raises the JBD and the Crusader is given the signal to stoke his engine again. The BARCAP leader is launched followed shortly by his wingmen and they turn right, join up, and climb out, their J-57s still roaring in full afterburner, looking for MiGs.

Everyone, not the least me, breathes a sigh of relief that the A-4 victim of the afterburner plume didn't flip over, explode, or catch on fire. I'm sure that pilot will have something to talk about now in lieu of how tough his last landing was. To my amazement, the subject of all the concern is spotted on a catapult and launched as if nothing has happened. After seeing the little jet tipped up like a Tonka toy I wouldn't have walked under its wing, much less flown in it. I guess these navy guys consider their planes as commodities to be used up. Maybe the dangers of landing on a twenty-foot pitching deck at night swamp any concerns about structural integrity caused by being body-slammed by jet blast.

★★★

It is finally time to meet with my host squadron and discuss Paveway laser-guided bombs. Back in the ready room, a group of eight or ten pilots is gathered in one quarter. They are all from the same squadron, save one. This loner has a different set of patches on his faded navy flight suit, a different color T shirt on under it, and a different, pissed-off look on his face. The other guys seem friendly enough but this lieutenant looks as if he was forced marched to our meeting at gunpoint. He won't look at me or speak to the others.

My steel trap mind instantly gloms onto the fact that there is something going on here I don't understand. I mentally switch my mental communications mode from "transmit" to "receive" and ask the guys how they intend to use the laser-guided bombs. They guys are only too willing to fill me in.

During the long, boring transit across the Pacific, it dawned upon the A-4 squadron they needed lasers to guide laser-guided bombs. The lasers were waiting for them at Subic Bay. The USN procurement community purchased several handheld, battery-powered lasers, probably from the lowest bidder. These units are about the size of a shoe box, with a leather strap handle on each end and a thumb trigger. On top of the box is an optical sight with aiming crosshairs. The laser emanates from a lens in the center of the box.

The current plan is to use the ship's one and only two-seat jet, a TA-4J Skyhawk trainer, as the illumination aircraft. The two-man T-bird will guide the Paveways dropped by the single-seat birds. It is a plan of breathtaking naiveté.

My first thought is, "How can I get out of this scene and escape being tarred with the fallout from the inevitable debacle. These guys are going to sprinkle wild Paveways all across Southeast Asia like falling leaves."

The illuminators in the backseats of our big USAF Phantoms are firmly bolted to the aircraft and are motion damped, operated by a tiny joy-stick. The accuracy of a laser-guided bomb is dependent on the pointing accuracy of the laser. The bomb doesn't know where the target is, only where the laser spot on the ground is. If the laser illumination is off the target, that's where the bomb will hit. It is hard enough to hold the laser spot precisely on a small target from the backseat of a large, stable aircraft such as the Phantom, even with the laser hard-mounted to the canopy rail.

There is no way a little bouncy jet like the Skyhawk can fly a flight path smoothly enough for illumination. Secondly, the laser is going to be handheld by a human being, with no support or damping. The laser spot is going to be all over the place and so are the bombs. Paveway has the ability to average out pointing errors of a few feet, but not hundreds of yards.

While I am considering hurling myself into the sea in despair, the situation gets even worse. I am told that the laser will be held and aimed by a F-8 Crusader pilot! This is the guy with the shitty attitude sitting grumpily out on the fringes of the meeting.

In the US Navy, there is a rigid hierarchy, a pecking order for pilots. At the top of the pyramid are fighter pilots who fly the single-seat, single-engine Crusader. They are strictly dedicated to air-to-air combat. They drop no bombs; indeed, the F-8 is presently incapable of carrying any external stores other than Sidewinder missiles. They always fly alone; there is no two-seat version of the Crusader. The fighter pilots flying the two-seat, twin-engine Phantom occupy the next rung down on the ladder. Phantoms are switch-hitters; they perform air combat as well as drop bombs. The single-seat attack pilots flying single-seat Skyhawks as well as the A-7 Corsair come third on the prestige ladder, followed by two-seat attack pilots in the A6A Intruder and so forth on down to lowly helicopter pilots and transport drivers.

The status ladder on the Hancock has but two rungs. The ship carries only the Crusaders and the Skyhawks; there are no two-seat jets on board, except for the TA-4J trainer.

Someone in authority has decided that a single-seat fighter pilot from the Hancock's Crusader squadron will fly in the backseat of the A-4 trainer and help deliver bombs, even if they are laser-guided. This is akin to sending a heart surgeon to work in a leper colony.

Evidently, the 1950s era Crusader aircraft are old and are broken a lot, giving their pilots lots of free time. You can't fly prestige; you have to have a working jet. In the interests of efficient utilization of onboard personnel, some command genius has decided to make bombardiers out of pure fighter pilots.

Thinking hard, I see I have been dealt a losing hand. Technically, tactically, and personality-wise, this USN introduction of Paveway laser-guided bombs is doomed to failure. My viable options are few. I can pretend to be seasick and hang over the rail vomiting until they take me off of this wretched boat. I can tell the USN its cockamamie scheme will never work and be dismissed as a lunatic crank from the USAF, probably an undercover agent from the Pentagon after Navy funding. I can help them all I can and hope for the best while expecting the worst. Or, I can dream up another plan that might just work.

I am having a big problem with my personal ethics. I can't just walk away from this situation, that would be UNSAT and cowardly. I strongly believe the destiny of tactical ground attack lies with guided bombs; these devices are the wave of the future. The results I see produced by Paveways from our base in Thailand are magical. We are destroying targets with surgical accuracy and in relative safety. Despite the naysayers, the traditionalists, the macho techno-phobes, and particularly guided munitions' long history of failure, we are proving terminal guidance works and works exceedingly well. Besides providing reliable target destruction, guided bombs save pilots' lives. Using Paveways, we fly many fewer dangerous combat sorties and we can stand off from the enemy's lethal defenses when we do go in harm's way. What can I do to fix things here and still be able to walk into the Ubon Officers' Club bar with my head held high?

My personal best bet is to quickly brief these guys and then get the hell off the ship before they try this unworkable plan. However, a highly visible failure of the USN Paveway program, however ill conceived, will set the cause of precision guided munitions back by years. I am a true believer in this technology and I just can't let it fail. The scoffers are still out there in their legions and will pounce on an abortive USN Paveway program to turn back the clock to employment of only dumb bombs. The USN brass likes nothing more than returning to the storied days of yore. So, I can't disengage, walk away, and still face myself in the mirror. I have to come up with a plan. It has to be good and it has to be now. I decide to enlist the help of the guy with the most to lose besides me. Starting slowly, speaking clearly waving my hands, and using simple words, I explain the physics of laser guidance and the absolute need for illumination accuracy. I forecast that a number of wild, unguided bombs will go ballistic if dropped under the current plan. I take a guess at the accuracy of the ones that do guide. I drop the hint that when things predictably go astray, the navy brass will start asking questions as to why the USAF is able to succeed splendidly with Paveways and the USN can't get its act together. I get shocked, worried looks returned from all hands present. They have been led to believe that these laser-guided wonders somehow find their targets with little human intervention. The disgruntled Crusader pilot takes the bait, hook, line, and sinker. He flatly refuses to be an operator of such a jury-rigged system. He now clearly sees a way out of an unpleasant situation he wanted no part of to begin with. The fighter jock leaves the meeting heading for his own crew room on the double. Undoubtedly, he will tell his skipper that those A-4 idiots are setting him up to be the fall guy. He has no intention in taking the blame for a failure of the technical community, a mistake fueled by the childish Washington area, inside the beltway rivalry with the USAF.

The guys remaining in the meeting give a visible sigh of relief, not having to deal any more with the departed prima donna. I go on with the second part of my hastily concocted plan. Why not let the USAF do the target illumination? The Skyhawk guys can rendezvous with one of my squadron's Paveway illuminators over the target area. We will do the lasing; they will do the bombing. We know how to aim lasers. They already know how to bomb and no one in the USN will have to learn anything new. This plan meets with relieved approval. If the bombs miss, they can always blame the failures on us USAF weenies.

All I have to do now is to get back to Thailand and sell the idea to our brass. Getting back to Thailand is a good idea in itself; I am tired of sailing. I am ready to have a drink in public, to have my chow served by a pretty Thai waitress instead of some Pilipino guy named Steward, and to fly instead of watching other guys fly. But, I have learned a lot while boating.

An aircraft carrier isn't a normal ship. It is large enough to be considered a place that moves to other locales. Living on board one is like inhabiting a giant, noisy, smelly machine full of other people, all of them ugly males. My helmet is off to these USN types who put up with their shipboard lifestyle like monks with no feminine company. I do respect the men who land back on the carrier; that looks way difficult. However, I am more than ready for a good ol' civilized U.S. Air Force base.

★★★

Back in Thailand, my plan is dashed on the shoals of bureaucracy. Once the idea of USAF Phantoms illuminating for USN Skyhawks is proposed and considered, the staffers and paper pushers in Saigon think of a myriad of reasons why it won't work and none why it will. How will they schedule the sorties? The USAF command elements have no direct lines of communication with the USN schedulers. The two bureaucracies live on separate planets despite being committed to fighting the same war. The navy isn't about to adjust its flight schedule for any reason; it is dictated by the rhythm of shipboard operations. The USAF isn't going to fly at the whim of the USN either. Who will get credit for the targets destroyed, the USAF or the USN? When a grateful Congress hands out the annual funding checks, whom will they go to? What happens if a bomb misses? Whose fault will it be? Does the USN really want everyone in the Pentagon to think they need the USAF for success? This sort of joint operation has never been tried before, therefore it must be impossible. If it were a good idea, we would have been doing it all along, say the staffers who didn't get their jobs because they were the sharpest knives in the drawer. If some junior officer up-country in Thailand can come up with a new and effective way of operating, then HQ doesn't need as many staff drones.

Given the insurmountable obstacles, all of which are bureaucratic, none are operational, the USN's Paveway project has been quietly shelved until it can be reconstituted as an all-Navy show, with purpose-built illumination hardware that actually works. The Bad Guys breathe a sigh of relief.

★★★

I am sitting at the bar in the Ubon Officers' Club, sipping a legal Bourbon and water, in plain view. I am watching how the Thai barmaid's trim, shapely bottom seems to have been poured into her skintight dress, realizing I can see more like her and more of her at any time I so desire. You won't find a vision like that on a US Navy ship. I'm also trying to remember what my last landing was like, no one taped or graded it. It must have been a good one as I walked away from it, but I can't for the life of me remember how it went.

THERE'S NO BUSINESS LIKE SHOW BUSINESS

I'm running the Vietnam War. Actually, I'm temporarily running the base Command Post, the CP, and thus the local outpost in that war. For the next six hours, I will be the Wing Duty Officer, or "duty pig" as exalted the position is affectionately called by one and sundry.

The CP is a windowless room in Wing Headquarters equipped with three desks facing a large wall of backlit Plexiglas. On that transparent wall is posted the current twenty-four hour day flying schedule for the entire wing, all five squadrons of it. Each flight's details are listed; squadron, call sign, takeoff times, missions, ordnance, and tail numbers of the aircraft in the flight. The board also lists pertinent facts about the status of actions under way on the base itself as well as the posted security posture, the DEFCON state. I have two sergeants with me who keep the big board current and assist in liaison with the non-flying units on base. Direct phone lines run to each squadron; the Wing Commander, the emergency fire and rescue crews, the weather station, the control tower, and Seventh/Thirteenth Air Force HQ in Saigon. My job is to make sure the daily flying schedule is accomplished without any hitches and to see any emergencies that arise are dealt with.

If all goes as planned, which it never does, I will have little to do on my six-hour shift but to sit and watch it all happen. I'm really not commanding anything, as the folks charged with actually doing the work know what they are doing far better than I do. All I can do is coordinate, communicate, and make sure there are no obstacles to them doing it.

I am pulling this shift to prepare me for higher command. The USAF believes in relentless promotion. You are either promoted on a fixed, predictable schedule, you are retired, or you are kicked out of the service. The USAF prepares each officer as he or she progresses up the rank ladder to be the Commander, the Chief of Staff USAF although only one of us will be the Chief at a time. Another canon of USAF dogma is you cannot achieve higher rank solely by flying. Many a failed officer's professional epitaph reads, "All he ever did was fly airplanes." Theoretically, the mission of the US Air Force is to fly, fight, and win. If you specialize in doing just that, your career is doomed. To progress up the chain of command, you must learn how to prosper in a bureaucracy, which means accepting assignments which put you behind a desk at times. Judging from the quality of command decisions made by our senior leadership, quite a few of them have spent far too much time flying those desks.

To prepare each and every one of us to be the Chief, we are assigned what are called "additional duties." Some of these duties are really necessary like my present part-time job in the CP, but the utility of other assignments is questionable at best. My roommate's additional duty is to serve as the acting commander of the sentry dog unit on base. He has a couple of dozen airmen and their dogs reporting to him. When he isn't flying, he is at the dog kennel supervising patrols, training men and dogs, doing veterinary checks, feeding, and watching dog shit disposal. I envy him; his additional duty is more enjoyable than mine and he is dealing with highly trained dogs and their expert handlers. My roomie gets to work in a more realistic environment than I do in the CP. He deals with more honest people than I do in working with the folks at Air Force HQ in Saigon. His sons of bitches really are dogs. My counterparts are human SOBs in training.

My shift runs from midnight to six o'clock in the morning. Usually, the tedium is pronounced, but not tonight. There is to be a major, secret, undercover mission conducted early tomorrow and I intend to make myself an integral part of what is to transpire. I am working at full speed to set things up, to schedule the aircraft, the tankers, the ordnance, to coordinate, not with those twits in Saigon, but with the pros at the US Embassy in Bangkok.

I wolfed down the pizza I had delivered earlier from the Officers' Club and set the greasy box on top of the Top Secret Rules of Engagement loose leaf notebook at the end of my desk. The ROEs govern everything we do at the war, who and what we can bomb and shoot down, and how we are to do it and not do it. The red-covered book is the CP bible. I personally sign for it when I come on duty and sign it off to my relief officer when I leave. Compromising the ROEs or giving the Bad Guys access to the Rules could seriously harm the war effort and could get more guys killed than currently predicted. I have to keep in mind the directives the ROE book contains as I plan and staff the extraordinary sortie I am putting on the big board for mid-morning next.

This secret two-ship sortie will be assigned to provide MiG CAP for a special mission aircraft flying up to Ubon from Bangkok. The passengers on that C-130 Herky Bird are to be safeguarded at all costs; no harm is to come to them. The flight schedule of the C-130 is classified Secret; the mission doesn't appear on my scheduling board, nor is it on the official daily flight orders from Saigon. There are perhaps a dozen folks on base, including me, who know when and where this aircraft is to appear and why. The Bob Hope show is coming to our base.

Everyone concerned, presumably including the Bad Guys, knows that losing this particular C-130 would be a devastating blow to American morale. Bob Hope is an American icon. He has entertained our troops since WWII. He was in Korea during the war there. Bob has traveled the globe to the far reaches of US Armed Forces deployments to put on his shows, usually around Christmastime.

If the North Vietnamese were able to enlist the support of the Communist Thais, known as the CTs, to mount a sapper attack on the base during the show, carnage could result among the assembled troops. If the North Vietnamese Air

Force were to fly south on a one-way mission to Thailand and shoot down the C-130, the propaganda and morale victory would be worth whatever it cost them. The North Vietnamese Air Force has never ventured over Thailand, but you never know what they might do. The dangers of an enemy appearance in Thailand pale in comparison to the risk at other venues where Hope's troupe performs, but the US Ambassador to Thailand is taking no chances whatsoever. He wants air cover, a MiG CAP, over the C-130 at all times.

My present CP challenge is to generate two additional sorties that are either off the books completely or not what they appear to be as listed on the schedule. I can't change the daily combat orders; Saigon won't stand for that. Ever mindful of the rabid stateside press, they are somehow afraid of a possible headline in the Washington Post, *"USAF Cancels Vital War Mission to Escort Hollywood Stars,"* The fact that 90 percent of the American public would applaud such a precautionary move escapes our leadership. Our generals' lack of understanding of the popularity of Bob Hope is indicative of their disconnect from US public sentiment about the war and of much else. I also sense a bureaucratic turf battle between the mandarins of Seventh/Thirteenth HQ and the U.S. Embassy in Thailand. The USAF, part of the Department of Defense, feels that it is its job to allocate fighter assets and not that of the U.S. Embassy, which of course is part of the State Department. But never mind, it is my intention to make both organizations happy and shine my own young ass as well.

I can't just schedule a dedicated sortie to do the job; the Thais are leery and understandably so, of us flying combat sorties operating only over Thailand. They feel the air defense of the Kingdom of Thailand is the job of the Royal Thai Air Force and they're right. However, both the Ambassador and the Wing Commander want Bob Hope to be escorted by Americans, not Thais. Also, the ROEs prohibit flying such a sortie or, to be more precise, inhibit planning and scheduling such a sortie.

As is usual, when a hot potato is tossed, it is a junior officer that gets assigned to catch it. That would be me. If this operation gets screwed up, the powers that be will sacrifice me like a voodoo chicken and continue on with their own careers. I sure hope the US Ambassador doesn't find out that the action officer on the Bob Hope MiG CAP project is the same guy who wiped out the Chinese cultural center in northern Laos. That flap is still blowing over.

The sergeant sitting beside me is in on the plan. He has found two jets that aren't committed to the morning schedule. I instruct him to have them loaded with dumb bombs for a cover mission as well as the necessary air-to-air missiles and to prepare the two Phantoms for an 0800 takeoff.

I call Saigon on the secure land line phone and tell them that I have generated two extra combat softies for next morning's combat action. I go on to say that as I am not allowed to schedule an airborne tanker, the flight will have to be un-refueled and work near the base in southern Laos. I am allowed to add to the daily flying schedule, all the better to fly more sorties than the US Navy, but not to subtract from it. Saigon is pleased that I am trying extra hard to win the war and will order a Forward Air Controller (FAC), whose call sign is "Nail," to work with us in southern Laos. They can't reassign a tanker over Thailand either, all that is done from Strategic Air Command HQ back in Nebraska. I suspect the Duty Officer in Saigon knows what I am up to, but I don't reveal my plan and thereby save him the embarrassment of telling me not to do it.

So far, I have two jets with ordnance, a FAC, and a slot on the schedule. Now I need a tanker. I can't count on those Hollywood types in the Bob Hope show to show up at the air base in Bangkok for the C-130's planned takeoff time. Entertainers take great personnel pride in not hewing to a precise military schedule. My "unofficial" MiG CAP needs to have enough flight time and gas to meet the C-130 whenever it leaves Bangkok.

I call the C-130 base farther up north, the home of the Airborne Command Post aircraft, "Alley Cat" (at night) and

"Cricket" (in the daytime). My ol' buddy Bruce is flying tonight, so I speak to his counterpart who is planning the daytime missions. He knows what is going down. The crew of Cricket in their role as the USAF airborne commander in Thailand will need to follow Hope's flight on the radio as it progresses. But the RoE's inhibit candor. I tell the Cricket guy that I will have a nonscheduled MiG CAP flight airborne tomorrow morning available for "special assignment" but the planes will need some gas. There is always extra jet fuel in some tanker somewhere.

All I need now is two crews. I call the desk officer at my squadron and tell him we are adding two sorties for tomorrow morning. I can sense his doubts over the phone, but I don't explain. I tell him to call the squadron officers' quarters and find three guys sober enough to fly tomorrow morning who aren't already on the flying schedule. He is to tell them to report at 0530 hours. He asks who will lead the flight. That would be me again. If I'm going to spend all night pulling strings to provide air cover for Bob Hope, I'm going to see the action up close and personal.

Only guys who are in on the plan know what is up with the planned show. Them and the whole base, that is. For three days, the civil engineering squadron and their Thai carpenters have been constructing a stage and setting up sound equipment in an open area on base. Everyone knows that Bob Hope and his entertainers are in the war zone and that a huge open air stage is under construction. This is the worst kept secret in the history of the war. I sure hope none of those Thai carpenters are CTs, it wouldn't take much subterfuge to stash a remote controlled satchel charge under the stage.

★★★

I get off duty at 0600 hours and I leave the CP with a wave to my relief after clearing away the mess of the night's action. The incoming duty pig also knows what is about to happen. The squadron desk officer has scheduled another pilot, call sign "Animal," to fly on my wing as Satan Two. Two navigators to work the rear cockpits of the Phantoms are also on tap. Their job will be to find the precious C-130 with our jets' radars and vector us in to a safe intercept.

We are briefing the flight at the squadron when I tell them what our real mission is to be today. I get three smiles in return; this is going to be fun. Suddenly the Duty Sergeant from the CP bursts into the briefing room without knocking. He is breathing hard and blurts out,

"Captain Cobleigh, you need to come to the CP on the double."

I reply that I am briefing a combat sortie and ask if this can wait.

He says, "No sir, the Duty Officer needs you right now, before he calls the Old Man and the Air Police."

That news gets my attention. I ask Animal to finish the briefing and say I will meet them at the aircraft in time to crank engines, if I'm not in jail. As I hurry to the CP, I ask myself, "'What could have gone wrong? Did someone in Saigon catch on and get cold feet? Has the C-130 flight been canceled or delayed? Did Cricket not find a tanker? Is the Ambassador wise to who is setting this special MiG CAP mission up? Has the U.S. Embassy in Bangkok declared war on USAF HQ in Saigon? None of the possible answers to those questions would have generated the panicked look on the sergeant's face or caused his lack of observance of military protocol. This must be really serious.

I punch in the combination on the cipher-locked door of the CP and enter. The Duty Officer, another captain, looks at me in panic, his face as white as a sheet. Has thermonuclear war broken out? He barks at me with the desperation of a man who is seeing his career go up in smoke.

"Where is the RoE book?"

I look quickly and discover it is not on the end of the desk where it should be. I am supposed to inventory the Top Secret book when I leave and sign a form stating that I did so. The incoming Duty Officer is to perform his own check, certifying that he is receiving the RoE book and is to sign the same form.

We have done none of this. I was in such a hurry to get to my flight briefing and the incoming guy had another separate crisis to deal with. Somehow in the chaos the crucial document has disappeared.

This is a court martial offense. "Top Secret" is the highest category of classification specified by the U.S. government. Misplacing the RoE book will certainly end my career with a dishonorable discharge and a large fine. If the book is lost or compromised, it means big trouble for all concerned. If the CTs and/or the North Vietnamese are thought to have had access to it, we all are looking at jail time in Leavenworth federal prison, making little ones out of big ones with sledgehammers.

The sergeant says, "We have to call the Air Police and the Old Man."

If he does, we all won't believe the shit storm that will instantly descend. I council caution.

"Let's all calm down and think. It has to be here somewhere. When did you last see it?"

The Duty Officer stammers that it wasn't on the desk when he finally got around to doing his inventory; he hasn't seen it since he arrived at 0600 hours.

I tell them, "It was here all night, right under the pizza box."

We all look at each other with the insight of a blinding flash of the obvious.

I ask, "When did the trash get set out?"

The sergeant tells me, "I put the trash bag out for the houseboy about 0630."

The Thai janitor/houseboy is of course not allowed in the CP, he picks up the bag of trash outside the security door.

Quickly, I probe further, "What does he do with it?"

The sergeant tells us that the houseboy dumps the trash in a large bin in the rear of the building where the Thai garbage guys pick it up and take it to the off-base dump.

I ask the Sixty-four Million Baht Question, "When do the garbage guys come?"

The sergeant doesn't know. As one man we sprint out the back door and find the open trash bin. Like people possessed by demons, we tear through the smelly mess with our bare hands. In a few frenzied seconds the sergeant finds the heavy brown paper trash bag from the CP and rips it open. Like a demented pearl diver, I plunge my hands and head into the sack. There, stuck to the bottom of a pizza box by melted mozzarella cheese is the most sensitive document possessed by U.S. Air Force in Thailand.

We instinctively look around to see if anyone has seen us poring through the trash bin. All's clear, and we take a deep breath. I scrape the glutinous white cheese off the book's red cover with my fingernails as we sheepishly try to nonchalantly stroll back into the CP as if nothing has happened. Once behind the locked door, we look at each other and silently ask, "Now what do we do?"

We are obliged to report any possible compromise of the RoEs. We are supposed to notify the security troops immediately if the book goes missing at any time. Official regulations dictate that if any un-cleared person, such as the Thai houseboy, ever has access to the document, a formal investigation must be launched. If any of this is discovered by the command authorities, they will take into account our failure to perform the required inventory in a timely manner. The whole caper will undoubtedly result in severe disciplinary action against the whole, sorry lot of us.

I look at the sergeant and the Duty Officer, "Sarge, was the garbage bag still tied closed when you found it?"

He confirms that it was, tightly.

I go on, "Then the houseboy couldn't have seen the RoE book, could he?"

The duty officer agrees. I reckon out loud that given the dangers inherent in flying daily combat, we will probably all be dead before any investigation can be conducted and concluded. That gets a laugh and I gently place the RoE book back in its accustomed place on the desk and tell the still-stunned pair that I have a takeoff time to meet. We all look at each other and turn to examine in great detail the floor of the CP as if we have never seen it before.

I am just able to meet Animal and the two navigators at the jets with my flight gear in time to pre-flight my F-4D Phantom. We take off, join up, and cruise east to Southern Laos; the flight is unremarkable and relaxing. It is calming to perform long-practiced routines in the cockpit and to forget about the near miss with disaster back at the base CP.

Satan flight arrives overhead the proposed target area on time and I contact the Nail FAC flying far below us in his OV-10 prop-driven bug smasher. On the radio he sounds happy to see us and to have extra, unplanned bombing support. He gives us the target area briefing and tells us he thinks there is a North Vietnamese truck convoy parked in a dense stretch of jungle alongside a dirt road. But, he isn't sure of the exact location of the convoy.

Nail's plan is to probe the green canopy of jungle trees with bombs, gradually stripping away the foliage with single explosions until the exact location of the trucks can be seen and they can be hit in force. He knows we each have twelve 500-pound bombs. I can sense from his voice on the radio he is going to enjoy watching this as we make pass after pass dropping one bomb each time until we hit pay dirt. The Nail isn't clued in on the real mission of Satan Flight.

The Nail finishes his radio briefing with, "Satan, how much time on target do you have?"

I reply, "We can give you one pass."

Without even a radio transmission, I can hear him thinking. "What's with these F-4 guys? I know they've just taken off with a full fuel load, we're near their home base, there is no ground fire, and they can only afford one pass?"

Resignation is apparent in Nail's voice as he accedes to our plan. The FAC launches a white phosphorous smoke rocket as a marker and tells us to hit the tree line on the other side of the trail from the smoke. I feel badly about cheating the FAC out of his expected success and I vow to put all twelve bombs right where he wants them.

Flying hard, I bear down even more than usual to achieve the planned dive bomb parameters in order to accurately deliver the twelve bombs to the point where Nail thinks the trucks are hidden. At forty-five degrees of dive, 450 knots and 7,500 feet above the ground, my navigator calls, "Pickle," and I salvo the bombs. I feel the jet leap upward, released from 6,000 pounds of cast steel and high explosives as the bombs fall away. I feed in the Gs with the control stick until the nose is well above the horizon, turn left, and look back over my shoulder. I see twelve instant brown mushrooms of dirt and smoke growing in a ragged line along the targeted tree line. For once, I have made good on a dumb bomb dive delivery.

Half a minute later, Animal's bombs splash through the green trees parallel to where mine hit but fifty to a hundred yards farther along the brown dirt road. I see the angry red flashes as his ordnance detonates and I take pride in Satan Flight's bombing accuracy. Despite being in a god-awful hurry we have put the ordnance right on target.

As I watch from on high, explosions continue in the Laotian jungle far below. These aren't bomb splashes, but secondary explosions caused by our bombs as the parked trucks ignite and burn. The black smoke of burning petroleum billows from individual trucks and merges into an angry cloud above the road. The truck park was hidden in the jungle just where the Nail suspected. Our bombs have set off a firestorm of burning trucks, torched fuel tanks, blazing supplies, and exploding ammunition. Everything that goes up in smoke here in Laos won't be used later at our troops in South Vietnam.

The Nail goes crazy on the radio, bursting with achievement and job satisfaction. His day is made. He thanks us for the good bombing as we climb out westward toward the Thai border. Normally we would stick around and admire our work, but we'll leave that to the Nail. I make a mental note to call the Nail pilot on the land line and explain our haste. Now, we have to find that bootleg tanker that Cricket has promised. We contact Cricket as we enter Thai airspace still climbing and throttle back to save fuel. Cricket gives us the tanker call sign and approximate location. It seems that a scheduled strike flight hasn't shown up, which is not uncommon, and this tanker has extra fuel to give away. Before we leave Cricket's radio frequency the controller working our flight, who obviously knows what we are up to, transmits to us a time-honored salutation.

"Satan Flight, you are cleared to tanker frequency. Good luck and good hunting."

The sarcasm fills my earphones; Cricket is telling us to watch out for those short-range MiGs between Bangkok and our base, hundreds of miles from North Vietnam.

My navigator finds the tanker on our radar and vectors us to a rendezvous. Animal and I top off our fuel tanks and I contact Lion radar on the air defense frequency. The Bob Hope C-130 is using the same call sign as the C-130 mail planes, "Klong," to confuse the Bad Guys. I ask for the status of Klong and am told that it hasn't left Bangkok's Don Muang Royal Thai Air Force Base yet. We are all dressed up with nowhere to go.

All we can do is wait. Animal and I hang on the tanker, flying loose formation as the KC-135 orbits over central Thailand. Our jets occasionally take sips of gas like enormous brown/green hummingbirds at a backyard feeder as we await our chance to break into show business.

Finally, Lion relays that the Klong is airborne. I thank the tanker crew for the bootleg fuel and turn to the vectored direction given by Lion to us as Animal joins up on my right wing. A few minutes later, both navigators acquire and lock on to the precious C-130 and we complete the intercept on our own radars. I pick up the Herky Bird visually about 10,000 feet below us, headed northeast. As we descend and turn in behind the Klong, Lion confirms there are no unidentified aircraft anywhere in northern Thailand. The skies are clean.

I transmit to Animal, "Satan Two, confirm missiles safe."

Animal replies, "Roger that."

Animal's annoyance at my reminder to deactivate his missiles is obvious on the radio, but we can't screw this up. I double-checked and made sure my own air-to-air missiles are totally safe, not armed, while directing Animal to do the same. Shooting down the Bob Hope show by mistake would be a worse career move than either losing the RoE book or trashing the Chinese cultural center. We would get a reserved seat in "Ol' Sparky" the electric chair for that foul-up and we would deserve it.

Satan Flight rolls out two miles behind the lumbering Klong and I contact the pilot on another radio frequency. I tell him that his MiG CAP flight is on the case two miles in trail and he need fear not the North Vietnamese Air Force. The Klong driver asks if we can make a slow pass by his turbo-prop aircraft so the distinguished passengers can see who is sweeping the skies for them.

I agree, but I have no idea how fast a C-130 flies at medium altitude, or rather how slowly. I pull the throttles back to slow down and my airspeed indicator stabilizes at 250 knots or about 300 miles per hour. The guy in the rear cockpit of my jet says his radar reads that we have 25 knots of overtake; that sounds about right. Flying at 250 knots gives me the creeps. I feel like a big sitting duck in the sky, even if these Thai skies are friendly. I am used to a minimum of 400 knots or faster when I can get it. With Animal on my right wing, we close on the C-130's right wing and I see the four big propellers thrashing their way through the Thai airspace. I rock my wings twice and Animal tucks his jet into closer proximity to mine and flies pretty parade formation as we slowly slide by the Klong's wing tip. The C-130 pilot compliments us on our tight formation as we accelerate ahead with more power to circle to the left around behind the Klong again.

The Klong pilot says Bob Hope's film crew, the guys who are recording the tour for the Bob Hope Christmas Special on state- side television, wants us to fly formation on the Klong for some stage-setting shots. They are setting up their camera on the flight deck of the C-130 to film from the cockpit. The C-130 guy asks us if we want to be on TV. Do we? This is our big chance to get discovered. Naturally I adjust the cockpit's rearview mirror with my left hand to check out my appearance as we roll out once more behind the Klong. What I see would scare little kids. No humanity is visible, only my hard, camouflaged helmet, my bug-eyed, mirrored visor, and my oxygen mask covers my face like a proboscis. Instead of a movie star, I look like a giant insect. It occurs to me that in every flying movie I have ever seen, and I have seen them all, stars such as John Wayne (*Jet Pilot* with Janet Leigh), or George C. Scott (*Not With My Wife, You Don't* with Virna Lisi), or William Holden (*The Bridges at Toko-Ri* with Grace Kelly) all fly with their visors up and their oxygen masks dangling loose. I assume this is to let the cameras record them acting. No real pilot flies like that. Without a visor, the high altitude glare would blind me and my microphone would pick up all the cockpit noise, of which there is plenty. I think about sliding my visor back and unhooking my mask on one side, but better judgment overcomes me and I leave them both in place. I would never escape the kidding that I would get from Animal and the guys about "going Hollywood." Besides, I don' have a matchstick to chew on like George C. Scott.

As we close again on the C-130, I reduce the power even more until we have matched airspeeds, enabling me to fly close formation on the Herky Bird's right wing. I can make out the camera crew in the cockpit of Klong, filming from the copilot's seat.

At 20,000 feet, we are above a layer of evenly scattered, small puffy clouds, like cotton balls in the sky over Thailand. In the States, these are called "summertime cumulus clouds." It's always summer in Thailand; I wonder what they call them here. Whatever their local name, the clouds accent the flat green rice fields of central Thailand far below. It is a good day for cinema photography with picturesque backgrounds .

In the tiny circular windows of the cargo plane I can see faces of what seem to be round-eyed American women looking out at our two fearsome war machines flying just outside. They are peering at us strangely clad Phantom aircrews. At least I think these are American women, it's been so long since I've seen one, I question my visual identification skills. I wonder if these Hollywood ladies expected to see us looking like John Wayne et al, as they did in the cockpits of all those movies.

Flying close formation on a C-130 is hard work. The transport cruises at 230 knots. That is the optimum wrong airspeed for a Phantom. Any faster and I would have more control authority. Any slower and I could put down the flaps for more low-speed responsiveness. At 230 knots, I have to make large control deflections to move the jet small amounts. I also have to stay out of the prop wash churned up by the big engines of the C-130. Also, at this leisurely airspeed, the engines don't respond to commands quickly and I have to constantly jockey the throttles up and back. . My navigator tells me it looks like I am killing snakes in the cockpit with the control stick.

I tell him, "Shut up, this is show business."

Animal is having it even rougher than I do; he has to fly formation on me while I bounce and wallow around on the wing of the Klong. Finally, I get the hang of it and settle down, flying some semblance of a stable position. Animal and I are able to float nearly motionless off the right wing of Bob Hope's plane. The C-130 pilot comes on the air and tells me that the camera crew thinks this is too boring and could we please do something exciting. Do something exciting! What I'm trying not to do is stall, spin, crash, and burn in the rice paddies below. Would they like to capture that on film?

I tell Animal to light his afterburners and do a split S. He departs as ordered, probably glad not to have to fly my wing for a while. I count to three and shove both throttles all the way forward. I feel the kick on my butt as the afterburners light and I roll the jet slowly (to the right, away from the C-130, not into it) inverted. As soon as I am exactly upside down, I pull the nose down with as many Gs as 230 knots and gravity can provide. When the nose comes through vertical, pointed straight down, I pick up Animal's jet below me and tell him to turn left to join up once again. That maneuver should have looked really cool from the C-130. I hope the film crew got it. It will probably end up on the cutting room floor with all my other best scenes.

We escort the Klong all the way to our base and it lands unmolested. Animal and I touch down shortly afterward and head straight to the hooch. we have to get some sleep before the big show tonight.

I am standing in a field that was populated primarily by water buffaloes a week ago. Now, every GI that isn't actually flying or guarding the base is here. Several thousand guys and a precious few American girls are watching the jury-rigged stage intently for the debut of the Bob Hope show. The enlisted people got first dibs on the places near the stage, which is only right; they are down front with us officers standing in the rear. I can't help but think as I wait about another show put on for American servicemen by the USO, the United Services Organization. The USO is a nonprofit group that organizes these morale-building live shows.

Recently, I was out sailing on a U.S. Navy aircraft carrier off the coast of North Vietnam. I was on board to instruct naval aviators how to drop laser-guided bombs. After duty hours, the pilots gathered in the ready room to swap what they called "sea stories" and they told me a doozie. The ship was abuzz with talk about a USO show recently held on board. It took place on a temporary stage built in the cavernous covered hanger deck. The U.S. Navy guys were only too happy to tell me in excruciating detail what they had seen.

Redheaded singer, dancer, actress, and patriot Ann-Margret and her backup band were there to perform for the troops. Ann-Margret jumped into her musical show wearing a frilly white long sleeved blouse, sprayed-on black slacks, and high heels. Evidently she was a big hit with the sailors (why wouldn't she be?) and as her performance progressed, she began taking requests for songs.

The audience got more and more enthusiastic, louder and louder in its approval. Ann-Margret got into the excitement of the moment, big-time. She was obviously turned on by the strong emotional response she was getting from her homesick audience and she worked harder and harder to please the adoring crowd and to grant their shouted requests.

One request led to another. First, she unzipped her skintight pants; that got a big cheer. A song or two later, she peeled off those black slacks, stepping out of them on stage. This unexpected strip show was enormously popular with the crazed sailors. After a few more songs, she used the palms of her hands to slide her panties down to her ankles, revealing to 3,000 sailors that she is a true redhead. Finally, Ann-Margret high-kicked her lacey undies off into the frenzied crowd. This impromptu act of ultimate feminine exposure on the raised stage met with even greater approval (again, why wouldn't it?). Ann-Margret danced, pranced, and sang her final musical numbers wearing nothing but her girly white blouse and high heels. As she left the stage wrapped in an official USN blanket, she told the nearly hysterical sailors that she wanted them to remember what they were fighting for. The word-of-mouth publicity and the amateur nude photos taken at the show couldn't have done her reputation any good, but now she has at least 3,000 more converted fans. I'm not sure this sea story is true in its entirety, but sure I hope it is.

On the ship, the navy flyers and I spent hours discussing how Ann-Margret thanked the sailors for their wartime sacrifices by taking nearly all her clothes off. We compared Ann's unselfish, if immodest, act with Jane Fonda's widely publicized trip to North Vietnam. There, Ms. Fonda encouraged the Bad Guys to kill more of us Americans. I wonder if Jane stripped for the North Vietnamese anti-aircraft gun crew she posed for pictures with.

Straight-laced Bob Hope won't stand for anything like impromptu female celebrity nudity tonight, particularly with a TV film crew on hand, but one can always dream.

To strong applause, Bob comes out on stage carrying a golf club and the show begins. His opening monologue features jokes from the Roosevelt administration, Teddy Roosevelt. Les Brown and His Band of Renown provide the musical background. Who dug up these fossils? They must have played at the Warren G. Harding inaugural ball.

Featured singer/dancer Lola Falana has more energy than talent. Her best assets stretch her white satin jumpsuit almost, but not quite to, the breaking point. She is backed up by a girl dance troupe called the "Gold Diggers" whom no one has ever heard of either.

The show features a corn ball comedy skit featuring Bob, the curvy, current Miss World, along with our very own Wing Commander. It is not a triumph for the Hollywood entertainment industry. About half the audience is one-third the age of the star and most have never heard any of the songs, but have heard all the jokes.

None of this matters one iota. The show is a howling success. Every hoary joke is a laugh riot. Each oldie song gets feet tapping and hands clapping. The girls in the show are ogled with laser focus. The production numbers go over big. The Wing Commander's skit with the blond beauty queen and Bob is a hit; the Old Man gets a standing ovation from the crowd. Even without a half-nude Ann-Margret, it is a show to remember. Regardless of the caliber of the entertainment, it is the thought that counts.

I don't know which is funnier, Bob's corny jokes or watching my squadron mates laugh at them. Each guy is going to great lengths to appear cool and not reveal just how much he is enjoying the show.

The audience is thrilled that a big Hollywood name like Bob Hope has come to our base on the northeast frontier of Thailand. Every GI knows that Bob entertained their soldier fathers in Korea and probably their grandfathers in WWII. Having seen this show biz legend in person puts an official stamp of legitimacy on our efforts in this miserable war.

There are two highlights of the show, each very different from the other. The first occurs after the comedy skit when the voluptuous Miss World takes a deep bow in a ball gown that seems precariously low cut, even viewed from my remote vantage point. No one here thinks it weird to see an international beauty queen in a clingy formal dress display most of her figure in a Thai water buffalo field. Bountiful cleavage is never out of line. If anyone thinks so, they forgo any doubts when she bends way, way over to take a bow. Two of her qualifications for her title are obvious and are almost on full display. Bob makes her straighten up, to loud boos from the crowd, the instant before she falls out of her dress. The second highlight happens when astronaut Neil Armstrong, the first man on the moon, is introduced to say a few words.

The rowdy crowd goes silent as Armstrong, without a prepared speech, expresses his sincere appreciation to all of us for what we are doing here. His unpolished monologue is all about us, not about him or his moon landing. It's about how proud he is of the folks surrounding the stage. Despite his readily apparent shyness, Armstrong comes across as articulate, intelligent, and patriotic.

Most of us fighter jocks consider those NASA civilian test pilot guys to be overly analytical pussies. However, a guy who strapped himself on top of a zillion pounds of explosive rocket fuel and flew a hand-built experimental spacecraft to the moon and back really gets our attention and respect. Having a real American hero like Neil Armstrong pay his respects to the airmen and enlisted guys brings a damp moistness to more than a few eyes, including mine.

Is this a great country or what (assuming that a water buffalo field in northeast Thailand can be considered for a few hours to be part of the USA) Where else could an elderly comic, a curvy bombshell, and the first man on the moon appear on the same stage and be revered as folk heroes?

The show breaks up and we all drift back to our quarters. My debut in show business is "in the can" until Bob Hope's Christmas TV show is aired back home. Tomorrow is another night and I'm back in the sewer.

TEST HOP

To record the flight time, I punch the stopwatch stem on the instrument panel; it's time to clock in at the job site. Release the brakes, shove the big throttles forward into afterburner, hold down the nose wheel steering button, pull the stick full back, and we're rolling. The Phantom, which was straining nose down under full military power against the brakes, leaps forward, eager to be shed of the ground.

The twin afterburners torch off with a thump and a kick in the ass, thrust is reporting for duty, a quick check of the exhaust nozzle gages, both full open, no warning lights. Speed is building quickly now as the two J-79 engines howl, blue afterburner plumes blasting the runway behind, pushing the F-4, lightweight for once, into the sky. One hundred knots, release the nose wheel steering, the rudder is effective now keeping us straight down the rapidly disappearing concrete. The runway is passing under the jet much faster now, the flat scenery alongside the strip is a green blur.

At 150 knots, the nose starts to rise, lift is overcoming gravity, stop it at ten degrees above the horizon until we lift off, which follows immediately, vibration from the wheels ceases. Slap the long landing gear handle up, retract the flaps with the small yellow lever on the left cockpit wall. The nose wants to keep climbing, stop it with forward stick and run the pitch trim nose down. Hold the big jet down over the runway, one hundred feet sounds about right, as the speed continues to build relentlessly.

The departure end runway flashes under the nose, followed in an instant by the airfield boundary, then the perimeter fence. Still more nose down trim needed to comfortably hold the nose steady, it wants to pitch up. 400 knots, 425, 450, time to go upstairs.

I let the stubborn nose climb past the dusty horizon and keep it coming up, up, up, I'm more letting it do what it wants than using back stick. Forty-Five degrees of pitch, sixty, then ninety, we're going straight up, Jack's and my weight is transferred from our asses on the ejection seat cushions to our spines on the metal seat backs. The Phantom climbs like a homesick angel, a brown and green angel that is, with fire spurting out of his/her ass.

Jack and I are off on a test hop, a Functional Check Flight, a FCF. FCFs are required whenever any heavy maintenance is done on the aircraft such as an engine change. FCFs are flown with a totally clean aircraft, no drop tanks, no missiles, no ECM pods, no wing pylons; the underside of the jet is as smooth as baby's butt. After flight after flight lugging iron to Laos and North Vietnam, flying a lighter, cleaner Phantom is a rare treat. We are limited to one combat mission a day, but we can fly FCFs over Thailand without restrictions. As the squadron FCF pilot, I fly these joy rides whenever I can.

I stood the Phantom on its tail and departed the airfield straight up. Why? Why does a dog lick his balls? Because he can. All FCF pilots perform the same spectacular departure because it's fun, but also to show off the Phantom's performance to the ground crewmen; it's an time-honored tradition. The crew chiefs, maintenance troops, aircraft mechanics, aka the Phantom Phixers, work long hours in the blistering Thai sun, in the monsoon rains, day and night. They see their jets depart loaded with ordnance and headed northeast. An hour or two or three later the same aircraft return, the ordnance gone and often something on the planes is broken, or shot up, which has to be fixed, by them. They seldom get to experience just what their precious charges can do, to see the Phantom really perform. Hence the vertical climb out.

Out of sight of the field, I lower the nose to a more sustainable climb angle, afterburners still at full blast, and continue climbing, turning westward, then south to stay in Thai airspace. Jack hasn't said much, as usual. He likes to fly these FCFs although there isn't much for a navigator to do, because he, like I do, enjoys having a jet to screw around with. Once we have determined the maintenance has been done correctly, that the jet isn't going to come unglued, we can use up the remaining fuel however we want. But today he seemed reluctant to come along. Jack is a hard guy to read; he packs a tight suitcase. He craves excitement, maybe a daring airplane ride to the edge of space will improve his mood.

20,000 feet comes quickly, then 30,000. The air gets much thinner the higher we go and the rate of climb slackens; less lift, less thrust. I have to lower the nose to maintain airspeed. 40,000 feet, maximum altitude for most commercial aircraft. 45,000, tops for the propeller-driven fighters of WWII and the SabreJets of the Korean War. 50,000 feet and I level out to gain some more speed. It's the maximum altitude we are allowed to fly without wearing full pressure suits like the one Neil Armstrong wore on the Moon, only without the gray, grimy moon dust.

Time for a quick look around. With all due respect to Rod Serling, Jack and I are in the twilight zone. Above us, the sky is a deep, dark blue, a more intense blue that anyone on the surface of the Earth has ever seen, starting its transition to the inky black of space. Below, the ever-present rice straw smoke obscures any discernible features of the flat plains of Northeast Thailand. There are no clouds, only a bottomless, brown haze. Serling's twilight zone was in the sunlit ocean, out of sight of both the surface and the sea bottom. Ours is much bigger, but the sensation is the same, total isolation. Out on the far-distant horizon, where the haze meets the blue, I think I can make out the curvature of the Earth, although I can't really.

Einstein said all speed is relative. He was right. With no clouds to fly past, no visual contact with any recognizable surface features, no other aircraft, we are up here all alone and there is no sensation of speed. The cockpit noise is constant, the engines continue to howl, the throttles haven't moved from full afterburner since brake release three minutes ago. We seem suspended motionless in the space/time continuum. Only the increasing mach meter read-out gives any indication of speed. It reads .9, nine-tenths the speed of sound and accelerating. As I watch, the Mach number climbs, .93, .95, .97, it hangs up for an instant and then jumps to 1.02. We are supersonic and still accelerating, the maniacal engines will not be denied. With nothing else to do, I watch the mach meter unwind; I want to see a number starting with a 2.

On the far side of the so-called sound barrier, the airflow around the Phantom has now changed radically. Shock waves are now attached to the nose and tail. In a few seconds, Thai farmers slip/sliding along behind stoic water buffalos plodding through their flooded rice paddies will be treated to a sharp boom marking our swift passage through the sky far above them. Supersonic, the flight controls are less effective, they seem stiff and unresponsive, particularly in pitch, the downward-slanting stabilators on the tail have less control authority.

There it is! Mach 2.0, twice the speed of sound. I could go on, Mach 2.4 is probably within reach. Instead, I ease the stiff stick back and the jet climbs again, trading airspeed for altitude, exchanging kinetic energy for potential energy, leaving the relative safety of 50,000 feet for the unexplored, ever-thinner air above us. 55,000 feet, 60,000. We aren't suppose to be up this high, but what the hell, I fly combat missions most days despite the Flight Surgeon's wise advice that bullets are not to enter my body at any time.

What did they teach us in aviation physiology? At 63,000 feet, coming up now on the altimeter, the boiling point of water is 98 degrees. If we lose cabin pressurization, not an unlikely event at this height, our blood will boil and our gooses will be cooked, literally. Yikes!

I roll the F-4 up on its left side and let the nose fall through the seemingly rounded horizon, starting back down. I dare not touch the throttles, the engines have little stall margin in the diasporas air up here and if we flame out the engines, we lose cabin pressure. The altimeter unwinds back to 50,000 feet and we can breathe easier again. I start a turn back to the northwest, our fuel is getting low. Still supersonic, I pull the throttles back out of afterburner to a more moderate power setting. With the stick full back, I can only get three Gs as I point the nose toward Ubon..... and oblivion. Everything goes black.

★★★

Is this what being dead is like? I am conscious but totally alone in an empty black void with no sensory inputs. No sight, no hearing, no feeling, just me and vacant blackness all around. Déscartés said, "I think, therefore I am." What if I can think but I am not? Slowly, slowly, I come to a heightened state of consciousness and I realize where I am and what has transpired. I can hear air rushing over the canopy somewhere out there in the void. Now, my vision is returning, but I am looking through a soda straw at my lap, my chin is resting on my chest. More sight comes and I can see my leather-gloved hands in that distant lap, not on the control stick. I know they are my hands by my big fighter pilot wrist watch, but I can't move them, they're still paralyzed and I can't raise my head to look around.

I know now what happened. When the jet came back through the Mach to the sub-sonic flight regime, the stabilators regained their purchase on the airflow, dug in, and my three G pull instantly became a seven G turn. The instant onset of seven G's, causing my body to weigh over 1200 pounds, blacked me out without warning as the blood drained from my brain, pulled downward by seven Gs. I've experienced this a few times before and it always seems an eternity until I can see and move again. While I'm waiting, all I can think is, "How long have I been out and what has the airplane been doing while I was gone?"

Finally, I can move again, I raise my head, grab the stick, and look outside. Above me, out the top of the canopy, is the ground, still far below. We are inverted, but still at altitude, I must not have been out long. Rolling the jet right side up, I take a deep breath of metallic-tasting oxygen from my soft rubber mask, get my bearings, pull the power back and start a long glide to base.

I ask Jack, "Are you OK?"

"I'm back," is all he says.

After a minimum fuel landing, we are taxing in, back to our jet's assigned revetment.

I tell Jack, "Maintenance forecasts there is another FCF scheduled for tomorrow, want to fly?"

"No," Jack replies.

That's a surprise, Jack always wants to fly. Unprovoked, Jack wields an unexpected verbal blade.

"I'll fly tomorrow, but not with you. You're getting too wild. You tried to kill us today. Twice. On a maintenance check flight."

That hurts, particularly coming from Jack, a man who knows no fear . I'll admit my adrenaline addiction has been getting harder and harder to fix, mere combat missions aren't enough anymore, but I thought Jack was there with me.

Jack goes on, shedding some of his own blood on the blade.

"I've been talking to a few of the guys, mostly back seaters. They're on board with me, you need to cool it."

I'm astounded that Jack would admit this feeling of peril and that he has spoken to other GIBs about his unease. Jack usually doesn't talk about anything, but this situation was evidently serious enough to provoke sharing with his, and my, squadron mates. Sometimes, insightful truth creeps into our consciousness bit by bit until we realize that it is time for a change; that our current life path is not sustainable or survivable. Other times, deep situational awareness arrives with all the subtlety of a custard pie slammed into our face. This is one of those second cases.

My year-long second tour is almost up, I'll be rotating out of Satan's Angels soon. A buddy at the US Embassy in Bangkok has offered me a new plum assignment. I could be stationed in the exotic Thai capital, working out of the Embassy, helping manage the CIA's covert Raven and Air America operations up-country. Part of the good deal is to be able to fly combat missions out of Ubon at least twice a month along with the occasional FCF. Given Jack's heart-felt input, maybe it's time for a rethink of that plan. An addiction to adrenaline probably can't be weaned away with a few missions a month. I've got to quit cold-turkey. Living in Bangkok but not flying would be the pits, particularly knowing that up-country, combat flying would be conducted without me. Also, it wouldn't be too long until someone in the Embassy connects the dots and discovers the war criminal who wasted the Chinese cultural center is working just down the hall. It's time for Plan B or maybe another Plan A.

AMAZING GRACE

I am in the busy, crowded San Francisco airport terminal waiting for my commercial flight to depart. Or at least I think that's where I am. I haven't had any real sleep in several days, since I left Bangkok on a military charter flight. Consequently, my sense of place and time is a little detached and worryingly groggy.

The civilian Boeing 707 bringing me home from Thailand was hired by Uncle Sam to return servicemen from the war to the United States, the fabled "Land of the Big Base Exchange." We stopped for an hour in Saigon to shoehorn even more GIs on board. To a man (and woman), the second group of passengers seemed uncommonly glad to be leaving South Vietnam. After uncountable, cramped, uncomfortable hours on board the crammed-full 707 and a short refueling stop in Hawaii, we landed at a USAF air base outside Sacramento, California. My fellow passengers were mostly US Army troops returning after their year's tour in Vietnam. Finally, the wheels of the big, clumsy jet squeaked down on the stateside runway and we were home at last. I thought the plane's hull would rupture from the over pressurization generated by a long and heartfelt cheer voiced by the returning troops.

I felt somehow cheated. After hundreds of combat flights and over a thousand hours of flight time, I didn't get to fly my own self home. Instead of seeing the United States from the panoramic cockpit of my Phantom, I had to squint out a tiny window at the Golden Gate Bridge while some weenie airline pilot getting paid three times my salary drove the airplane.

Sleepily, I caught a bus to 'Frisco and somehow found the airport. Prolonged sleep deprivation is now causing me to feel disconnected from reality. I am a zombie in a wrinkled USAF uniform. I do know I am in route to my next service assignment in Las Vegas, Nevada. The success of the Paveway laser-guided bomb program has generated an urgent need to train other fighter pilots on how to best deliver these new wonder weapons dispatched from the future. I am to be an instructor at the famed USAF Fighter Weapons School.

The 'Frisco airport is crowded with civilians getting on and off airplanes, arriving from and departing to places unknown. They take no notice of a red-eyed guy with a two-day beard in a drab brown summer uniform and green flight jacket. That would be me. I recognize them though; these are a few of the folks I have spent two years fighting for in combat against godless Communism. After two years in exotic, oriental Thailand, immersed in the pressure cooker of war, I feel not of this place and not at one with my fellow US citizens. These folks are different; they haven't seen the bright lights nor heard the loud noises of war. They fully expect to be alive at the end of each day. Why does defending my country make me feel not a part of it anymore? Perhaps that's the price one pays to see the things I've experienced. I've done things that civilians can only dream about. Or is the proper word "nightmare"? Dreams or nightmares, that's a close call and I'm too sleepy to make it.

A few minutes ago, I was killing time and trying to stay vertically upright when I saw a sign that read "USO Service Personnel Lounge." That sounded homey so I reported here, showed the nice elderly volunteer lady at the desk my military ID card and now I'm in like Flynn. The coffee is standard US government issue mud, the doughnuts aren't Krispy Kreme, but the price is right, i.e. free and I'm a happy camper, back among my fellow GIs and away from the unknowing, uncaring, oblivious civilians outside the lounge in the terminal.

I'm not too keen about hanging around the public areas of the 'Frisco airport anyway. In the Bangkok Post I have read the great City of San Francisco is the epicenter of antiwar protests.

I am a good target for protesters, in my light brown USAF uniform, officer's flight cap, and my flight jacket with its fearsome squadron insignia patches. Normally, I would relish opportunities to confront peaceniks, but not after a couple of days without proper sleep. It's not fun trying to talk sense to people who have decided not to listen. I'm not really sure how much sense I could make now anyway.

The lounge is busy, but I find a seat on a worn, cracked leather sofa and try not to fall asleep and miss my flight. It is hard to prevent my mind from dwelling on the concept that a major phase of my life is over and I'm moving on. I always wanted to fly in combat in fighter aircraft for the US Air Force and I have done just that. After 375 combat missions spread over two years and 1000 hours of combat time, my direct involvement in this crummy war is at last over. I have seen many wonderful and terrible things. I have watched my friends die and I believed that it wouldn't happen to me. I have dived to the low altitudes of despair and soared to stratospheric heights of elation. I have been tighter with a group of guys than I have ever been in my life and probably will ever be again.

Life in a combat fighter squadron is like none other. Absurdities follow on the heels of hard realities and contradictions abound. Nonsense is intermixed with life-or-death decisions. I made lifelong friends of guys whose chances on surviving the war aren't good. I strove to win an unwinnable war. I flew missions that were relatively safe and complained that nothing happened. I lived comfortably and I fought for my life. While our troops in South Vietnam were enduring rain, mud, heat, bugs and sharp, shit-covered punji sticks, I complained about getting served chocolate ice cream on apple pie. I lusted after women that I couldn't bring home to Mom and with whom I couldn't bring myself to stay.

Despite the intensity and the excitement of the last two plus years, I really don't think that my career and my life will run downhill from here; there will always be challenges to meet on the ground as well as in the air. It is sad to think that I will never again feel the degree of emotional passion I experienced during these two years. On the other hand, my prospects of living to a ripe old age have just improved markedly.

Others haven't been so lucky. On my last mission, once again I used a piece of blackboard chalk to write on the rough cast-steel surface of a 2,000-pound laser-guided bomb. On the bomb I scrawled the names of USAF friends that are now dead, captured, or missing in action. Not merely acquaintances, these were guys who I knew well. They were men whom I drank with and whose wives and girlfriends I called by their first names.

When I was finished, the olive-drab warhead was overall a dusty white color, like a ghost bomb. Or perhaps a bomb carrying the names of spirits, of lost souls.

An hour later, that bomb detonated on the soil of North Vietnam. Maybe the force of the explosion vaporizing the names of my unlucky friends will somehow give their souls a measure of peace. I know watching the fiery bomb splash made me feel better. With any luck, the bomb might have taken out some of the folks responsible for my losses. But that was days and worlds ago.

In front of me is a beat-up stereo. Maybe some musical entertainment will keep me awake. I click the power knob on and without any hesitation whatsoever I am rewarded with instant music. No commercials, no introduction, no gap, just a clear, pure female voice without instrumental accompaniment pours forth from the stereo. It's as if the song was already cued up, waiting for me to turn it on.

I recognize the voice of Anita Bryant. I don't really care for her style of music, but something keeps me listening, something that says, "You need to hear this." I recently read that Anita is embroiled in some controversy concerning her stands in favor of Florida orange juice and against homosexuality, or is it the other way round? Anyway, she seems to be now singing soprano for me and me alone in the servicemen's lounge. No one around me appears to be listening; can't they hear her?

Amazing grace, how sweet the sound
That saved a wretch like me.

I once was lost, but now I'm found.
Was blind, but now I see.
Through many dangers, toils and snares,
I have already come,
'Tis grace hath brought me safe this far,
And Grace will lead me home.

I know well the song's words from my childhood church-going days. The classic hymn seems to be coming from another long-ago time and a faraway place. It was last heard by a kid, me, who doesn't exist anymore; he grew up. The allegorical words from the past seem aimed at the present, my present. The music's mental image hits home deep inside and I listen intently until the high, lonesome voice finishes the last verse. As the last note fades and dies, I turn off the stereo. I am getting strange looks from the other GIs in the lounge. Haven't they ever seen a fighter pilot cry?

ACKNOWLEDGEMENTS

I would like to acknowledge the contributions which various folks made, making “‘War for the Hell of It” a reality.

The following people helped me by checking facts, scouring their memories for details of flight operations occurring during the time frame of the book as well as suggesting improvements to the tone and to the accounts and descriptions herein: Colonel Larry Casper, U.S. Army Aviation; Colonel Phil Comstock, USAF; Lt/ Commander Broc McCaman, USN; Major Tom McKinney U.S. Marine Corps; Lt. General Jim Record, USAF.; Commander Bill West, USN; Lt/ Colonel Doug Holmes, USAF..

Also, Donna Beddie’s word processing contributions were invaluable. Doris Badger attempted to pound some proper English grammar into the manuscript. I wrote the bulk of this book while employed by the Hughes Aircraft Company, but I swear none of it was written on company time.

Finally, special thanks to my wife and best friend, Heidi Cobleigh for her tolerance of my late-night work at the computer and her strong support for this book.

CPSIA information can be obtained
at www.ICGtesting.com
Printed in the USA
LVHW092151120219
607352LV00001B/120/P

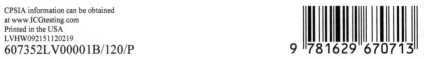

9 781629 670713